PARENTAL DEATH

IT HAPPENED TO ME

Series Editor: Arlene Hirschfelder

Books in the It Happened to Me series are designed for inquisitive teens digging for answers about social issues, certain illnesses, or lifestyle interests. These books feature up-to-date information, relatable teen views, and thoughtful suggestions to help you figure out stuff. Besides special boxes that highlight singular facts, each book is enhanced with the latest reading lists, websites, and other recommendations.

The following titles may also be of interest:

Adopted: The Ultimate Teen Guide, Revised Edition, by Suzanne Buckingham Slade
Bullying: The Ultimate Teen Guide, by Mathangi Subramanian
Creativity: The Ultimate Teen Guide, by Aryna M. Ryan
Dealing with Death: The Ultimate Teen Guide, by Kathlyn Gay
Depression: The Ultimate Teen Guide, by Tina P. Schwartz
Divorce: The Ultimate Teen Guide, by Kathlyn Gay
Eating Disorders: The Ultimate Teen Guide, by Jessica R. Greene
LGBTQ Families: The Ultimate Teen Guide, by Eva Apelqvist
Living with Cancer: The Ultimate Teen Guide, by Denise Thornton
Self-Injury: The Ultimate Teen Guide, by Judy Dodge Cummings
Shyness: The Ultimate Teen Guide, by Bernardo J. Carducci, Ph.D, and Lisa Kaiser
Social Networking: The Ultimate Teen Guide, by Jenna Obee
Substance Abuse: The Ultimate Teen Guide, by Sheri Bestor

PARENTAL DEATH

THE ULTIMATE TEEN GUIDE

MICHELLE SHREEVE

ROWMAN & LITTLEFIELD
Lanham • Boulder • New York • London

Published by Rowman & Littlefield
An imprint of The Rowman & Littlefield Publishing Group, Inc.
4501 Forbes Boulevard, Suite 200, Lanham, Maryland 20706
www.rowman.com

Unit A, Whitacre Mews, 26-34 Stannary Street, London SE11 4AB

British Library Cataloguing in Publication Information Available

Library of Congress Cataloging-in-Publication Data

Names: Shreeve, Michelle, 1984– author.
Title: Parental death : the ultimate teen guide / Michelle Shreeve.
Description: Lanham : Rowman & Littlefield, [2017] | Series: It happened to
  me ; No. 56 | Includes bibliographical references and index.
Identifiers: LCCN 2017036144 (print) | LCCN 2017055958 (ebook) | ISBN
  9781442270886 (electronic) | ISBN 9781442270879 (hardback : alk. paper)
Subjects: LCSH: Teenagers and death. | Parents—Death—Psychological aspects.
  | Bereavement—Psychological aspects. | MESH: Maternal deprivation.
Classification: LCC BF724.3.D43 (ebook) | LCC BF724.3.D43 S47 2017 (print) |
  DDC 155.9/370835—dc23
LC record available at https://lccn.loc.gov/2017036144
  The paper used in this publication meets the minimum requirements of American National
  Standard for Information Sciences—Permanence of Paper for Printed Library Materials,
  ANSI/NISO Z39.48-1992.

∞™ The paper used in this publication meets the minimum requirements of American
National Standard for Information Sciences—Permanence of Paper for Printed Library
Materials, ANSI/NISO Z39.48-1992.

Printed in the United States of America

To God; my husband, Chris; my late mother, Kathy;
my father, Dave; my brother, Mike; my grandparents;
my extended family; my in-laws; and my closest friends:
Thank you for guiding me along this journey
after losing my mother at a young age.
Your love and support enabled me to write this book.

To parentless teens everywhere:
May there finally be a book that speaks directly to you
and that can help you understand what you are going through.

Contents

Acknowledgments

I have to be honest with you. I am not the sole author of this book. It has been compiled through twenty-four years of research and my own experience coping with my mother's death in 1993 when I was nine years old. It contains advice, research, and lessons I have learned the hard way, research and suggestions from experts, as well as insights from parentless children and adults I have come across and teens I have mentored; it was written with the love and support of God, my husband, my family, friends, coaches, teachers, and peers I met during this journey. In a way, I feel like this book has been written by the world, and I feel like I should not get credit for it. Many people have had a hand in this book—you know who you are, and I just wanted to thank you all for helping me write this.

With the limited amount of space I am given to acknowledge those who had a part, I do have a few I would like to thank. First, I want to thank God for believing in me to carry out this task and for thinking I was strong enough to handle the responsibility that came with writing this book. God, you also guided me over the last twenty-four years of coping with my own mother's death, and I just want to thank you for never giving up on me, even though I may have felt like giving up on myself at times.

Many thanks go to my wonderful and very supportive husband, Chris, my best friend. You have literally witnessed the stress, the frustration, the lack of sleep; dealt with the microwaved meals, the tears, the tooth with a hat, and everything else that has gone into writing this book—not to mention the late nights where you helped me with the tech side of the book and many other tasks. I feel like your name should be going on the cover as well, as you being there for me makes you a part of this book. Thank you for always being my rock during this writing experience, every day in our lives together, and for supporting me going after my dreams of becoming an author who can help others, especially children and teenagers. Thank you for being a wonderful husband, for always looking out for me and guiding me. I love you with all of my heart.

To my mother, the late very sweet and incredibly kind Kathy: I only was able to spend nine years with you, Mom, but I will be forever grateful that I have those nine years to hold onto. You were such a fighter and a strong woman; I will always admire you and how you still mothered me even while you were dying. I wish I had more years with you. I miss you every day, and I want you to know how much I love you. Thank you for being my mother.

To my father, Dave: Thank you for being my father and thank you for sticking around after mom died. You had one of the hardest jobs possible, and that was deciding to stay and raise Mike and me after mom died, despite how hard that probably was. Thank you for wanting to be our father, for always being there for us, and for always taking care of us. Thank you for loving us as much as you always have throughout our lives and for always being in our corner to offer us support. Thank you for always encouraging me to go after my dreams. Thank you and mom for teaching me how to read and write, and for initiating my love for books, by buying them for me as a kid. I love you.

To my brother, Mike: Thank you for being a great brother to me and for looking out for me after mom died. You didn't have to do that, but you stepped up to the plate. Even though I didn't realize you were protecting me from the shadows in every single situation and with every single person I met, I hope you know how much I appreciate you doing that for me. You are the best brother a sister could ever ask for. I love you.

To my stepmother, Trish: You also had a very hard job trying to raise two teenage stepkids shortly after they lost their mother. You could have walked away from the job, but you stuck around, despite how hard I imagine the job truly was. Thank you for that. I love you.

To my "sisters," Sam and Ashlie; my nieces, Hailey, Victoria, and Kathryn; and my nephews, Cameron and Braxton: You all have brought great joy to my life over the years. Stay who you are, and I just wanted to thank you for letting me be a part of your lives. I love all of you.

To my grandparents: Thank you for always trying to guide me on a positive path despite being over 750 miles away after we moved. You lost your daughter, and I am sure the million questions I have asked you over the years have not been the easiest to answer. It took me a while to realize that you two were grieving around the same time the rest of us were; while I was grieving the loss of my mother, you both were grieving the loss of your daughter. Thank you for being great grandparents. I hope I have been an OK granddaughter to you guys. I love you both.

To the Arana, Brooks, Elder, Gigliotti, Hazard, Janiga, and Nash families: Thank you for all of the support you have given me over the years. Aunt Jean and Uncle Bob, your cards have meant the world to me; you have always been there to offer advice. Uncle Dan, Aunt Cindy, Uncle Tomas, and Aunt Price, thank you for all of your support over the years. Aunt Lynn, thanks for always making me smile and for always offering positive words. Aunt Chris, you have reminded me of mom over the years; I appreciate how much you and Aunt Wendy have acted like second mothers to me. I can't thank you enough. Uncle Jim, thank you for all of your book and author advice over the years. Part of the reason why I wanted to become an author is because I always looked up to you. Uncle Dave and Aunt

Mary, Aunt Vicki and Uncle Don, thank you as well for all of your support over the years. Thank you also to all of my cousins. I love you all.

To my in-laws, the Shreeve and the Lincicum families: Thank you all for welcoming me into your hearts and homes, as if I have always been a part of your family. You all have made me feel loved, welcome, and cared for, and I thank you all for that. Mama Judy, Terry, Cheryl, Steve, Becky, late Grandma Lincicum, late Grandpa Lincicum, Matt, Grant, Amber, Heather, Josh, Amy, Shawn, Kristin, Brea, Mackenzie, Linda, Gary, Diane, Taylor, Abreanna, and Ellie Ray: Thank you all for sharing Chris with me to be my husband. I love him more than anything. I love you all.

To Chris Putman, Connor Putman, Emily Putman, Ron Camacho, and Vicky Camacho: Thank you for being like a second family to Chris and me. You guys have always been there for us, and I can't thank you enough for everything you do for us. Chris Putman, your friendship over the years has meant the world to us, and we appreciate how you welcomed us into your family so many years ago. I love you all.

To Cody, Jody, and Meagan Jenkins: You guys are living proof that something positive can come out of a negative situation. Your friendship has meant so much to me after all of these years, and I can't thank you all enough for always being there for me. I love you all.

Due to space issues, I can only list the names of some other people I would like to thank and who have had some sort of a positive impact on me throughout my life and my parentless journey. If your name is not on the list, please know that I recognize and appreciate you. It is simply just a matter of space requirements. I love you all, and I am very grateful for each and every one of you: *Ahwatukee Foothills News*; the Akay family; Mrs. Alston; the Amoroso family; Eric Angeloff; Justin Angeloff; Lisa Angeloff; Mike Angeloff; Ryan Angeloff; Violetta Armour; Debbie Armstrong; Annie Arnke; Lauren Arnke; the Arnke family; Ms. Balbi; the Banchero family; the Barber family; Lenny Barranti; the Bell family; Rachael Bell; Daniel Bergeron; Señora Boatright; the Bondan family; Barb Boschetto; the Buick family; Chad and Elvia Cagle; Theresa Canizarro; Kristen Caruso; Debbie Casey; Ron Chavez; the Chelini family; the Chelone family; Tom Chow; Nicole Clanton; Brandie Clark; Robert Cohen; Charlene Curiale; Regina Curiale; Stephanie Curiale; Brenda Dailey; Don Dailey Jr.; Diego De La Cruz; Larry De La Cruz; Lorenzo De La Cruz; Margaret De La Cruz; Monica De La Cruz; Daniele Wilks DeMartini; Sara DeMartini; Katie Desserres; Gabe DeWitt; Ginny Dias; the Donati family; the Earnshaw family; *East Valley Tribune*; Rich Eckley; Hope Edelman; Luana Ehrlich; the Ellison family; Lauren Ellison; Aimee Erickson; Jose Esquivel; J. P. Esquivel; Kathy Esquivel; Rachel Esquivel; Sarah Esquivel; Lee Farinas; Kirk Fauske; Elyna Feist; Jane Flanagan; Jessica Forsgren; Kevin Fortune; Melissa Fortune; Lydell and Marissa Francisco; Mario

Frontierro; Maria Garcia; *Gilbert Sun News*; Allison Gilbert; Doug Gordon; Kelly Green; Lenore Griffin; Kelly Griffith and TAPS; JoAnn Hammen; the Hanke family; Chris Hanna; Aaron Hardy; Julie Hardy; David Harrison; Dr. Marlen Harrison; Lynette Barber Haskins; Jenna Innes; Taji James; Jamie Jones; Chris Kane; Brandie Kayal; Dave Klecka; Denny Kruger; Joanie Kruger; Susanne Lambdin; Georgianne Landy-Kordis; Randy Lane; the Laneri family; Andrea Laneri-Martin; Señora Lassen; Patricia Leavy; the Maciejewski family; the Maka family; Francis Maka; Eddie Mancini; Adam Martini; Jo and Pola Martino; Paul Maryniak; Kenny Mathis; Stacy Mathis; the McDonald family; the Middagh family; Kelly Mixer; Glenn Morishita; Rex Morrison; Mountain Pointe High School; the Moyer Foundation; Robert Nadzan; Stacy Nadzan; the Original Burrito and Company; Lindsay Orosco; Ricardo and Lauren Ortiz; Brad and Michele Parres; the Potter family; Marlene Price; Mrs. Rafalski; Jeremy Ramirez; Tony Ramseyer; Eric Reese; Janet Roberts, the Centering Corporation, and *Grief Digest Magazine*; Carol Ross; Shane Ross; Doug Ross; Carumba; the Rossi family; the Rudee family; Nick Saethre; Anna Saunders; Paulette Schmidt; Dr. David Schonfeld; Rebecca Schuller; Derek Schultz; Kelly Schultz; Donna Schuurman and the Dougy Center; Laura Sena; Jennifer Shattles; Keith Shaw; Kasey Shobe; Andrea Sinclair; Elizabeth Singleton; Sara Slone and COPS; Larry Smith; the Soriano family; Jessica Soriano; Southern New Hampshire University; Laurie Stricklin; the Strohecker family; Mrs. Sullivan; Jody Swanson; Danielle Thompson; Times New Media; Liz Toma; Rick Tribuzi; Adrienne Trier-Bineiek; Billy Venturini; Ruth Venturini; Nick Wagner; Ronald T. Waldo; Deborah Ware; Jonathan Weeks; Robert Whitney, MSW; Jenn Woodward; Ms. Worley; Scott Worthington; Carol Zakula; the Zaninni family; Dan Zevallos. For those who were brave to share their personal story of parent loss in this book: Adriana, Aedan, Autum, Barbara, Beth, Carissa, Catherine, Chase, Christina, D. B., Elizabeth, Ella, Ellen, Eric, Erin, Isabella, Joella, John, Julie, Katie, Kaylene, Kristen, Larry, Laura, Lindsay, Lori, Louise, Maggie, Mahala, Mary, McKenna, Nancy, Nicki, Rachel, Rebecca, Richard, Sharon, Stacy, Taylor, Thomas, Tiffany, Wendy, and all those whose stories were not selected for the book, as well as those who emailed me tips and suggestions from the newspaper articles. Arlene Hirschfelder, thank you for the time, patience, and energy spent guiding me through my first book; for letting me be a part of this much needed series for teens, and for taking a chance on a first-time author. Elaine Schleiffer, Stephen Ryan, Jessica McCleary, Gail Fay, Bethany Davis, and the folks at Rowman & Littlefield, thank you for recognizing how much this book is truly needed, and for giving me the extra time to make this book the very best it could possibly be.

To everyone who had some hand in this book, from the bottom of my heart, thank you. I love you all.

Introduction

In 1993, I lost my mother when I was just nine years old. She had been sick for a while and in and out of the hospital; however, she always came back home. Although I knew she was sick, I did not see her death coming. The day that she died, December 3, 1993, changed my life forever. At that point, I was no longer a nine-year-old little girl, but a nine-year-old little girl trying to navigate life without a mother. After that day, I didn't know what my future was going to look like, let alone each day. A lot of change took place the moment we found out, and the lives of my family members and me were never the same again.

In dealing with the loss of my mother, I had to take it in life stages. For example, my childhood years and teen years presented entirely different challenges. Each phase was new territory for me, and I always felt like I was trying to navigate my life blindly. I still had my father, my brother, and my extended family members, but not having my mom anymore made everything more challenging on a whole different level.

You see, back in the nineties, I could only find one book on growing up motherless. And although I was an intellectual bookworm at age nine, the book was not easy to read and didn't seem connected to the situation I was going through. I basically read half of the first chapter and tossed the book aside because I could not relate to the tone and language. To this day, I have not read that book all the way through. It did not speak to me on a preteen or teen level, which is what I desperately needed back then. At that point, I realized I was on my own.

Sure, I had friends, family members, mentors, teachers, and even coaches who helped me along the way; however, not everyone could be there for me 100 percent of the time. As a result, I had to teach myself to be there for myself and to figure things out on my own. With that came a lot of mistake-making on my part. Did I mean to make mistakes? Does anyone ever mean to purposely make mistakes? No, but I learned a lot by making quite a few mistakes over the years. Yet, looking back on when I lost my mother twenty-four years ago, I really wish there was a book that could have helped me get through the difficult challenges I was going to face.

Growing up, I ended up doing a lot of mentoring of my own. If I came across others who had lost one or both of their parents, or just lost their way in general, I was always the first one to want to help them out. I also joked with my family members, stating that I could write a book about all of the mistakes I had made by the time I was twenty-five years old. Yet somehow, some way, I made it through my teen years, mistakes and all. It may have taken a lot of help from a lot of different people, to whom I am very grateful to this day, but I made it.

And so can you.

I want this book to speak to you and to help you get through those tough times ahead and even the ones you are already experiencing. I want this book to be the type of helpful resource I wish had been around when I was your age. This book should prove that you are not alone and that you don't ever have to feel that way, as there are many teens out there who are going through what you are. There are lots of resources—support groups, nonprofit organizations, books, movies, and even TV shows—that can help you make positive and wonderful choices in your life despite the challenge you now face growing up without one or both of your parents. All the information found in this book is here to guide you. And for you, I want this book to be the ultimate teen guide for parental death.

THE FIRST YEAR

The Day That Changes Your Life Forever

Suffering the loss of a parent is no small thing, especially when it happens during childhood. "According to clinical psychologist Maxine Harris, PhD, in her book, *The Lifelong Impact of the Early Death of a Mother or Father*, the loss of a parent before adulthood has a profound effect on the rest of that person's life. The loss affects adult personality development, a sense of security, and relationships with the surviving parent and significant others."[1] Whether you realize it or not yet, the day your parent died changed your life forever.

Maybe your parent was sick, and you had a little time to prepare. Or maybe your parent was home and everything was fine that morning before you left for school, and suddenly he or she was gone by the time you got home. No matter the case, "for children, a parent's death can never be fully anticipated, regardless of how impending the death."[2] Suddenly, you get the phone call, or you get pulled out of class, or you somehow receive the message that your parent just died. And that's it—you cannot say you are sorry for the fight you had earlier that morning; there is no fulfilling the shopping plans you made with your mother for your annual mother-daughter weekend; there will be no going to the football game with your dad next week. If you forgot to say, "I love you" before you left for school that morning, you can't say it now. If you had a fight with your father—what's done is done. The day that you find out the news is the day your life changes forever; nothing will ever be the same again. You are now wandering into uncharted waters, where change will most likely confront you every day, no matter how hard you try to fight it. Your emotions will now probably come in waves depending on the length of time that has passed since you lost your parent.

Your first day you may experience shock. You can't believe it happened. You almost think it didn't happen, until you wake up the next day and face the reality that it indeed happened. You are probably going to feel extremely overwhelmed. That's not even counting the part when your friends and family members crowd your house to start making funeral arrangements, or the number of phone calls

Finding out that your parent has died is one of the hardest moments you will ever have to face. ©iStock / KatarzynaBialasiewicz

you and your surviving parent and/or siblings are going to receive as support—it is all going to get overwhelming and happen so fast, whether you are ready to deal with it or not.

What to Expect during the First Year

Living without one or both of your parents is most likely new territory for you, and you are probably wondering, "What happens now?" Family members or your surviving parent might try to talk to you about how your parent's death is going to impact your daily school routine, life events, and more. Let's break it down into smaller sections to help you prepare for what might be coming around the corner.

The First Week

The first week will probably be as overwhelming as the first day you found out the terrible news. Funerals and celebrations of life are typically planned within the first week or two after a person passes away, so in addition to dealing with your emotions, you will probably be bombarded with plans for and decisions about the funeral. It's not something you can avoid; the funeral can't be postponed until you are ready. Because, well, let's face it—do you really think you would ever be ready to bury your parent?

You may want to remember your parent privately and not have to deal with funeral plans during the first week. Other family members, especially your surviving parent, may feel strongly about preparing a meaningful celebration of your parent's life. Try to remember that everyone grieves in their own way. Authors David Schonfeld and Marcia Quackenbush say, "It is natural for people to want to

"In January of 2014, I got the flu. I was so sick, I couldn't even show up to work. My grandmother made me stay at home to recover. My cell phone suddenly rang, and I saw that it was my aunt calling. I didn't answer, because I was too weak to talk. I saw that she left a voicemail. 'Hey Erin, it's auntie. Do you happen to have your mother's cell phone number? She hasn't been answering her house phone.' I called my aunt back and gave her my mom's cell phone number. I then tunneled back under the covers and continued to sleep. My phone rang again and my aunt stated that she still could not get a hold of my mom. I told her I would call my best friends Vania and Jennifer to see if they could go over and check on her. Jennifer told me she was at work, but she would go when she could, and Vania said the same thing. Around 9 p.m. Florida time, Vania stated she had reached my mom's house. She knocked and rang the doorbell, but there was no answer. She looked through the windows and could not see anything. I begged her to burst open the door. She opened the door and there was my mom. I heard Vania scream that she was gone. My mom and I had shared so many differences, we hadn't spoken in five years, and we did not have the best relationship, and so a wave of emotions just swept over me. I forgot I was sick, I forgot I had a fever. I fell to my knees in such great emotion screaming and crying. I could hardly speak when I had to tell my grandparents—her parents. I couldn't even breathe. All I could do was hold my daughter and pray.

"I had to go to Phoenix to deal with my mother's affairs. I had just begun nursing school. I went to class the following day and tried my hardest to participate. At break, I told my teacher that I would have to leave and catch a flight, because my mom just passed away. My teacher was shocked that I was even in class at all, and told me to leave right away. I was numb at this point, and I had no emotions. I told her I was OK, and then I thanked her for the condolences. My grandma and grandpa chose not to come with us and they instead wanted to keep my daughter. I told my grandma that I needed her with me for strength. We flew out that afternoon and I met my aunt, cousin, and her daughter at the hotel. They kept asking me if I was OK, but I did not know how to respond to that. I had not spoken to this woman, my mother, in five years, due to our last fight . . . she can't possibly be gone.

"The next morning, we went to the funeral home to start making arrangements for her. I asked them if we could view her body, and they stated that they would have her moved the following day. All of the decisions were left up to me, because she was my mom. I remember my mom told me she wanted to be cremated, and so I abided by her wishes. We then left to start securing her house.

"Seeing my mom lying in that funeral home was finally the realization that she was gone. She looked just as I had remembered her. I touched her, and she felt cold. I missed her so much at that point. That was the first time my daughter had seen my mom in person, and I did not want it to be in that way. I broke down, I cried, I lost it. My daughter did not understand. I replayed in my head the last conversation we had, the last words which were all bitter and in anger. I just wanted to hold my mom again. I just wanted to have one conversation with her again and tell her how sorry I was, and that I didn't care that she was wrong. I just wanted my mom back!

"The next couple of months were hell. I flunked two of my nursing classes, because I couldn't cope. My doctor started me on anti-depressants that took all of my emotions away, so I just felt blah all the time. My anxiety went to another level, and so then I was prescribed Xanax to help control the panic attacks. I was an emotional wreck. I would find myself crying for no reason and had a difficult time coping. It did not help that my mom and I's last words and last time together was on bad terms. I just tried to throw myself into my schoolwork, job, and daughter, in order to keep myself distracted from the pain.

"At my mom's memorial service in July, at this point I thought I was fine. The panic attacks were less, the crying was less, my doctor had taken me off of my anti-depressants, and I was starting to function again. Listening to everyone at the service just brought back so many emotions, but from all of the stories I heard, I realized that my mom loved me more than anything. People told me stories of her that I never heard of before, and people even came from various states to be at her service. That right there let me know that she was truly loved.

"I find peace now knowing that she is in a better place, and I feel as if she is watching over my daughter and I. From time to time, I still cry when I think

> about her. Actually, by writing this, it's the first time I have ever confronted a lot of the emotions that stemmed from the situation. Now, I mainly try to stay busy and work hard, because I know that she would be proud of what I am doing. I still struggle with anxiety, but instead of using medications, I try to cope with my anxiety through practicing relaxation techniques, as well as I talk out my issues a lot more now."—Erin[a]

remember, honor, and reflect on those who have died. We do these things through funerals, events that commemorate the deceased, the placements of memorial markers [a marker that usually commemorates a site where a person died suddenly and unexpectedly], and similar activities."[3]

Just like the first day when you probably received lots of phone calls and had lots of visitors stop by your house, the first week will most likely be filled with the same. People will want to help you and your family get ready for the funeral, notify other family members and friends of the death, and take care of other planning. On top of that, people will probably ask you and your family tedious questions regarding the arrangements, the schedule of the celebration of life, what to wear to the funeral, what food will be served at the funeral, and many other things you will be trying to find some importance in—because all you can think of is the parent you just lost.

Be aware that planning and attending the funeral or celebration of life will probably be stressful. Some of you might feel so stressed that you wonder if you should even attend the funeral. According to the Coalition to Support Grieving Students, most of the time, it is better for you if you do attend.[4] Attending will help you feel more included in the whole process of laying your parent to rest; you can be comforted by your friends, family members, and in some cases your teachers and classmates; and you can learn about your own grief as you watch others grieve and receive support.

> "I wasn't overwhelmed after she died, as I was only twelve, and I was too young to process anything. When our family members and friends heard the news, many people stopped by our house, called us, and some family even flew in to try and offer us support. My mother was gone and there was nothing. I was simply too young to process an overwhelming situation like that. I wasn't old enough to understand the gravity of what was going on. It was a sad situation, but I didn't understand."—Mike[b]

"At one of my dad's viewings, I remember one of my friends asking me if I had touched my dad to say goodbye. I remember how disturbed I was by the cold, hard feel of his skin. His face was bruised by falling into the tree, so he didn't look like how I wanted to remember him. I had nightmares for over a year about death—two predominant, repeated nightmares plagued me in those early months. One nightmare, was that he had been buried alive and was scratching at his coffin lid and calling for me to help him. The second, which I experienced for about three years after his death, was that I was walking down the basement stairs in my house and on one side it was really dark and red and scary, and the other side was light and bright. I heard voices call from both sides of the stairs and then would wake up. These dreams and experiencing the death of a loved one at such an early age resulted in an increased thought of my own mortality. I struggled to want to sleep at night.

"My mom was so amazing during this time. She cried with us, but wasn't inconsolable. She was strong. She actually reached out and ministered to all the students and family members who were struggling. She said she and dad had talked about what they expected of each other should one of them die unexpectedly. She worked very hard to demonstrate her faith in action. She and I actually went on a mission trip to the Dominican Republic (in place of my dad who was leading the trip) two weeks after his death. Serving others and seeing people, who despite my grief were more destitute than I, was actually quite cathartic."—Julie[c]

Some of you might want to participate in the funeral arrangements or the funeral ceremony itself; experts say this can provide support for young people: "Children can find helpful support through commemorative activities. These activities or events help them express and cope with difficult feelings that might otherwise seem overwhelming to them. They can draw on the support of a caring community—their peers, teachers, and school or community based counseling staff. They can learn from others who are also facing these challenging feelings, and everyone can share techniques for coping. A commemorative activity can give children a framework for further discussion with their parents or other family members."[5] Some teens may want to read a goodbye letter to their late parent, recite a poem, play their late parent's favorite song, or say a few things on behalf

It Happened to Me: A Note from the Author

The week after my mother passed away was basically a blur. At the same time that I was dealing with what I was personally feeling, we also had many people coming in and out of our house. My school was made aware of what happened, so many of my friends' parents brought us over pans of lasagna, meat loaves, and other dinners to help get us through that first week. Our family members came over to help my dad with all of the funeral arrangements, and there were a few trips made to the funeral home in preparation as well.

During this first week, a few family members and friends came over and talked about what would happen during the funeral. My dad was really busy and dealing with his own grief at the time, but he did set expectations regarding what the funeral was going to be like. He (and the school) let a lot of my class-mates come to the funeral. That really helped me.

During the funeral I read a letter about my mother (also known as reciting a eulogy) in front of everyone who attended. I was nine years old, reading a letter to my mother who just passed away, but to this day, I am glad that I did that. In many ways, I felt like I honored her by doing that. Other family members and friends also read letters or spoke on her behalf, and by doing so, we really honored her that day.

I'm glad I attended the funeral and that I knew beforehand what to expect on the day of the funeral and later during the cemetery burial phase. Being prepared like this, reading the letter to my mother, kissing her on her forehead one last time after she passed away and before the funeral home prepared her body—these things all helped me during my grieving journey, especially at the beginning.

of their late parent. It's perfectly OK if you don't want to or you are not comfortable doing any of these things.

Know that you might feel uncomfortable when you attend the funeral and that you might cry or become very upset. This is normal; it is OK to express your emotions. You might want to take a friend or trusted adult such as a coach or teacher to the funeral; talk with your surviving parent or guardian to see if this is OK. Doing so allows you to have your own support system at the funeral in case you need it. The Coalition to Support Grieving Students suggests that you have an

"During the first week after I lost my father, everything was very overwhelming with deciding what songs to pick for his celebration of life, funeral arrangements, and family pressures for deciding the funeral arrangements. I was actually the first person to give the eulogy at my father's celebration of life. Four hundred people showed up to my father's celebration of life. There were so many people, that not everyone could fit into the building."—Catherine[d]

adult explain beforehand the events that are going to take place when you attend the funeral. This way you are aware of everything that will happen, which might help you cope better than if you go to the funeral unaware.[6]

If you think things will get easier after the funeral is over, that's probably not accurate. The whole first year will most likely present many new challenges for you, which will come in waves during different time frames. Everyone handles the first year differently: "some children go through an acute period of grief and gradually feel better over time. Others do well for a period of time and face challenges later."[7] If you accept that the first year is going to be a hard one, then you are off to a better start than if you refuse to believe that it will be tough.

"The first week after my dad died I went and stayed with my grandparents. I remember my grandpa being a great influence in my life from that time forward. My grandma was also very supportive and always there for me. I took about three weeks or so off school to spend time with my family and get away from normal day-to-day life. Going back to school was a hard transition because everybody in my class wanted to talk to me about what happened, but I didn't want to. I had quite a few tearful breakdowns the first few months. After the first year passed by, my sadness slowly began to taper off. It was still very difficult to think or talk about it, but I started to be able to focus on everyday things again. Now, as the decades pass by, I am able to look back fondly on the short time that I was able to spend with him with a smile. I still miss him very much, but I have reached the acceptance stage of the grieving process and no longer feel intense emotional pain when I think about what happened."—Thomas[e]

"After my mom's death, everything changed. We went from the four of us to just the three. My dad was now a single father raising two kids. My brother and I no longer had our mom to wake us up and walk us to school every morning, to help out in our classrooms or with homework, to cheer us on from the sidelines at our sporting events, or to make us dinner and tuck us in at night. The first week was insane. Our family from back home flew out immediately for her service and to help my dad out with my brother and I. We did not return to school for what seemed like a few weeks. It was hard to process what had happened with all of the chaos. The first few months was a blur. I felt like I was outside my body just watching myself get by. Life started to get easier as time went by. I still miss her every day. And at times the pain comes rushing back. It never really goes away.

"My dad tried counseling for my brother and I. It didn't work. We hated it as kids. What worked for me was talking about my mom, smelling her Victoria's Secret Vanilla body spray, looking at pictures, and watching home videos to hear her voice. I would talk to her when I was alone."—Lindsay[f]

The First Month

At this point, after the funeral is over, you may think things will go back to how they were before, just with one important person missing from your life. Unfortunately, that's not really going to happen. Although you and your siblings and surviving parent or guardian will probably try to put everything back to the way it was before, you sadly won't be able to achieve this, no matter how hard you all

"The first week or two after his death were strange. Lots of family that I had never seen together at any one time came into town, but then we had to get back to our old lives. With the exception of the first day or two coming back to school as the kid whose dad just died, I'm shocked at how quickly I at least got back into my normal childhood. I didn't realize at the time all the work our mom did to keep things as similar as possible to before our dad died."—Eric[g]

"During the first month after my father's death, everything was hectic. There was no down time; other family members were constantly surrounding us. His first birthday was tough, but it wasn't as tough as some of the other holidays were. He died on December 14th, so that first Christmas was really rough. People bought him presents before he died, so it was really difficult to see them under the tree, never going to get opened by him. We instead, opened them on his behalf."—Catherine[h]

try. How can everything go back to being how it was before when one person who played a huge role in your life is missing?

During the first month, you will probably need to adjust to many changes. Just think about it—if you lost your father and he used to drive you to school, now you might have your mother take you, but it won't be the same. She probably won't listen to the same music that your dad listened to, and she might not stop at the donut place like your father used to; you won't hear your father's goofy laugh in the car or smell his particular aftershave. You can try all you want to re-create everything as if he is still living and spending time with you (spray his aftershave in the car, listen to the radio station he did, etc.), but deep down inside it is going to sting when you acknowledge the reality of the situation. He is gone, and you can't bring him back.

The first month will probably be an emotional roller coaster. You might seem OK at first, but the second you see a daughter and mother fighting at the mall, you might become enraged when you realize you will never be able to fight with

"After my mother's death, my paternal grandmother had come to stay, usually for a couple nights at a time, before heading back to her home (about an hour or so away from where we lived) and then would usually be back the next day or the day after. After my father had passed, she moved in to the house, and once every two weeks, we would head back to her house for the weekend so she could tend to her life. One of my friends at school, and still best friend to this day, his family would house me for a couple weeks at a time, in order to make it easier for my grandmother to figure out the estate situation and my living arrangements. I now currently live with my aunt, my legal guardian, and have lived here for four years now."—Aedan[i]

"I think one of the major things that changed after my dad died, was that many friends stepped in to help our family. We had people step up to drive us to and from school or sports practices. Not much changed within our household as we stayed in the same home until my mom remarried."—Julie[j]

your mother ever again. Or grief might flare up when you suddenly realize the yearly father-son camping trip that you and your dad took together is no more. These are known as grief triggers. According to the Coalition to Support Grieving Students, a grief trigger is a sudden reminder of the person who died that causes a powerful emotional response. These triggers are most common in the first few months after the death, but may happen at any time. They can catch you off guard, you can suddenly get really sad in class or start crying.[8] Your sadness can suddenly turn into anger, and you might even find yourself trying to blame others for your loss.[9]

Whether you want to deal with your feelings or not, it is imperative that you do so, and in a positive way. You are going to need as much support as you can get, especially during the first year. Allison Gilbert, author of *Always Too Soon:*

Joining a support group, such as a religious congregation, can really help you channel your emotions, especially during the first year. You might meet other people who have suffered a loss similar to yours. ©iStock / KatarzynaBialasiewicz

"During my mother's death, I really didn't know how to cope. Going through routines, like school, and all of the extra-curricular activities definitely made things easier, but it was still hard to cope at times. After my father's death, I, again, did not really do anything to internalize the situation or make sense of it, at all. It wasn't until much later, that I was able to cope through music. For the first portion of my life, my father drank alcohol excessively (eventually quit, but it was not until later, a few years before he died), and after watching the unintended effects that prescription drugs had had on both of my parents, I was turned off to even the idea of unhealthy coping mechanisms. I bottled in my emotions for a while, and they would come out, occasionally, through short, explosive bursts of emotions. It's sufficient to say that coping mechanisms did not work at all, and still will, on occasion, cause me to overreact in high stress situations."—Aedan[k]

Voices of Support for Those Who Have Lost Both Parents, says, "Many times we feel powerless after a loss. Seeking support restores some of that power because you're making a conscious choice to reach for what you need."[10] According to the Coalition to Support Grieving Students, school professionals who aren't personally affected by the death are often the most ideal sources of support. They will better be able to attend to your needs while you are grieving.[11] If you have a favorite teacher or a coach you feel comfortable around and trust, try not to be afraid to talk to them, as they are all most likely willing to be there for you during your difficult time of need.

During that tough first month, you might start looking for positive ways to distract yourself to help you deal with everything you are feeling. Play a sport, sign up for a class at church, volunteer—you need to stay busy, but by doing positive and constructive tasks only. If you don't give yourself a positive outlet, you can accidentally find yourself going down a negative path. Stay busy doing healthy and constructive things, and surround yourself with positive people who have your best interest at heart.

Your First Birthday without Your Parent

Your parent has probably been to every single birthday party or dinner you have ever had in your life. He or she has most likely never missed your birthday, from the day you were born—that is, until this year. Suddenly when you look down the table where your parent has always sat for the last twelve years, or fifteen years, or even eighteen years, the chair is empty. And your day that is supposed to be happy suddenly turns into a gloomy one. This birthday is probably not going to be fun like it always has been because you miss your parent. Though your birthday has always been a day of celebration on your behalf, the first one without your parent is going to be a reality check, that you will never have your parent physically present at your birthday ever again.

Though it might be hard, remember to address your feelings on that first birthday. Cry, look at old photographs, watch old videos of you and your parent. You might even hold something that your parent gave you on a past birthday. Holding a special gift or keepsake can "evoke a sensory-laden memory of, and communion with," your parent, and give you a close sense of connection.[12] Celebrate just like you would on a typical birthday, but there is nothing wrong with celebrating their life as well. If your parent always used to bake you a cake on your

Creative Outlets

During the first month and beyond, many teens turn to creative outlets to help them cope with their parents' death. One website says that when young people "draw or color, words are not needed. There's a connection between the head, the heart, and the hand which helps them express many feelings that had previously been trapped inside. Creativity helps children put those emotions outside, so they can see their experience from a different perspective, making things clearer and giving them distance. Creativity gives children a sense of control and allows them to tell their story over and over again so they can let go and make sense of it. It is an important coping skill that can serve them for the rest of their lives."[I] Creative outlets you might want to try include playing a musical instrument, writing poetry, writing stories, drawing, pottery, sculpting, singing, recording music, graphic designing, building model airplanes or cars, playing video games, reading, woodworking, coloring (you are never too old to color!), painting, playing with Play-Doh, or playing with sand in a Zen garden (in this case a miniature garden filled with sand and rocks. The sand is raked to represent the natural movement of water, and the motion of raking the sand can be very relaxing and therapeutic).

Here's a unique creative exercise to try, compliments of What'sYourGrief.com:

Found Poems: A found poem is when you take existing text (from anywhere) and eliminate or rearrange words to make a poem.

Step One: Freewrite about your grief. You may want to choose to write about negative feelings like guilt and regret because in step two you get to cover those words up and turn them into something beautiful. Write for as long as you like, but you will probably want to write a page at the very least.

Step Two: Now experiment with removing or crossing out sections of your text. You can reread your text first and make a plan for the emotion or theme you want to convey in your found poem, or you can just dive in and keep the words and phrases that feel most pleasing. Don't worry about rules, form, or punctuation. You can use text of any length, but for your first try, it may be easiest to use a small amount of text.[m]

birthday, why not get the whole family over and bake a cake together to honor your parent? If your parent always took you to the same restaurant each year to celebrate your birthday, keep the tradition alive by making reservations again as if your parent were still here. By keeping traditions alive, you are keeping your parent's memory alive. In keeping your parent's memory alive, you also learn how to push forward in life, something your parent would most likely want you to do. You don't have to break traditions because he or she is no longer here. Your parent's memory can still be present if you let it.

No matter how you celebrate that first birthday, remember this: Your parent's life changed the day that you were born. You made a difference in his or her life! As you are now learning, life is short and can be over in a minute, with or without

"Children sometimes worry that they will forget the person who died, especially if they were quite young at the time of the death. Stories, pictures, and continued mention of the person who died can help children sustain their memory of the deceased. This reinforces their sense of having known and been known by this person."—Schonfeld and Quackenbush, authors of *The Grieving Student*[n]

"Going back to school after my mom passed away was very difficult because everyone knew what happened. My dad said I was very brave, and everyone showed their support by making us dinners, giving us cards, as well as their condolences. The headmaster of our school even had a grief counselor come in to spend time with our third-grade class since everyone knew my mom.

"After my mom died, my dad and I continued to go to grief counseling after the grief counselor visited my class at school. While I would join my support group for losing a parent, my dad would join his group for the surviving parents.

"At the time, I was the only person at my school who lost a parent. So, when my dad and I went to the grief counseling support group, we found other people who could relate to what we were feeling and going through. I actually looked forward to going each week. I didn't feel alone, and neither did my dad. My dad and I went together. I liked the joint counseling with my dad and that he was a part of my grief journey just like I was a part of his . . . and we still are."—Taylor°

warning. Your parent would want you to continue trying to live your life to the fullest. I know right now it seems impossible, but as time goes on, you will get better at coping as long as you address your feelings. "Grief changes over time, but for most of us, the death of someone we care about stays with us in some way throughout our lives. This is especially true for children. As they continue to develop and grow, they are able to bring more complex understanding to their experiences. As they revisit the death over time, it will have new meaning to them."[13]

"The first year of celebrations was definitely the hardest. The first birthday without him. The first Christmas. It was hard to feel much like celebrating in those days. I remember, though, wanting to really bless my mom and show her extra love during those days. My mom turned forty just a few months after his death, so I remember my brother and I trying to throw her a party. The first Christmas, I wanted to buy my mom a special gift (a watch) because the one she had had broken that year."—Julie[P]

Your Parent's First Birthday

Perhaps each year, you and your brother would make a banner for your mother on her birthday. Maybe you would then surprise her with a cake, and then you and the rest of the family would always end your mother's special day with dinner at her favorite restaurant. Except this year, you won't be able to see the look on her face when you guys surprise her with the banner or homemade cake. And then it hits you again—your mother will never open another birthday present from you.

Although celebrating won't be the same as it was before, there are things you can still do to celebrate your parent as if he or she were still here. You might still go to your mom's favorite restaurant in her honor, or leave presents at your father's gravesite. If you were going to surprise mom with a spa day package at the salon, why not grab the women in your family, or a few of your best girlfriends, and still book the spa day? If you were going to surprise dad with tickets to go see his favorite musician, why not still get the tickets and go with other loved ones? No, it won't bring your parent back, but you will be honoring and celebrating your parent as if he or she were still here. Remember, it's about keeping your parent's memory alive.

It Happened to Me: A Note from the Author

My mother is buried in another state, so her gravesite is not easily accessible. Each year, my family sends my mom flowers to her gravesite in California, and we always attach a note with all of our family member's names on it. This year, I also cooked my father's favorite meal, which was the same meal my mother always used to cook for my father on his birthday: ribs, mashed potatoes, and corn on the cob, topped off with his favorite dessert of lemon meringue pie.

So, there we were, gathered around our kitchen table, eating my dad's favorite meal and dessert that my mom used to cook for him; we listened to Italian music (my mother was Sicilian), talked about my mom, said an honorary speech in her memory, and ended the night with a very comforting grief movie for us, *Collateral Beauty* (which I highly recommend). At the end of the night, we all felt like we honored my mother in new ways, combined with old traditions we have done in the past. I think it is safe to say that we will do something similar for her birthday again next year.

The First Mother's/Father's Day without Your Parent

Perhaps you used to spend hours working on some special gift or planning a surprise party for Mother's Day or Father's Day. However, again, this is the year of firsts for you, and not having your parent happily open your handmade gift or not seeing the look on your parent's face when he or she walks through the door is going to sting. It is not going to sting a little either—the first year will sting a lot, especially if you worked hard to make your parent something or worked hard to plan something special, and your parent died before he or she could open it or experience it. Just because your parent is no longer physically here doesn't mean you can't still make your parent something or do something special to honor him or her. In fact, it can actually be very therapeutic for you and your family to continue the traditions. If you are not comfortable doing that just yet, you can make something for your surviving parent or caregiver instead. You can also make something special for someone else who is in your life who is helping support you during this difficult time for you and your family.

If you can keep an open mind, especially during your first year, you will most likely thank yourself later on in life. For one day, you will look back, and you will appreciate how strong you were during the first year and also how strong you became overall.

❗ Honoring Your Parent All Year Long

Though you may not be able to fulfill the traditions you once had with your parent—on Mother's Day, Father's Day, or any other holiday—you can still start new traditions with the remaining members of your family. There are even ways to incorporate your late parent into your current everyday life as if he or she were still here. You can write a letter to your parent, place the letter in a balloon, and let the balloon fly away, as if you were mailing your parent a letter to heaven. You and your family can visit his or her headstone at the cemetery—grab some lawn chairs, pack a lunch, and visit with one another by your parent's grave, as if you are eating lunch with your parent. "Honoring or remembering the person in some way, such as lighting a candle, saying a prayer, making a scrapbook, reviewing photographs, or telling a story may be helpful. Children should be allowed to express feelings about their loss and grief in their own way."[9]

> "The first Mother's Day after my mom's death was something I'll never forget. That day in class we were supposed to make crafts for our moms. I panicked and asked my teacher what I was supposed to do because my mom was gone, and she told me to just make it for my dad. Every Mother's Day following, my gifts were made out to my dad, and he was always happy to receive them."—McKenna[4]

The First Holiday Season without Your Parent

Most families really get into the holiday spirit and have lots of family traditions when it comes to Thanksgiving, Chanukah, Christmas, Kwanzaa, and New Year. I am not going to lie to you—the first holiday season without your parent will probably be hard, especially if you have already bought Christmas or Chanukah presents, and they are under the tree, wrapped and waiting to be opened. You will probably be upset when you look at that unopened present and acknowledge that you will never get to see the look on your parent's face when he or she opens your present. Be prepared for a not-so-jolly holiday season during the first year without your parent.

The trick to your first holiday season is to act as if your parent is still present. Set a place at the table for your parent, as if he or she is still going to eat your annual Thanksgiving turkey with the family. Put up your parent's stocking over the fireplace. Add a family picture with your parent in it for your Christmas card—he or she is not physically here anymore, but that does not mean he or she has to be emotionally or spiritually absent. Your parent is still a big part of your life, and he or she always will be. A parent has a strong and permanent bond with his or her children—a bond that can't even break because of death. So why not still talk

> "Mother's Day each year can be challenging especially at school since all of the classes typically do Mother's Day crafts and activities. For the first couple of years after my mother's death, Mother's Day at school was really uncomfortable for me. One year though, my 3rd grade teacher had me make a necklace to remember my mom instead of doing what the other kids were doing to celebrate Mother's Day. That made me feel comfortable when she suggested that to me."—Taylor[5]

One coping mechanism is to write notes to your late parent to tell him or her what you are doing in your everyday life. Placing your letter in a balloon and letting it fly away can be very therapeutic. *©iStock / Andreka*

to your parent? Write to him or her? Do the things you used to do with your parent? Keep this in mind during the holidays of the first year, and you might make it through a little more easily.

The First Anniversary of a Parent's Death

The first year will most likely go by really fast, and that can be a good thing as you try to adjust to all of the changes you will most likely be experiencing. A fast year means you probably kept busy, and hopefully did so with positive and constructive distractions. The end of the first year also means you have reached the first anniversary of your parent's death.

> "The first Christmas was the hardest, as she died three weeks before Christmas of 1993. It was very noticeable that she was not there that year for Christmas. My dad and the rest of our family did a good job trying to make Christmas a good one for us that year, but my mother was the one who made Christmas what it was for us. It wasn't the same without her there."—Mike[t]

The first death anniversary will likely be a unique experience. You have missed your parent throughout the year and have probably had to adjust to numerous changes, but you might also realize that you accomplished something big: you just survived your first year without your parent. Although it may have been extremely difficult and painful, you just showed yourself that you are a strong individual.

I want you to know something, however. You might have been doing OK for the past few months, but be prepared that the death anniversary might trigger some strong emotions for you. It might be a good day to plan something with close friends or loved ones to help you get through it. Everyone reacts differently, so you may want to go out and do something fun, or curl up on the couch and watch parent-child movies. Only you know what you truly need, so please take care of yourself.

You Will Grow in Your First Year

Losing a parent at a young age can fast-track your growing-up process. While your friends might be worried whether they have enough time to watch their favorite TV show tonight, you might have to make dinner for your younger sister. Most likely, your priorities will change, needs will change, wants will change, and

> "My dad passed away a few weeks before Christmas, on 12/7/16 to be exact. Since this was our first Christmas without him, it was really different and really noticeable this year. The schedule changed for my sister and I this year, as normally we would spend time with my dad on Christmas. Now, we live full time with my mom and stepdad, so Christmas wasn't our normal everyday routine this year."—Chase[u]

Processing the Death of a Parent

Processing the loss of your parent is not an easy task. It is a "painful process. There is nothing that anyone—family member, teacher, therapist—can say or do that will take away the pain or make the loss less powerful."[v] It is not a quick process either. "Children who have lost a family member or friend will feel the effects strongly for some time. The trajectory of grief is different for every child, and how this influences school and family life will also be different."[w]

Experts also say that "a child generally sustains more losses than an adult when a parent is lost. A child not only loses the loved one, but also the provider of nurturance." A parent supplies support and help that children need for "continued psychological growth and development. Thus, the work of mourning is greater for a child than an adult who loses a parent, and the child has fewer inner resources with which to cope" (Cohen, Phyllis, K. Mark Sossin, and Richard Ruth. *Healing after Parent Loss in Childhood and Adolescence: Therapeutic Interventions and Theoretical Considerations.* Lanham, MD: Rowman & Littlefield, 2014, page 49). This all means that if you're really struggling with your parent's death, there's a reason for it; it's completely normal. It will take some time to work through this grieving process.

According to psychologist J. W. Worden and the Harvard Child Bereavement Study, children have to accomplish four mourning "tasks" to process the death of a parent:

1. "They must accept the reality of the parent's death.
2. They must experience the grieving and emotional pain of the loss.
3. They must adjust to the world in which the deceased is no longer there.
4. They must find ways to memorialize the deceased, and relocate the lost parent within his or her life in a different way."[x]

If you can keep these four tasks in the back of your mind, you can use them as a guide for coping with and processing the death of your parent.

"Probably for me, one of the biggest changes was how other children treated me. There were many acquaintances that didn't know how to relate to me. The experience felt awkward and would isolate me. Not everyone, for sure, but I did find that people who had dealt with a death of a grandparent or other loved one were much more compassionate during the early years. I was only in third grade when my dad died, so that is a lot for any child to process or know how to deal with."—Julie[y]

your overall life will change. Losing your parent will most likely teach you a lot more about the real world and about yourself.

Your Parent's Death Can Alter Your Behavior

Before your parent(s) died, you might have been a straight A student who got along with everyone. Suddenly, after he or she passed away, your grades slipped and you aren't able to get along with anyone, even your teacher. This is completely normal. The authors of *The Grieving Student* write, "Children who are grieving sometimes act in ways that challenge teachers. They are experiencing many powerful emotions. They may express anger, act selfishly, or say things that are hurtful to other students. They might break or carelessly lose things. They might speak insolently to school staff."[14] Behavior changes can happen to you as a result of how you are dealing with your parent's death. A study in Sweden was done to

"It has only been about 60 days after my father passed away, but I have already learned to really put things into perspective a lot better. My dad wanted to be a message to people about drugs and alcohol. This has made me be more aware about life.

"None of my friends have lost their parents, so I don't really get a chance to talk to my friends about how I am feeling. I feel like if I tried to talk to them about how I am feeling about his loss, they just wouldn't understand.

"I don't like attention, so I don't really like to bring up the loss to anyone, especially at school. My school has been really supportive throughout all of this."—Chase[z]

"When he died, things in my life got really overwhelming. Everything happened so fast. He died the night before, and the next day everyone started planning the funeral, talked about where to spread his ashes—there was no time to be sad. At the funeral itself, I was numb. I was sad, but I didn't cry at all. At the time, I thought it was bad that I didn't cry at my own father's funeral. His death was so sudden and shocking, that it took a while to really sink in for me.

"Since my dad's death, my grades have slipped a little. Sometimes I need to leave class for a few minutes to regroup, and when I do that I miss lessons, especially in Spanish. My dad was fluent in Spanish, and it's hard because I already need help with a Spanish project, and now my dad's not here to help me anymore.

"With all of these feelings, it is both a blessing and a curse. It is a curse because I am feeling the way that I am, but it is also a blessing because I can use how I am feeling to help others."—Ella[aa]

determine what can happen from an academic standpoint once a parent is lost: "The extensive study from Sweden finds that after a parent's death, kids tend to struggle with lower grades and even failure in school. If the tragedy was caused by something external—such as accidents, violence or suicide—the impact seems to be even more pronounced."[15] It is important to talk to someone—whether a counselor, teacher, friend, or family member—immediately after your parent dies to try to ensure you stay on a healthy, positive path while you are trying to cope.

What Is Counseling and Should I Go?

You have probably heard of counseling before, but maybe you are not familiar with what it is.

Counseling is defined as assistance and guidance in resolving personal, social, or psychological problems and difficulties, especially by a professional; it is similar to therapy, which is defined as treatment intended to heal or relieve.

A lot of people, especially teens your age, are afraid of counseling. If you have never gone to counseling, it is understandable why you might be scared or nervous about going. Many people get nervous when they don't know what to expect. You might be scared to talk to someone you don't really know. Sometimes, however, it can be easier to share our feelings when we talk to someone new, like a professional counselor.

"I struggled with feelings of insecurity and fear a lot in the first couple of years. This was pre-cell phone years, so any time my mom was late coming home, I was afraid she had died too and wouldn't be coming home. I think my greatest fears during this time were becoming an orphan. I picture myself as a young child sitting on the porch looking for my mom's car to come up the road.

"I also struggled with depression/attention-getting behaviors. I didn't want to do basic self-care activities (like wash my hair, wash my face, etc.). I ended up cutting off my long hair into a boyish cut. To get attention—I wanted glasses and purposely tried to fail the eye exam twice. I wanted an arm cast, and would frequently amplify my falls/injuries in the first year or so trying to get attention.

"Because of these behaviors in the first year, I worked with a counselor to talk about my feelings and work out why I was doing the things I was doing. Thankfully, we were able to work through them and express the hurt I was feeling and channel it into more productive avenues."—Julie[bb]

The goal of counseling is exactly what the definition tells us—to provide guidance and assistance to get through something we are struggling with. In this case, you might be struggling with dealing with the death of your parent. You are not alone in this; many teens struggle with this, especially at first. There is nothing wrong with you if your surviving parent or caregiver takes you to see a counselor. In fact, in many cases, counseling can be very helpful. It can set up a game plan for how you can cope in a healthy and positive way. It can also ensure that you are getting the support *you* need, in case your surviving family members cannot tend to your needs because they are trying to tend to their own needs while grieving.

"I had refused to get counseling initially, and was eventually forced into it. I lied for the first couple of months, because I felt like it was a waste of my time, and that I should try and end it as soon as possible. Starting around my ninth grade year, I believe, I went to my aunt, and felt that I actually wanted to take counseling. Ironically, the initial reason was my turmoil over the end of a relationship, rather than my parents, but it evolved beyond the first problem, and delved more into the lasting effects of my parents' deaths."—Aedan[cc]

There are many different types of counselors offering many different counseling styles. However, there are many similarities. On average, here's what you can expect: On the first day, you will meet the counselor. In some cases, you might have the option to go by yourself, or, if you are not comfortable going alone, your surviving parent or caregiver can go into the session with you until you are ready to go on your own. Your counselor will introduce himself or herself and try to get to know you; think of it as a conversation with a close friend or family member. But, remember why you are there. You are there to work through your grief and develop healthy coping mechanisms to guide you in your life post-parental

Identifying If You Are Having Trouble Coping

Here are some signs that might indicate you are having trouble coping with your loss:

- A sharp drop in grades or other problems at school
- Refusing to go to school or refusing to participate in activities you used to enjoy
- Trouble eating, sleeping, or concentrating
- Physical problems for which doctors can find no medical cause
- Never or rarely talking about the person who died
- Withdrawing from friends and family members
- Only feeling safe when people are around
- Going back to behavior that you had outgrown (such as clinging or bed-wetting)
- Getting into trouble with the police for stealing, vandalism, or other acting out or attention-seeking behavior
- Developing anxieties or phobias (such as excessive hand washing or an intense fear of becoming separated from the surviving parent)
- Abusing alcohol or drugs
- Frequent angry or emotional outbursts or tantrums
- Continual fear of dying or of becoming sick or of others dying or becoming sick

Have you been experiencing any of these things lately? If so, reach out to an adult for support. Please know that there is nothing wrong with you if you are experiencing some of these behaviors. "Many parentally-bereaved children experience anger, anxiety, apathy, confusion, dysphoria [a state of unease or generalized dissatisfaction with life], guilt, and frustration for a year or more after their loss." Many young people also experience "pains, changes in energy, sleep, and appetite, as well as lost prior masteries. Behaviorally, they may withdraw, act out, or regress."[dd] If your signs have been persisting for more than a few weeks, talk to a professional such as a pediatrician or therapist, who can help you decide what to do next.[ee]

death. So, expect the counselor to ask questions regarding your late parent, your surviving parent, your siblings, how you are feeling, and so on. The key is to be completely honest in your responses. If you don't feel comfortable answering one of the counselor's questions, let your counselor know that you would like to come back to that question later. Or you can say that you are not ready to talk about certain subjects yet, but you are comfortable writing about them instead. In the book *Healing after Parent Loss in Childhood and Adolescence*, the authors write, "When a teenager is in therapy, the therapist and teen find a way to interact with a balance of verbal communicating, nonverbal communicating, and not communicating about the loss. As that way of interacting becomes comfortable for the teenager, there is a greater chance to do the work of mourning."[16] However you choose to communicate, be open and honest so your counselor can guide you in the best way possible for *you*.

Each time you visit your counselor, it is called a session. Your sessions might take place weekly, monthly, or every three months—whatever your counselor, and your surviving parent, think is best to get you on a positive coping track. And that's basically what counseling is. You will get to know your counselor more and more during each session, and you will work as a team to try and get you on track to cope in a positive way. It's OK to cry, get mad, get really sad, or even laugh while in your sessions. Be as open as you comfortably can be, know that the counselor is there to help you, and be honest with what you are feeling.

Complicated Mourning

When your parent died, you probably witnessed many different emotions not just within yourself, but in your family members as well. Maybe your surviving

"On the day that my father died, my father's girlfriend's daughter showed up at my house, and said there was an accident and that my dad was at the hospital, but the paramedics said he would be fine. I was fifteen years old. As I was in the back seat of the car around 3:00 a.m., I was wondering what the hell was going on.

"We arrived at the hospital, and the receptionist had me fill out an emergency contact form for my dad. I figured he was all right. A moment later, a doctor in a white lab coat and two women on each side of him said, "Is this his family?" We said *yes*. He replied by saying, "I'm sorry to say, but your dad has passed away." His girlfriend fell to the floor crying hysterically. I couldn't believe it. I felt frozen. Stuck. They asked if we wanted to see him. Of course, we said *yes*. I remember going into a room with very bright lights, and saw him lying there in a metal gurney with just a pair of Hawaiian style shorts, and his black curly hair was sweaty. He still had the breathing tube down his throat and I will never forget the tear he still had in his eye. I just looked at him in disbelief. My world as I knew it had changed. What I had experienced was a living hell.

"After my dad's death, I was numb and shocked. The first week I stayed with several family members, and got passed around between each one of their homes. My mother was out of the state taking care of my sick grandmother and didn't make it down to the services.

"My parents had been split up since I was two years old. I was spiraling out of control. I ended up moving to Kansas to be with my mom. She was waiting at the airport looking for me. She didn't recognize me because I had shaved my head after settling in. I had this overwhelming sadness.

"I had started walking around downtown, and I met some friends. Months after, I was very angry and afraid. My grandmother had passed away six months after my dad. I went over the edge. I started to go out a lot, smoked pot, and realized drinking seemed to take the edge off of things. It made me numb and not want to think about it all.

"As time went by, a year had passed and suddenly I was sixteen years old. I was more angry at that time. I had developed anxiety and I thought I was going to die all of the time. Fear was taking over and I couldn't even sleep at night if there was not a night light on. I continuously kept on getting into trouble as a teen. I had to finish school later on because I dropped out of high school.

"When I got my GED, I was sad that my dad couldn't see or know I graduated, and as the years passed by I kind of got used to him not being around. I think that I was afraid to get close to people for a long time because I couldn't trust that they would stay around."—Tiffany[ff]

parent cried nonstop for a few days or maybe he or she was extremely quiet. Maybe your uncle dealt with the loss of your parent in an angry way, or perhaps your sibling just kept to his or her room. Everyone goes through grief differently. Most will progress and transition through from one stage to the next. You will probably notice the emotions are strong at first and may fluctuate later on. Sometimes, you may notice that someone is stuck in a certain stage of grieving. This is known as complicated mourning: "Instead of gradual improvement, the situation may become increasingly difficult. That is, the feeling of positive movement—of change or progress—is still absent months after the death. Individuals may also demonstrate unusual or particularly severe reactions, such as intense guilt. They may be unable to draw on inner resources or external support. They cannot adjust to the reality of life without their loved one."[17] If you are experiencing any of this, please reach out to an adult immediately for help and support.

What to Take Away from the First Year

Your first year will probably be very difficult, possibly the hardest year of your life so far. You will likely learn more about yourself during those twelve months than you have at any point before this. You will learn a lot about your strengths and weaknesses, the ways that you successfully and not-so-successfully cope with your grief. You might find that your group of friends changes during the first year, and you might find different hobbies and interests. This is all normal.

As you go through the year, you will probably experience a wide variety of grief triggers: "listening to a song, hearing a piece of information on the news, certain smells and sounds, special occasions like birthdays, holidays, Mother's and Father's Day, graduations, and lost opportunities such as recitals, sporting activities, father-daughter dance, and prom"[18]—all of these things and more have the potential of sending you into profound sadness. But that's OK. You will learn to recognize grief triggers for what they are, and know that you can get through them.

Experiencing the death of a parent is not something that every person goes through, so people around you may not know what to say to you. They may try to comfort you in ways that don't work. During the first year, you will start to learn what works for you and what doesn't in terms of support, comfort, positive coping mechanisms, and more. Remember: grieving is a process. You will probably have good days and bad days. You will likely find that certain events and situations set you off that you didn't think would. You might think you can handle going on a fishing trip with your buddy and his father, only to realize how incredibly upset you suddenly feel when you realize your dad can't be there this year. Or you might rejoin your volleyball team thinking you are done grieving, only to break down the moment you see the team mom bring everyone snacks on the day that it was supposed to be your mom's turn. You might have a big test that six months earlier you would have aced, but now you find yourself emotionally distracted and unable to focus and as a result, you end up failing. Many things will happen during your first year—you will be faced with changes, new emotions, new questions. Know that it is OK to cry, it's OK to have hard days, it's OK to miss him or her. It's OK. This is how the first year will most likely be for teens who just experienced parental death. You will probably make mistakes, but try not to be too hard on yourself. It's a learning process; you've never had to navigate life without the support and guidance of your late parent. It takes time and practice, so be patient with yourself.

You might be afraid that as each day, week, month, and year go by, you will grow further and further away from your late parent. However, there's another way to look at it. Have a glass-is-half-full attitude and realize that as each day goes by, you are slowly moving forward with your life.

You are also becoming a stronger person. After you survive the first year, you will probably get a little bit better at dealing with all of the milestones the next year—birthdays, anniversaries, holidays, and so on. You will never fully get over your parent's death. In fact, you will re-experience the death of your parent in different ways as you get older. Authors Schonfeld and Quackenbush explain that "feelings of loss are re-experienced in many ways as children grow, mature, and gain new insights. Children commonly have these experiences during the following: holidays, transitions to a new grade or school, special events, awards, and graduations, and rites of passage."[19] Each year, you will most likely learn more about yourself and begin to acknowledge your strength. The goal is to get progressively better at using coping mechanisms. One day, you may get so good at it that you can give back to other parentless teens to help them along their coping journey.

CAUSE OF DEATH

Many things in this life are out of our control. Events happen that cannot be explained or understood, and they may leave you with lots of unanswered questions. That's just how it is. Accepting that there are going to be unexplainable events doesn't make it any easier when tragedy strikes, but it can emotionally prepare you to cope with a devastating loss like the death of a parent.

There Is No Harder or Easier Way to Lose a Parent

Some teens who suddenly lost their parent to illness think that they have it harder than those who lost their parent to suicide or a car accident. Those who lost their parent to an unexpected crime might think that their case takes the cake as the

Losing a parent to a lingering illness can be just as traumatic as losing one suddenly. ©iStock / KatarzynaBialasiewicz

hardest type of loss. The truth is that no matter how you lost your parent, it's hard; you now have to proceed through life without your mom or dad.

To help you understand what other parentless teens have gone through, here's a brief look at the most common types of parent loss.

Parent Loss: Disease

Thankfully, medicine has advanced since ancient times, yet that doesn't guarantee a cure for every single disease. Nowadays, we have to deal with diseases that weren't even heard of during ancient times. Men and women are affected about equally by two diseases in particular: cancer and heart disease. Most parent deaths by disease result from one of these two illnesses.

It Happened to Me: A Note from the Author

As my mother was nearing the end of her life, I witnessed things a child should not have to witness. Some of the things I saw still haunt me to this day. Looking back and thinking about everything my mother went through, my heart breaks because I realize she suffered, especially toward the end. Bless my mother's heart, she was still parenting me up until her very last day. I will never forget her strength or courage.

While my mother was sick and before she died, I constantly had nightmares. In one dream, my whole house filled up with water, and everyone made it out safely except my mom. In another reoccurring dream, a certain tea kettle—the one my mother always used to boil hot water and make us Cream of Wheat— started a fire on the stove, and again, everyone else made it out alive except for her. I would wake up terrified, and my mother would always be halfway down the hallway toward my room by the time I realized I just had a nightmare. Those last few months of her life when I had those nightmares, as sick as she was, my mother would always crawl into bed with me to comfort me, until I calmed down and fell asleep.

After my mom passed away, the dreams stopped, and I have been begging God to allow me to have one dream with her ever since—just one, where maybe I can talk to her about how my life is going. Twenty-four years later, I am still not giving up hope. I still pray for at least just one more dream with her, but this time it would be a nice mother-daughter visit, instead of the dreams I had before.

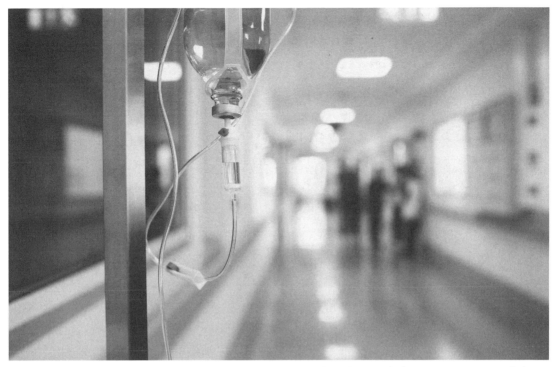

Hospitals can haunt teens when the last memories they have of their parents are of them sick or dying. ©iStock / sudok1

"With my dad, he had always been strong and healthy (as far as we knew at least, he never went to the doctor). He worked long days (ten to twelve hours) to provide a good life for me, and later on, my son as well. In early 2012 (I was twenty-two, my son was three), he began experiencing urinary problems. I kept urging him to go to the doctor, seeing his symptoms escalate from what seemed like a UTI to a bladder infection, but he refused. When he finally went to the emergency room, they found that his kidneys were near failure and his blood pressure was extremely high. They placed stents in his kidneys and sent him home with instructions for setting up at home dialysis and a special diet. He did not follow those instructions, as much as I tried to make him, but because they had sent him home, I felt that it was hopeful it could be treated and he would improve. Not very long after coming home from the hospital, I woke up one weekend morning and my dad was not up yet, which was very unusual for him. I brushed off the uneasy feeling in the pit of my stomach and pushed it to the back of my mind while my friend and I (who had spent the night) worked on baking for a co-worker's baby shower we were helping with that afternoon. As it grew later into the morning, I couldn't stifle the nagging feeling in my gut and decided to check on my dad in his room. I had been avoiding doing so all morning because I think subconsciously, I knew something was wrong, but didn't want to face it. When I opened his bedroom door after he did not respond to me knocking, I immediately saw him kneeled down on the floor and quickly closed the door because my son was right behind me, eager to say good morning to his Papa. At that moment, I felt like I went into a state of shock and survival mode. I stayed composed, scooped up my son, took him to my friend in my bedroom at the back of the house and asked her to keep him distracted in the bedroom until I came back in. I went back into my dad's bedroom and called 911, telling them that my dad was deceased. Then, I called my ex-boyfriend's parents who I was close to and who lived nearby and asked them to please come get my son before the ambulance and medical examiner arrived at our house because I did not want my son to be alarmed. They came to pick him up, I told him he was going to go play at their house for a little while, and they took him to get ice cream while I stayed to handle everything. After he left, I told my friend was what going on, I asked her to leave, and I waited for authorities to arrive. The images of finding him next to his bed and watching him be carried out of the house in a black bag are burned into my memory and I still often have flashbacks of that day."— Kaylene[a]

Parent loss by disease often includes another factor: your parent might have been sick for some time leading up to his or her final day. This means your parent's sickness affected you before he or she died, and now you are dealing with the aftermath. The authors of *Healing after Parent Loss in Childhood and Adolescence* write, "If the child knows that the parent is dying, there is anticipatory dread, fear, anger, and sorrow, depending on the circumstances. After the death, there can be a period of numbing and denial, but then ache, loneliness, blame, sadness, guilt, and some chaos as family life changes."[1] Watching your parent become sick and suffer can be harder or just as hard as dealing with the aftermath of their death.

There is no easy way to watch your parent get progressively sick, knowing that the disease has already taken over him or her. Surviving children might be afraid that they too will contract whatever disease the late parent had. If you are

"With my mom, she had been fighting the cancer for years and had been very ill in the hospital for weeks, if not months. She was in a coma in the ICU. She had developed a staph infection in the hospital and her body was too weak to fight it. I was fifteen years old (in 2005), and had been her primary caregiver for years, so I had witnessed the decline of her health. I knew it was coming and had time to mentally prepare myself. I did not want to remember her as the frail, unresponsive woman in the hospital bed hooked to machines, so when I felt convinced that she was not going to improve, I chose to stop going to the hospital, so I was not there when she passed. My aunt called me to tell me when she was gone. I remember feeling numb, as I had in a way already been processing the feelings of losing her for quite some time."—Kaylene[b]

concerned that you will end up with the same disease, go see your doctor; it might give you some peace of mind.

Some young people experience guilt after a sick parent dies. You might feel guilty that your parent died but you are still alive; this is called survivor's guilt. Or maybe while watching your parent suffer, you thought it might be better for him or her to die and be relieved of that physical and emotional pain. Now that

"I remember my mother's passing like it was yesterday. I was eleven years old. My mother was in a hospice center. My mom was sleeping all of the time. I gave her a hug and a kiss and told her I would see her tomorrow not knowing it would be the last goodbye I gave her. I remember staying the night at my friend's house and playing in her room. Celine Dion's 'My Heart Will Go On' song came on the radio, and I immediately felt my heart break and couldn't stop crying. I knew something was wrong. I felt it. The next morning my friend's mom took me and my brother home where we met our dad in the driveway. He knelt down and hugged us both. That's when we found out she had passed away while we were at our friend's house. I remember crying . . . a lot. I didn't want to believe it. It didn't feel real to me, but it was."—Lindsay[c]

"My mom had developed throat cancer and at that point had been living in the city already. She started radiation and chemo—the outlook was good, or should have been. Clearly, this was a result of years of smoking, yet she continued to smoke as she went through treatments, which was how she coped. It was difficult to watch, even more so when I myself had attempted to quit smoking in the winter and was struggling, but successful. Also, because of the location of the cancer, she'd had a feeding tube installed in her tummy, which is where she was supposed to feed herself. She resisted this as well, and instead counted on a liquid diet of coffee, hot chocolate, and those Ensure drinks that were meant to be vitamin supplements for older people. She was losing too much weight, and getting so small, and insisted it was just the cancer doing it, not because she wasn't feeding herself. One afternoon in March, the 28th to be exact, she called me with such excitement in her voice. The doctor had called to say that the treatments had worked—the cancer was GONE, and all that was left was a tiny bump that they would inspect to see if it would be necessary to surgically remove it (for comfort purposes) or not. She was given the 'okay' to eat again to her comfort level, and her roommates had chips and guacamole, and she was in heaven with being able to eat again. She was already making plans to start cooking the next day—we were so happy! I left the house to go to work and promised I'd call when I woke up the next day. She died that night, in her sleep. She had just gotten too little, and I believe the excitement got to her heart and it was too much for her. It was peaceful, but so unexpected and sudden and just so—cruel?"—Stacy[d]

your parent is gone, you might feel guilty for having those thoughts.[2] Some young people experience such strong guilt and emotional distress that they want to harm themselves: "Self-reported self-injury, a manifestation of severe psychological distress, was twice as common in youths (aged eighteen to twenty-six) who, as teenagers, lost a parent to cancer as compared with their non-bereaved peers even when controlling for well-known risk factors."[3] If you are having an extremely difficult time trying to cope with the death, if you feel guilty for being a survivor, if you are severely depressed, or if you feel like you want to harm yourself, reach out to an adult or counselor immediately.

"In January of 2009, when I was four years old and in preschool, my mother was diagnosed with breast cancer. My mom wanted to be with me as long as possible, so she chose an aggressive treatment plan which included surgery and five rounds of chemotherapy. She lost her hair, but proudly wore fashionable head gear as the class Mom when I started kindergarten in August 2009. She also started a Girl Scout troop for me and my friends that year. The second half of 2009 her doctors said she was cancer free. That fall, she had breast reconstruction surgery which was hard on my mother. My mom's attitude was remarkably upbeat and positive throughout and everyone admired her for it. We thought everything was okay.

"When I was seven years old and in second grade, my mother was then diagnosed with leukemia in January 2012. My mom was fifty-one when she died on December 10, 2012, two weeks before Christmas. I was eight and in third grade when she passed. During that year, my mom was in the hospital most, but not all, of the time. Because of concerns for a weakened immune system, leukemia chemotherapy required that she be in the hospital three weeks of each month through May. Despite the chemo treatments, there were serious complications that started in July and by October we knew that she probably would not survive much longer. The doctors told us that the leukemia was more than likely caused by the chemotherapy treatment she received from her breast cancer.

"During her last year, she was hospitalized most of the time. Her death was not sudden, as her last year was a year of illness and difficulties relating to it. I had a year of my mother being gone most of the time before she actually was gone in the end—a gradual transition that led up to her death— a gradual one-year adjustment.

"During the hospitalized time in 2012, I would visit my mom in her hospital room at least twice a week, working on homework, girl scout projects and crafts, and having lunch or dinner. This was very challenging, as I wanted to be with my mom and, as important, I knew my mom wanted to be with me; but I was scared by the hospital, in general, and the oncology ward in particular.

Seeing the other very sick patients and my mom with tubes hooked up and looking unhealthy was extremely difficult. My dad and I cried every time we left the hospital, for many reasons. Not until the last ten days or so in December, when my mom was moved to the intensive care unit, was I no longer 'allowed' to visit my mom. We were sleeping when my family member called at about two o'clock a.m. to let us know 'it was over.' We cried for the rest of the night.

"My mother was only fifty-one when she died. She was cremated, and we have her urn in our home along with a picture of her and other various mementos to help keep her memory alive."—Taylor[e]

"I remember her death like it was yesterday. My dad came to my room and I remember right when he opened the door I looked at the clock and it was 6:30 a.m. Although I had just woken up, I was very alert because I knew something had happened, but I didn't know exactly what happened. My dad, while holding back his tears, said three words that would change my life forever and they were, *Mom has died* (my mom slept downstairs in a hospital bed at our house and we had hospice care taking care of her, plus it allowed my brother and I to see her all the time). So, right as I heard the news, I rushed downstairs to see my mother dead. I came to find my grandmother, grandfather, brother, and dad crying, and for some reason I did not cry when I first saw my mother dead. I knew what death was, but I never had experienced it in my family prior to my mom's death.

Being the Catholic family we are, a deacon came over and we prayed around my mom. I believe some neighbors came over and they were all in tears as well. Then it came time for the people from the mortuary to take my mother's body. I remember someone telling my brother and I to go upstairs and in that moment, they took my mother away and took her body to the local mortuary. That's all I remember from that day."—Adriana[f]

"My dad was always sick. Well, that's not necessarily true. But, he was sick for as long as I was capable of making memories. My dad made some bad decisions when he was young and wild, and he had a virus hiding in his body that was causing him serious damage. Compounded with a drinking problem, and you had the perfect storm. All of this was unknown to little four-year-old me. I just remember the murder scene that the bathroom looked like when he got an esophageal bleed and his blood couldn't clot. All that red splattered on the white porcelain. That's when we found out he was sick. I remember leaving him at the hospital for an overnight stay, and I couldn't understand why daddy wasn't coming home with us. That's when the diagnosis was dropped. My dad had Hepatitis C, and compounded with the drinking problem, his liver was severely damaged.

"We managed as best we could. My dad quit drinking and was put on the transplant list. My dad eventually could not work and my mom became the sole provider for our home. Having a SAHD (stay-at-home dad) wasn't very common, but my dad was great at it. He clipped coupons and made dinner, and took me shopping for shoes and school supplies. He also was the first person I went to after a friendship fell apart or a boy broke my heart. We were a team. My parents separated sometime when I was in the eighth grade, and my mom moved out. We stayed as close to a family as we could. As I got older, his condition slowly got worse. I became more self-reliant, and took on some of the chores. Once I got my driver's license, I would take my dad to doctor's appointments, pick up my brother from his friend's house, or grab some groceries on my way home from school. My dad got to see me graduate from high school and see my acceptance to ASU. I'm so thankful for that. I remember a conversation my dad and I had about a wedding and the topic changed to my hypothetical wedding in the distant future. He said he didn't think he would be able to walk me down the aisle. I don't remember my exact response, but I was dismissive and told him he was being silly.

"One day, my dad asked me to take him to the hospital for a routine test. It required an overnight stay. I told him I loved him and gave him a kiss on the cheek. That was the last time I saw him coherent. My dad had a bowel obstruction and his body was poisoning itself. They couldn't operate because he couldn't clot, and he wouldn't survive the surgery anyway. His overnight stay turned into a week, and I took my little brother and we visited him. He had lucid moments where he recognized us and made silly jokes and called us by our nicknames. This is where the brain does funny things to one's memory. I can't recall an exact timeline or specific details. Maybe it's an act of self-preservation to reduce the amount of trauma, I'm not sure. My dad was in a coma and on life-support. Family came in surprisingly fast to visit, and I remember being irrationally angry that they suddenly found the time to visit. Why now? The hours in the special ICU family waiting room stretched and became one long day. The doctors pulled my mom and brother and I into a break room to tell us to say goodbye. He hadn't wanted to be on life support, and his body was in full system failure. He didn't look the same. With all those tubes and machines attached to him, he didn't look like my dad. I kissed his forehead and held his hand, and I promised him I'd take care of my brother and told him he could let go. I don't remember how I got home. I called my best friend and she broke every traffic law to get to me in record time. She held me in my bed while I cried and eventually passed out from exhaustion. The next morning, we were running late. My mom and my uncle had gone ahead to the hospital. My friend and I were in the elevator on the way to his room when my mom called and told me he was gone. They had taken him off life support and I wasn't there. As an adult, I understand why my mom chose to do it without me present. As a teenager/young adult, I was livid and devastated. I finally worked up the courage to go see him. The thing that struck me the most was that he looked more like my dad than he had in a while. He looked peaceful in all the quiet and without all those machines. I smooched his forehead and held his hand. Leaving that room and going on with life without him was one of the most difficult things I've ever experienced. It felt like a betrayal to walk away."—Christina[9]

AIDS

In the 1980s and '90s, a new disease surfaced that doctors didn't know how to treat. It was called Acquired Immunodeficiency Syndrome, better known as AIDS. This disease is caused by the human immunodeficiency virus, better known as HIV. People can contract HIV through sexual contact with someone who is infected, by sharing drug needles with someone who has HIV, and through contact with infected blood—whether by blood transfusion or during childbirth.

Not everyone who has HIV gets AIDS, and not everyone who has HIV or AIDS dies. Since the 1980s and '90s, many advances in medicine have been made to provide medications for those living with HIV and AIDS to help prolong their lifespan and quality of life. Unfortunately, when this disease first surfaced, millions of people lost their lives, as there was no medicine to cure them or reduce the symptoms, pain, or long-term effects that occurred.

According to the US AIDS website, "HIV and AIDS have exacted a terrible toll on children and their families. During the 30 years of the global HIV epidemic, an estimated 17 million children lost one or both parents due to AIDS.[h] Children who have lost one or both parents to AIDS are widely known as AIDS orphans. According to the National Resource Center for Family-Centered Practice and Permanency Planning, "Children who have lost parents to AIDS, unlike those whose mothers have died from any other disease, have often been labeled as 'AIDS orphans' due to the lack of adequate plans or support systems in place for the care of these children in the event of a parent's death."[i]

Although medical advances have been progressively made over the last few decades of this epidemic, the world has forgotten that AIDS orphans are still out there, in need of help. Some of you reading this book might be considered AIDS orphans. You might have noticed that you are having a stronger reaction to how your parent died compared to your friend who lost a parent to an accident or other type of illness. "Bereavement factors differ for different populations. Death from AIDS is often accompanied with trauma as these losses cannot be openly acknowledged and socially validated. The dominant feeling of shame attached to these losses complicates the grief process and compounds reactions of guilt and anger in bereaved survivors especially in light of the AIDS."[j] If you are in need of support, please reach out to a trusted adult, or a counselor.

"On the second day of January, my dad went out running (as he did every morning), leaving a note for my brother and I on the kitchen table that he was running to the barbers to get his hair cut and would be back by nine o' clock. I was never much of a morning person and liked to sleep in, so I was actually still in bed when I heard the phone ringing in the kitchen. My brother rushed into my room yelling, 'Julie, Julie, get up. Dad's in the hospital.'

"I jumped out of bed, and my brother (Ryan) helped me pull out all the curlers that were in my hair. Hastily I got dressed and ran to the front door to wait for our ride. The superintendent of the high school, where my dad was an assistant principal, picked us up and drove us to the hospital. We waited in a room silently until my mom, who was a med-tech and was working that morning at the same hospital, came into the room. She hugged both of us and told us, 'Kids, dad has gone home to be with the Lord.'

"Beyond shocked. Tears flowed rapidly. I felt numb. He was only forty-two and was healthy and athletic. How could that happen to him? I remember how strong my mom was for us. I remember her holding us and praying over us and assuring us that we were going to be okay. She asked if we wanted to go see my dad to say goodbye and explained that he looked a bit bruised and different. I declined, but my brother left with my mom to see my dad's body. I felt guilty that I didn't go then to say goodbye. Later, my mom told us more of what happened. My dad had 90 percent blockage in two of his coronary arteries, so while he was running, he had a heart attack and fell, hitting his head on a tree. Some stranger noticed him outside of her house and called 911. He was taken to the hospital where they unsuccessfully tried to resuscitate him."— Julie[k]

"I remember when I found out my dad went into the hospital. I was in shock and felt like the world had stopped, but I still believed he would be fine. I remember it was a hot sunny day and I was sitting on campus waiting for my boyfriend to pick me up to go to the hospital, and I felt so distant from all the activity around me. The day my dad died was a week and a half after we realized there was very little chance he would survive, and we took him off the ventilator. We had been told that he would be able to breathe on his own for a while, but we got the call from hospice early the next morning. I remember going there right away and spending the day in the room with him while we called people and arranged the funeral. I remember also how our rabbi came to be with us. It was extremely surreal. I remember giving my dad one last hug before we had to let him go."—Beth[1]

Parent Loss: War, Law Enforcement, First Responders

Thousands of parents have left their hometowns and their families to fight for their city, country, and community. It is a very noble action, to potentially risk one's life in this way. Sometimes parents are gone for twelve-hour shifts, for four-day shifts, or for two to three years at a time. If your parent lost his or her life while fighting a war, patrolling the streets, fighting a fire, whether local or overseas, know that your parent made the ultimate sacrifice—not just for you, your surviving parent, and your siblings, but also for your country and community. This is something you can be proud of, even though losing your parent is still hard.

When parents are lost to war or in the line of duty, surviving children sometimes experience post-traumatic stress disorder (PTSD), anxiety disorders, and other disruptions in neuropsychological functioning.[4] According to Harold Cohen, PhD, PTSD happens when "the mind is unable to process information or feelings in a normal way."[5] The trauma of your parent's death can cause you to struggle mentally and emotionally in ways that regular day-to-day teen struggles don't.

PTSD symptoms include having trouble sleeping, depression, headaches, angry outbursts, and irritability. According to the *American Journal of Orthopsychiatry*, the age of a child or teen when their parent died may be related to the intensity of PTSD symptoms.[6]

Losing a parent to war is difficult, but you can be proud of your parent for serving your country. ©iStock / alancrosthwaite

If you feel like you are experiencing symptoms of PTSD, or other related complicated grief reactions (being absent mentally or emotionally; having excessive, distorted, exaggerated, or unending feelings of grief), talk to your surviving parent about seeking counseling or help, as you begin your coping and healing journey. There are also some amazing organizations out there specifically for you and your family members that can offer extra support if you need it. Check out the TAPS organization, Tragedy Assistance Program for Survivors (www.taps.org/), or C.O.P.S., Concerns of Police Survivors (nationalcops.org/) to name a few.

In case you ever feel alone in having lost a parent to war or in the line of duty, consider this: "It is estimated that when World War II ended, there were 180,000 children in the United States who had lost their fathers. The United States government officially called them World War II Orphans even though their mothers were still alive, and financial support was provided for them through their teen years."[7] Even though it doesn't make your loss hurt any less, it might help to know others have made it through and so can you.

Parent Loss: Suicide

The most confusing way to lose your parents is probably suicide. If you have lost a parent to suicide, you may still have unanswered questions floating around in your mind. The main thing to remember, as hard as it may be at times, is that your parent did not die by suicide because of you; your parent chose to die by suicide because of something in him or her.

Often, we don't have the answers to why our person died by suicide. This can be very upsetting and you might think about these questions for a long time. If these questions become overwhelming or if you find these questions taking up a lot of space in your mind, it may be helpful to talk to an adult you trust. It's hard not to think back on things you could have done or should have said or not said to your person who died. These thoughts can make you feel like you had a part in your person's death. This is called magical thinking. You feel that your words or actions have enough power to influence someone to suicide. These thoughts can be very harmful to you. If you feel this way, please talk to someone you trust.[8]

Even if your parent left a note explaining his or her reasons, the note could leave you more confused and hurt. You will drive yourself crazy trying to figure out why your parent left in the way that he or she did. If you accept that those questions will probably remain unanswered, that will be key in your healing process.

This acceptance will most likely not happen overnight. It will take a lot of time and patience. The best way to work on this acceptance, and to properly deal with all of the emotions that come with it, is to work one on one with a counselor.

Celebrity Jane Fonda

Actress Jane Fonda lost her mother when she was twelve years old. At first, Jane was told that her mother died from a heart attack. A year after her mother's death, Jane found out from a magazine article that her mother actually died by suicide. On her mother's last day, Jane was asked to come downstairs to see her mother but she refused to come down; she stayed upstairs playing with her brother. After she found out what really happened to her mother, Jane felt extremely guilty for not coming downstairs that day to see her mother. "I thought, if I had gone downstairs and seen her that day that she came to the house, then she wouldn't have killed herself," Jane says. "It was my fault."[m]

Although Jane apparently blamed herself for losing her mother to suicide, she didn't need to, as it wasn't her fault. Just like our late parents would not want us to blame ourselves for things we may or may not have said or done right before they passed away. How were we supposed to know that was the last moment we had with our parent? My feeling is that our parents would not want us to feel guilty about anything that happened in our final moments with them.

> "My father died at night. In the morning, I woke up and realized it was past the time I was supposed to wake up for school. I found a note saying that we were staying home from school that day in my room. When I found out my father died, I was shocked and sad. I saw signs of something bad happening with my dad during the last weeks leading up to the day he died. When I would go to his house, I could tell there was something wrong. My dad started to get a lot quieter than normal, and I noticed that he just wasn't the same happy guy he used to be. There were times when I would actually hear him go in his room and just cry."—Chase[n]

"Children need age-appropriate support—that is, counseling and support that correlates to the way a person processes death at a certain age—to deal with the effects of the loss of a parent and the ensuing grief. Since people understand death differently at different stages of development, the emotional support they receive needs to reflect the child's ability to process the information."[9] Regularly meeting with a counselor will help you work on healing from losing your parent to suicide. Although you may never heal 100 percent, the counselor can provide you tools for working through your grief and can guide you to accepting how your parent died. This will be highly beneficial to you as you get older and become an adult.

> "My dad was really depressed, and would often throw things and cry at night. Hearing him cry would make me cry at night. He was slowly getting worse and worse. One time we had a friend over, and my dad just suddenly started crying. I eventually had to leave the house because his crying got to be too much for me to deal with.
>
> "On the day that he died, I had a hard time sleeping that night. I woke up and heard my mom crying downstairs. She had taken my phone away so my alarm wouldn't wake me up, and when I found her she had told me my dad died. I knew my father was having issues prior to the night he died.
>
> "Knowing that my father was no longer in pain anymore helped me cope after I found out the news. I also look at photo albums to try and remember the good times."—Ella[o]

"My mother died when I was twelve years old, and my brother was ten. Her death was unexpected, as she committed suicide, to where I even found a letter later. This letter was from my grandmother's pastor stating that they knew it was going to happen. Everyone knew my mother was battling daily, and that the day was coming when she wasn't going to be here anymore, but no one knew when that day would officially come. My mother had back surgery, and I was told that the doctor suggested that she have a glass of brandy with the pain pills, which over time turned into an alcoholism problem for her. She would often lock my brother and I in the basement and would drink. For many years I never knew this until my father told me and even then, I rationalized that it was to protect us.

"The weekend that my mom passed, my dad and stepmom were out of town and my grandparents were watching my brother and me. I was picking out my church clothes with my grandma, when my grandma looked over at me in pain. I could see sadness and pain in her eyes, but at the time I didn't ask her what was wrong (I eventually made this connection later). My dad and stepmom came home that night and told me that my mother had committed suicide. My mom had left a note and asked my dad to tell my brother and I that she died in a car accident, but my dad was honest with us and I appreciate that each day.

"Every summer, I remember going to the Detroit Zoo with my mother as well as Boblo Island, which was an amusement park. She would also put my brother and I on a farm for one week each summer. My mom and I shared a love for animals. She loved horses and owls, and at the end of being on the farm, we would all go horseback riding together. Those were the good memories with her. I know she did her best.

"Only seven (looking through her sign-in book) people showed up to my mother's funeral, which included my father, brother, grandmother, and myself. She had an open casket, and it was only a viewing, as the counselor recommended it for us to have closure. Then she was cremated."—Rebecca[P]

"My father had to deal with a large amount of mental health issues since his childhood, the stress of no longer having a job due to the economy in 2008, the sickness of my mother, and the poor financial situation we were in due to it. He later attempted to kill himself, and then again was successful in killing himself a month later.

   "With my father, it was almost expected, more of, not really relief, but that he was no longer in so much pain. For previous context, my father, due to a plethora of issues, pre-existing and newly arisen due to the death of my mother, had attempted to end his life almost a month prior. He had been admitted to the inpatient mental institution at the local hospital for a few weeks, to detox off of the medicine he had used to end his life, and recover mentally. The summer before my mother passed, he had been diagnosed with an inoperable cyst on his Pineal Gland—a tumor in the middle of his brain, essentially. Shortly before, and especially after my mother's death, my father had slipped into a depression, previously struggling with suicidal tendencies and mood swings, and while not, to my knowledge, officially diagnosed, the constant miserable anecdotes and hopelessness was damaging enough. After arriving home from summer camp, and learning that my father was not there, I thought nothing of it. After getting out of inpatient, he expressed to us how he hated being cooped up, and missed being able to drive and go places. My family mistook his long leave of absence as merely enjoying the freedom of being able to drive. The police officers told us that they had found his car in front of train tracks, with his wallet and keys in the front seat, and that he had stepped in front of a train earlier that afternoon. The announcement didn't really have the shock in the stomach feeling, that movies and books describe, nor the sense of dread that came over me with my mother's passing. It was blank, and I was unable to muster any reaction, whatsoever. I vividly remember not crying, or not being able to cry. And in all honesty, it really didn't feel any different the days after. I have since talked and concluded with my brother, that ever since my mom passed, the father we knew and grew up with wasn't really with us, and the person that passed away was just a shell of who he was. But the unfortunate fact is that it was him. We tend to not remember people for their worst moments, and especially with my father, out of fear of tarnishing the previous memories, but it's equally as important to remember they were flawed people. I catch myself using exact phrases he had said, and using mannerisms almost identical to his, and it's really startling, but it's good, that instead of idolizing him, that recognizing that the last portion of his life was filled with so much delusion, that it allows me to catch myself and deter the unhealthy mannerisms.

"The last thing my father said to me was, 'Have a great day at camp, I'll see you later, I love you bud,' and I said, 'Thank you, have a good day, love you too.' We had previously gotten into an argument, when he was impatient, and I told him I hated him. He called me on July 4th, and asked me why I wasn't visiting. I told him that I was having fun with my brother, and that I'd visit him soon. A part of me feels like he may have believed I no longer needed him or wanted him around, and that I was the cause for his suicide, but with all of the events surrounding it, I usually conclude that with or without my doing, he no longer desired to live."—Aedan[q]

Famous Parental Suicides

Parent loss by suicide has happened to those we read about in textbooks and those we see on the big screen. It might seem like something as tragic as a parental death by suicide would only happen to the average person, but celebrities and public figures have had their share as well. For example, in ancient Egypt, Cleopatra chose to die by suicide and left her ten-year-old daughter, Cleopatra Selene II, motherless.[r] Author Sylvia Plath chose to die by suicide and left her two-year-old daughter, Frieda, behind.[s] Actress Jane Fonda's mother chose to die by suicide when Jane was just twelve years old.[t] Singer Chester Bennington chose to die by suicide in 2017, sadly leaving behind his six children.[u]

Parent Loss: Accidents

Accidents are another cause of death that cannot be predicted or foreseen. Maybe your dad was driving to work, and he ended up in a car accident that took his life. Or maybe your family was having a nice trip at the lake and a terrible boating accident took your mother. No one can usually see an accident coming, and the shock that comes afterward can be devastating.

"It was May 14th, and my dad and my mom were going to a birthday celebration for my mom's friend. They knew it was going to be a late night, so they planned for my sister and I to sleep over at the house of one of her day care kids. My sister and I were excited because they were having a pool party the next day, but I always had a hard time leaving them, so I was upset.

"When my mom and dad were on their way back in the early hours of May 15th, they had witnessed a crash on the other side of the freeway. My dad decided to pull over to help, and he told my mom to stay in the car. My dad made it across safely and called 911, but my mom followed. She made it to my dad safely, but he told her to go back. On her way back, an oncoming car failed to see her crossing, and she was killed on impact.

"I don't remember much of what we did the night of the sleepover, but the next day is still vivid in my mind. My sister and I woke up the next morning to our grandparents at the door. We were really confused and I was upset because my mom knew there was a pool party that day and I didn't want to miss out. You could tell by their faces that something was wrong. My sister was old enough to pick up on it and asked, but I was just crying because I had to miss the pool party. We pulled up to our house and there were a lot of unfamiliar cars outside, and when we walked in, our house was filled with family. My grandparents led us down the hall to my parents' room where my dad was sitting on the bed. As soon as we sat down my sister asked, 'Where's mom?' and my dad said that there had been an accident and mom had died. The three of us sat there hugging and crying, with our family around us."—McKenna[v]

Actress Natasha Richardson's Skiing Accident

Natasha Richardson, the actress who starred as Elizabeth James, fictional mother to Annie and Halley Parker on *The Parent Trap*, tragically lost her life as a result of a 2009 skiing accident in Quebec, Canada. Natasha fell a few times while skiing. She thought she was OK and didn't get her head checked out right away after she fell. Tragically, she passed away from her injuries. She left her husband, actor Liam Neeson behind, along with their two teenage sons, Daniel and Micheál.[w]

Parent Loss: Unexpected Tragic Events

There is no way possible to prepare for a parent's death by unexpected tragic circumstances—murder, terrorism, shootings, or even natural disasters. While all parental death is shocking and sad, it is "especially traumatic if the child has lost several family members at once, or the death was untimely, unanticipated, or violent." When a parent death involves violence or some other tragedy, children tend to experience high levels of anxiety in addition to sorrow and grief.[10]

Maybe your dad went to the store to get ice cream for family night at your house, and he never returned home because he was robbed and killed at the store. Or maybe your mom went to work at the North Tower in New York City like she normally did and was part of the casualty list of people who tragically lost their lives on September 11. Or maybe your parent got caught in an area where a devastating earthquake hit or a hurricane rolled in. Whatever the case, if your situation falls into this category, you couldn't see it coming, you didn't get to say goodbye, and because of someone or something else, your parent is now no longer here.

Movie Spotlight: Extremely Loud and Incredibly Close

In the movie, Oskar is convinced that his father, who just died in the 9/11 attacks, has left him a message somewhere in New York City. Not being able to relate to his mother who is also grieving, Oskar sets out on a journey to follow clues he feels his late father left behind for him. What he finds instead can help any parentless teen who is struggling from losing a parent to an unexpected tragic event. Adventure/drama/mystery, 2011. 129 minutes.

"I thought I had a happy childhood. My thirty-year-old parents tried to keep things happy for us, though I believe they may have been struggling with their own unhappiness. I have memories of many times before they died. Most of the times I remember them individually, but in some memories we are all together. I was especially close to my father, and my brother was more connected to our mother. So, the influence was a little different for each of us. My mother was the type of person who wanted to do 'what was right' and my father was more of the 'how do you feel' person, which I believe both to be important, so I appreciated both of them. They were very different in some ways. My mother was very intelligent, skipped three grades in school, taught classes in a college when she was only sixteen years old. She was an accountant. She was very social, religious, ambitious, and very active in life. She was very loved by many. My father was talented with his hands (he was an auto body fender man), and was a genius at it. He made full fenders on my trike that was the talk of the town. But, he was shy, reserved, and introverted. The army released him after six months because they said he was truly not capable of military life. I came to understand this as I grew up and my brother did too. We have difficulty with socialization. Preferring deeper relationships with few close people rather than groups. My mother was very church oriented and they belonged to a very social religious group with leadership as qualification for pleasing God. My father stumbled at this one. And he was not capable of earning the amount of money for the lifestyle they both seemed to think they needed. This, I believe, was the biggest of their problems. Also, my father had been very bullied by an older brother from childhood and never learned how to cope. He belonged to a church that also bullied him, and then married into a family that ended up bullying him because he could not live up to their expectations. I believe he was drawn to my mother because she was a very strong person and she would somehow provide cover and protection for him. But, he didn't realize that at some point that her strength would be used against him. A gun was the last power he had, after everything fell apart. My mother left him, got a job, took my brother and I to a big city, and put him in a mental hospital. It was all tragic, senseless, and useless. But, I do have some understanding of it all.

"The day of the event was the morning of January 5th. Christmas was over and it was back to school for me. We were getting ready for the day. The mental hospital had let my father out for a few days with his own family for Christmas and he had been able to get a gun. Then he came to where my mother, brother, and I were living. I believe, he did this to try and help my mother understand from his point of view, but she could not see and could not agree. So, he used the last and only power he thought he had left. He shot her and then he shot himself."—Katie[x]

If your parent's death resulted from tragedy, family members may try to shield you from the details. However, experts say, "Children must understand the truth about the death of a loved one. The best possible place for them to hear that truth is from within the family. Some deaths are disturbing, such as homicides, suicides, and random acts of violence. Understandably, parents hesitate to share the details of these kinds of deaths with children, especially if they are young. As difficult as it may be, honesty is essential."[11] If family members seem hesitant to share all the details, keep asking questions, even though it might be hard to hear what happened. In the long run, it will help with your healing.

This type of situation may make you question your faith, wonder why this happened to you and your family; it can cause you to be very angry at the party responsible for your parent no longer being alive. It takes great strength to forgive someone who caused your parent's death, whether they did it intentionally or not. "Remember that anger is simply energy, waiting to be harnessed, used or ignored. If we can harness it and use it appropriately, great things can happen."[12] You can choose how to handle your emotions. Although it may be difficult, try to forgive and live peacefully, turning your anger and other negative feelings into something positive, rather than going down a path of anger, frustration, and resentment for the rest of your life.

These types of traumatic circumstances can complicate your grieving process as well. "Traumatic grief, following the death of a loved one under traumatic circumstances, hampers the process of mourning. Symptoms include: re-experiencing the loss physiologically [in the body] and psychologically [in the mind], especially in the face of reminders, through intrusive and distressing thoughts, memories, and images; extreme avoidance, emotional numbing, estrangement from others, exaggerated fears, such as those of other loving people dying too, and denial of any resemblances to the deceased for fear of sharing the same fate or, instead, over-identification with the deceased parent."[13] If you feel as though you might be suffering from traumatic grief, reach out to a trusted adult immediately for support.

If you have lost a parent to an unexpected tragedy, it might help you to remember you are not alone. Other teens have lost a parent in a similar manner and understand how devastated you feel. Think of 9/11 for example, where nearly three thousand children lost a parent in one day: "September 11, 2001, was a tragedy unparalleled in the United States, resulting in the largest number of parentally bereaved children from a single terrorist incident."[14] It's important to realize that you are not alone in any of this. In fact, many organizations created after tragedies have striven to help promote healing and coping with the aftermath effect and to connect survivors to other survivors. For example, after September 11, 2001, organizations such as Tuesday's Children (www.tuesdayschildren.org/) and Children of September 11 (www.foractioninitiative.org/children-of-september-11) were created to offer support for families affected by the terrorist attack that day. Having the support of others who have gone through something similar can actually help you both out in your grieving and coping journey.

The Only One Who Has Lost a Parent

There will probably be times when you feel like you are the only one who has ever lost a parent at a young age. During these times, it is important to remember that you are not alone. There are thousands, millions even, of other teens who have lost

The Five Stages of Grief

According to Dr. Elisabeth Kübler-Ross, esteemed psychiatrist and author, the five stages of grief identify the different phases a person goes through when they are grieving. These stages are denial, anger, bargaining, depression, and acceptance.

1. *Denial:* If he or she died from an illness, you might think that someone somewhere along the way made a mistake—that your parent is still actually alive somewhere out there in the world, or that the medical staff or someone else involved didn't catch something in time or diagnose your parent correctly.

2. *Anger:* In this stage you suddenly feel angry that this happened. You wonder why it happened to you, to your loved one, and realize how incredibly unfair this is. You might become angry because you realize your parent isn't coming back.

3. *Bargaining:* You reach out to your higher power or just the universe in general, offering something in exchange if someone just lets your loved one come back. You try to negotiate or make a deal that you will live your life better if your loved one is allowed to return.

4. *Depression:* You start to feel like what's the point of living your life if you are eventually going to die like your loved one did. You realize you are sad all the time, you have given up, and you don't really care about much anymore.

5. *Acceptance:* You start to believe in life again and want to fight for it, or make a difference, often in the honor of the loved one you have lost. Your depression starts turning into a newfound strength to start living your life again.[y]

One key note about the five stages of grief: they do not necessarily happen in a nice, neat order. "Although these models may help us understand something about the range of experiences people have in relationship to grief, they do not by themselves accurately predict the sequence of reactions most people go through most of the time. In fact, people, including most children, experience many of these kinds of feelings at different times throughout grief."[z] Still, by understanding Dr. Kübler-Ross's grief model, you can figure out what you are currently feeling and gain awareness for feelings that are still to come.

Do you know which stage you are experiencing right this minute?

a parent at a young age just like you. Motherless and fatherless teens come from all walks of life, from different backgrounds, from different parts of the country, and from all around the world. In fact, you have lots in common with other parentless teens from around the world—especially in regard to different moments throughout the year when you might feel the sting of your parent loss the most. For example, if you're a guy, that time might be football season. Your mom might have been at every game cheering you on, and now you don't hear her voice in the crowd. Maybe you and your dad used to get together for football games with your friends and their dads. Now, however, you look around the room, and all of your buddies are eating wings around the TV with their dads, and you are the only one there without a father. For daughters, that lonely time of year might be spring and the annual father-daughter dance. Your dad used to love playing your date, but this year, he's not there to take you. Or maybe it's softball season, and your mom isn't sitting in the first row of the bleachers holding a sign with your face on it.

These situations and others might bring up that feeling of being the only teen in existence who has lost a parent, but you aren't. Try to find the courage to find those other teens and stick with them. Although your pain will never truly go away, having others who have been through a loss like yours can definitely help your healing process.

Leaving Things Unsaid with Your Parent

Dealing with the loss of your parent can be even harder if you left things unsaid with him or her. Let's say you stayed out too late on a Friday night, and Saturday morning your parent grounded you for a week; obviously, you guys probably weren't on good speaking terms. Then Monday when you got home from school you learned your parent passed away from a heart attack. Guilt, sadness, anger, confusion—all sorts of feelings might fill your mind because now you remember the last thing you said to your parent was something terrible, as a result of him or her grounding you.

You can't take back what was or wasn't said right before your parent passed away, but you can hold onto the fact that your parent loved you very much, even though things ended in a frustrating way. Most likely your parent would not want you to move forward in life with guilty feelings. It will be hard at first, but through time you can learn to forgive yourself.

Life and time are precious; we never know what the next moment holds. As you may have learned the hard way, it's good practice to not leave the house angry and to not leave things unsaid or done.

> "I did not leave on good terms with my mom, which is something that I think I will always regret. We fought and argued a lot as I entered my teenage years. We both said things we didn't mean and didn't get a chance to mend those wounds before it was too late. I was on much better terms with my dad. We rarely fought and I remember my son and I hugging him and telling him we loved him the night before he passed."—Kaylene[aa]

"My mom and I have not always had the best relationship. Childhood was rough, and when I became a young adult, we really did not see eye-to-eye. When I was twenty-four years old, I decided that I was going to venture out to Florida to start my adult life post-college. Regrettably, my mom and I had a terrible fight. Our fight was so bad, that we ended up not being on speaking terms for the rest of her life. I missed my mom during this time because I could not share little life moments, such as having my daughter, or getting motherly advice."—Erin[bb]

Where Do I Go from Here?

So, it happened to you: you are a teen and you just lost your parent, possibly in one of the ways described in this chapter. I am so very sorry for your loss. Everyone probably keeps telling you this, possibly to the extent that you are now sick of hearing it. You know everyone is sorry, but you also might be at the point where you realize "sorry" is not going to help you get through the rest of your teen years or the rest of your life. You need something more than apologies. You need your parent, and sadly he or she can't be here anymore.

At this point, you may be thinking about your future, wondering, "Where do I go from here? How am I going to make it in life and be successful without someone to guide me?" Believe it or not, there are plenty of men and women out there who grew up parentless and became very successful in today's world (you'll read about some of them in the next two chapters). You can still be successful, too. You just need to remember to be kind to yourself, be patient, and always believe in yourself.

Bereavement experts Schonfeld and Quackenbush acknowledge that "puberty can be a very challenging time for students who have lost a loved one. The loss of a same-gender parent can be particularly troublesome at this time. Puberty can be more difficult for girls without a mother or boys without a father."[15] The next two chapters have been written to address the specific challenges you might be experiencing as a teenage son or daughter going through parent loss. The next chapter is written specifically for daughters, and chapter 4 is just for sons. We can all meet back up again in chapter 5, where we will discuss how the family dynamic at home can change after the death of your parent.

"My father was diagnosed with cancer when I was nine years old and died a year later when I was ten. My mother was never the same again after that. One night, my mother and I had a talk about my fear for losing other loved ones, including her. I ended up spending that particular night somewhere other than my own home, and in the middle of the night I woke up suddenly needing to talk to my mother. I couldn't understand what I was feeling, but my intuition was telling me that something was wrong. My mother died suddenly and un-expectedly of a pulmonary embolism in her lung that day.

"What frustrates me now as the years are going on is the fact that I do not know a lot of things that I feel I should know. Things that other mothers have probably taught their daughters to do—I feel like I have a disadvantage. The other day I was at the grocery store and I did not know how to buy an ear of corn. On applying to jobs, I have trouble with understanding taxes, and I find that I struggle with putting on makeup, doing my hair, etc. This can be very frustrating, but I try to push forward. I have accepted that I am going to have some bad days every now and then.

"I turned to God a lot throughout all of this and I realized that God is giving me what I need. Although I may not understand why all of this happened to me or why God is or is not providing me with certain things, at the end of the day, I know He is giving me what I need."—Joella[cc]

DAUGHTERS

A mother and a father both have many things to offer a daughter. They provide support and encouragement for becoming a strong and good woman, and they help the daughter learn responsibility and how to pick the right guy. "Parents help their adolescent daughters navigate transition by maintaining a firm but flexible hold—containing, remaining emotionally available in the face of ambivalence, scaffolding [demonstrating the problem-solving process, then offering support as needed], encouraging the negotiation of a balance between autonomy and exploration," and helping daughters understand other points of view in problem solving.[1] Often, the roles of mothers and fathers are interchangeable. No matter, daughters need support and guidance from both of their parents.

Losing a parent is the most devastating event that can happen in a child's life. You may have already heard this in one form or another. Aside from hearing it, you are probably acknowledging that the loss of your parent is the worst thing that has happened to you so far. You may be wondering how you are supposed to navigate life now that one or both of your parents are gone. You probably have a lot of questions; you may be wondering what you are supposed to do, how you are supposed to feel, and where you are supposed to go. Although you are in uncharted territory, I do believe deep down inside, you have the strength you are going to need. You just have to believe in yourself.

For starters, let's get you familiar with how you are probably feeling, what you can expect, and recommendations on how to proceed from here. You're probably thinking long term about how the loss of your parent is going to affect your future as a teen growing up to become a woman. You may have already thought, "If my mother is not here anymore, how will I learn how to cook, put on makeup, or do other female-related things?" If you can accept now, early on, that you are going to make mistakes along the way and that you are going to have some really hard days, and if you can determine that you are going to try your best to stay as positive as you possibly can as each day comes barreling through, then that is half the battle. To stay strong throughout all of this, you need to believe in yourself, not be so hard on yourself, and start each day fresh, not beating yourself up for any lost battles from the day before.

There are going to be days when you may accidentally snap at one of your friends out of frustration while you are grieving. Or days when you might get in a fight with your surviving parent because you are not seeing eye to eye like you used to. You are probably going to wish you could take certain days back, but you have to fight the pain and learn how to forgive yourself. Be prepared that days like these are probably going to happen. No matter what happens or how hard the day before was, leave it behind. Start each day with a clean slate and don't ever give up. Keep pushing forward and know that over time it does get easier to deal with the new life changes you will experience while you are grieving the loss of your parent. The pain of losing your mother or father will never completely go away, but I will help you find ways to fill the void and get back on your feet when you experience difficult days.

What I can recommend is to start helping yourself now, right away. Don't wait until ten years from now before you start dealing with your grief. Experts agree that "experiencing parental death in childhood is expected to result in emotional distress, increased anxiety and depression, a decrement in physical health, and an emotional detachment resulting in social estrangement."[2] If this is the case, then the sooner you start dealing with your grief, the better—whether you currently think you need to or not. Not doing so could result in increased physical, mental, and emotional struggles later on in life.

As you get older, you will get better at regularly tending to your grief. I personally have been dealing with the loss of my mother for the last twenty-four years, and looking back, I have come to realize it has been quite the journey. The one thing I wish looking back? That this chapter was written for me during my time of need. Now I am glad that I am able to write it for you, fellow motherless and fatherless daughters.

Your parent, up to this point in time, has most likely been there for you every single day of your life. Your parent may have helped you with your homework, given you advice about your friendships at school, made you breakfast, and in many other ways showed that he or she cared for and loved you. Now that your parent is not here anymore, you are probably wondering how you are supposed to proceed in life. You might be asking yourself, "Who is going to help me with my homework now that dad is gone, and mom is always at work? My mom didn't teach me how to wear makeup; how will I learn now? Who do I ask for dating advice?" Before you let your mind go off into all possible scenarios, take a minute and just breathe.

From one parentless daughter to another, the key to being able to get through each and every day of the rest of your life without your parent is to take one day at a time and to learn to give yourself a lot of credit. You are not going to solve all your problems in one night. Take everything step by step and learn how to be patient with yourself.

Benefits of Writing in a Journal

A journal, also known as a diary, is a place where you can record your innermost thoughts and feelings on a regular basis. Authors Cohen, Sossin, and Ruth say that keeping a journal "leaves behind a representational keepsake—a memorial space in which the past is both remembered and actively mourned while the future is imagined in the present moment." They also say that because people often write journal entries to someone, writing can provide a sense of comfort and connection during a time of loss.[a] Journals are typically private, so no one else reads what you are writing except for you, unless you give someone permission to read your private thoughts.

Writing your thoughts down in a journal can be very therapeutic. It's a way to figure out what you're thinking and feeling about the past, present, and future. Sometimes, you might want to vent or tell someone what you're thinking and feeling, but you struggle with feeling comfortable enough physically speaking the words. Other times, you might get really upset when you try to share, or the words just don't seem to come out. This is where writing in a journal can really benefit you.

Being a parentless daughter can make you a stronger young woman. Maybe you have other women in your life who can support you along the way (aunts, grandmothers, your mom's friends, older sisters). Maybe it is just you and your dad or just you and your mom, because you don't have any siblings. Maybe you are now surrounded by men—your brothers and your dad—ever since your mother's loss. Whatever the situation, you can find strength in knowing parents have a special love for their daughter that can never be broken, even through death.

Some of you might experience side effects from the loss of your parent. You may suffer from post-traumatic stress disorder, depression, or anxiety. A 1999 study in the *Journal of Youth and Adolescence* titled "Children's Psychological Distress Following the Death of a Parent" stated, "Girls were more likely to experience depressive symptoms after the loss of a parent than boys."[3] If you feel like you are experiencing sad, anxious, or really confusing emotions, seek help from your school or guidance counselor or an outside counselor, or tell an adult close to you so you can get the help that you need. There is nothing wrong with you if you are feeling like this. It is better to start working on the obstacle now before it gets worse.

It is no secret that a parent shares a special love with his or her daughter. Although your mom or dad may not physically be here anymore, your connection lives on forever, and in some ways, your parent is actually really still here.

Motherless Daughters: The Importance of Having a Mother

Mothers are important to daughters in more ways than a daughter could possibly calculate throughout her lifetime. According to author Gregory Lang, "Daughters need moms to help them understand what is happening to their bodies, to teach them how to make sound decisions regarding boys, to show them how to care for themselves, how to care for their children, and how to care for their marriage. Daughters need moms because they understand that sometimes tears come for no reason, that bad moods may simply mean nothing at all, that chocolate is a neces-

---

It Happened to Me: A Note from the Author

I was nine years old when my mother passed away. Although my mother was sick and in and out of the hospital, I still wasn't fully prepared to lose her.

My dad, brother, and I went to visit my mom in the hospital that Thursday night, December 2, 1993, just like we often did. We were getting ready to say goodnight and head home, but we noticed that there was something different about my mother on that particular night. She was usually in positive spirits and tried to be strong for all of us, but that night she had little patience and tried to rush us out of the hospital room to make us go home earlier and faster. We left confused as to why she was acting that way, went home, and fell asleep.

The next morning, I woke up realizing we were late for school and went to find my dad in the house. I found him in the living room, just putting the phone down on the coffee table. He asked me to come sit on his lap as he had something to tell me. I looked into his eyes as they filled up with tears and he suddenly burst out, "Mommy passed away last night." That moment changed my life forever. That is the day I was forced to grow up.

Successful Motherless Daughters

Did you know that celebrities and notable women all around the world have also experienced mother loss? It could be one of your favorite actresses or a woman you really respect. The fact that it happened to them and they still were able to make something out of their lives proves that you can do it too. It takes time to get to that point, but as the years go on, you will learn more ways to cope with your mother's death, while also reaching your dreams and goals along the way.

Here are a few famous women who lost their mothers at a young age:

Coco Chanel (1883–1971)
- Fashion designer and perfume creator who started her own business
- Mother died when Coco was a child[b]

Jacqueline Cochran (1906–1980)
- Pilot who set many aviation records
- First woman to break the sound barrier
- Mother died when Jacqueline was an infant[c]

Marie Curie (1867–1934)
- First woman to win a Nobel Prize and to win in two different fields, physics and chemistry
- Mother died when Marie was eleven years old[d]

Ella Fitzgerald (1917–1996)
- Jazz singer, music icon
- Mother died when Ella was a teenager[e]

Ruth Bader Ginsburg (1933–)
- Second woman to be appointed to the US Supreme Court
- Mother died when Ruth was a teenager[f]

Mary Todd Lincoln (1818–1882)

- US first lady
- Mother died when Mary was six years old[g]

Eleanor Roosevelt (1884–1962)

- US first lady, human rights speaker, newspaper columnist, civil and women's rights leader, author
- Mother died when Eleanor was eight years old[h]

Maya Rudolph (1972–)

- Actress and comedian
- Mother died when Maya was nearly seven years old[i]

Harriet Beecher Stowe (1811–1896)

- Philanthropist, author
- Wrote famous anti-slavery novel *Uncle Tom's Cabin*
- Mother died when Harriet was a child[j]

Anne Sullivan (1866–1936)

- Gifted teacher who taught Helen Keller how to communicate even though Helen was deaf and blind
- Mother died when Anne was eight years old[k]

sity, that being silly is fun, and that everything does not have to be practical or in accordance with a schedule."[4]

And right about now you are probably thinking, "Gee, thanks, Michelle. Now I am worried even more about this situation as you just so kindly listed all the reasons why I need my mother and she cannot fulfill them anymore." That is not at all what I am trying to do. What I am trying to do is to prepare you for what lies ahead on this challenging journey you now must face. I know you can do it, because I once did it.

Being a daughter and losing your same gender parent can bring up some challenges as you continue to grow and develop; for example, "girls who have lost their mothers may not have a comfortable source to turn to for information about how to manage menstrual periods and the physical and emotional issues that often accompany them."[5] You can handle this lack of motherly guidance in two differ-

Writing down thoughts and feelings is a positive coping mechanism to help channel your emotions. ©*iStock / petrograd99*

ent ways: you can learn how to turn to others for advice and support or even seek out answers yourself by researching at the library or online trusted resources, or you can use your mother's death as a handicap for the rest of your life, stating that you never learned this or that, which is why you aren't good at this or that. Likewise, you can either develop healthy coping mechanisms and get involved in positive and constructive activities such as clubs, sports, or volunteering; journaling; and/or going through counseling. Or you can cope with your loss by turning to drugs, alcohol, or other destructive activities that can harm you physically, mentally, and/or emotionally later on down the road. Which will you choose?

While learning about yourself on your grief journey and what works and doesn't regarding coping mechanisms, you might become interested in conducting personal research on the matter. There are some helpful tools out there: websites, books, TV shows, and movies that can help you cope. These resources can provide support in various ways: novels might have fictional characters you can relate to, nonfiction books such as this one can provide practical tips and information, movies and TV shows can depict parentless circumstances or situations with a parent that you miss. Michelle Hart, a writer for BookRiot.com, says, "I got into comics while my mother was in the hospital. The large, colorful, exciting images were the ultimate distraction—and after she died, I became even more obsessed with them. Neil Gaiman's two part send off for the Dark Knight, focusing on Bat-

One Woman's Pioneering Journey to Help Motherless Daughters Everywhere

In 1994, Hope Edelman published *Motherless Daughters: The Legacy of Loss*, the first book targeted toward daughters who'd experienced early mother loss, to help them cope with their significant and devastating loss. Edelman lost her own mother at seventeen and that experience has led her to write about this subject for the last twenty-four years. I interviewed Hope Edelman regarding what new motherless daughters will experience upon the death of their mother, and this is what she shared:

> During the first week after a daughter loses her mother there are no rules. Anything goes for the daughter because her emotions will be all over the place. The daughter may experience anger, grief, crying, sleep disturbances, and feel like she is on an emotional roller coaster that is out of her control, and that she's only along for the ride. This feeling is normal. There is nothing the daughter can do but ride those waves and reach out to people that care about her.
>
> After the first thirty days or so, she's still trying to get things back to normal but will start to realize that her old normal has changed into a new normal. For example, her living situation might now change, change in finances might impact her, she will now have to adjust to a new daily routine, and the daughter will possibly come across people trying to tell her she should be over the loss by now. This in return makes the daughter feel disconnected to people since she will clearly not feel "over" the loss yet. The best thing a daughter can do during this time is to expect change, and embrace the loved ones she can. It is perfectly okay for the daughter to feel angry towards all the new changes that are taking place.
>
> During the first year after the loss of her mother, the best thing for the daughter to do is to find a special place where she can express her

emotions freely. Often times this will be with a person outside of family members such as a teacher, a coach, or a neighbor for example. Joining bereavement support groups can also help, or just to have a place in general where she can express what she truly feels.

The first year is also the hardest year, because a daughter will go through the first set of milestones without her mother—her birthday, her mother's birthday, holidays, first Mother's Day without her mother, and the first death anniversary. Having someone to talk with freely at those times is key.

Hope Edelman has since helped thousands of motherless daughters worldwide with their struggles. Edelman has published other books, some of which deal with early mother loss:

Motherless Daughters: The Legacy of Loss (1994)
Letters from Motherless Daughters (1994)
Mother of My Mother (2000)
Motherless Mothers (2007)
The Possibility of Everything (2010)

Reflecting on her own personal mother loss, Hope Edelman shared, "The one thing I have learned since I wrote my first book is how much my mother is still a part of me even more than thirty years after she died. I still think about her often and I'm grateful that I had her for as long as I did, even though it was only for seventeen years. It took a long time for me to get to this place I am now. She still influences me to this day with decisions I make as a mother, a wife, and as an author."

Motherless Daughters was reprinted in a third edition on its twentieth anniversary. You can find out more about support groups started by Edelman, her books, and the overall subject of mother loss by visiting her website, www. hopeedelman.com.[1]

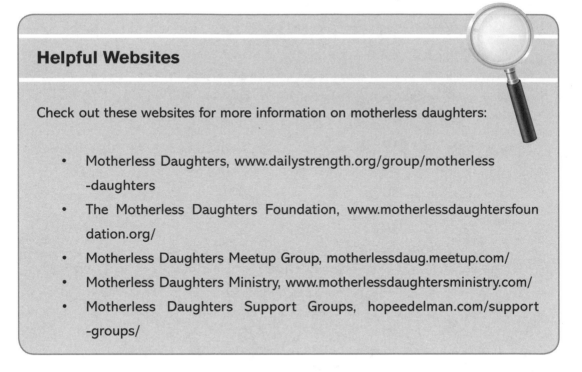

Helpful Websites

Check out these websites for more information on motherless daughters:

- Motherless Daughters, www.dailystrength.org/group/motherless
-daughters
- The Motherless Daughters Foundation, www.motherlessdaughtersfoun
dation.org/
- Motherless Daughters Meetup Group, motherlessdaug.meetup.com/
- Motherless Daughters Ministry, www.motherlessdaughtersministry.com/
- Motherless Daughters Support Groups, hopeedelman.com/support
-groups/

man's lasting legacy, blew up the notion of what people leave behind when they die to superheroic proportions. I always saw my mother as a kind of superhero and mythological figure, and Gaiman's story reified that idea for me."[6]

Something that has really helped me cope over the years is watching TV shows or movies that deal with a motherless daughter–type situation or that show a warm and cozy mother-daughter situation. When I have my hard days (which I still have every now and then just like you might and maybe do already), I often turn to one of these movies or TV shows and feel comforted. For me, at least, they usually do the trick.

Movies and TV Shows with Mother Loss

Here are some motherless daughter and mother-daughter documentaries, movies, and TV series that might comfort you and make you realize you are not alone:

- *Aladdin*. Animation/adventure/comedy movie, 1992. 90 minutes. Jasmine lost her mother at a young age and now lives with her father in his palace. She also grew up to be a very strong and independent woman.

- *Beauty and the Beast*. Animation/family/fantasy movie, 1991. 84 minutes. Belle lost her mother at a young age and assumed the caretaker role for her father. She grows up to be a strong and independent woman.
- *Bride Wars*. Comedy/romance movie, 2009. 89 minutes. Liv and her brother Nate lost both of their parents at a young age and have to deal with their parents missing all of their milestones in life.
- *Casper*. Comedy/family/fantasy movie, 1995. 100 minutes. Kat lost her mother unexpectedly and now moves around the country with her father. In this movie, she actually gets to see her mother again, but in a different form.
- *The Dead Mother's Club*. Documentary, 2014. 75 minutes. A documentary about three women who grew up motherless.
- *Frozen*. Animated/adventure/comedy movie, 2013. 102 minutes. Anna and Elsa are sisters who lose both their mother and father in a shipwreck accident during their teenage years. Now they are forced to move on without them and run a kingdom at the same time.
- *Full House*. Comedy/drama/family TV series, 1987–1995. 30-minute episodes. DJ, Stephanie, and Michelle all lost their mother at a young age and are now being raised by their father and two uncles. The show depicts their journey through life without their mother.
- *Harry Potter and the Order of the Phoenix*. Adventure/family/fantasy movie, 2007. 138 minutes. In the fifth installment of the Harry Potter series, we get introduced to Luna Lovegood, a witch who lost her mother when she was young. Luna now lives with her father and aside from dealing with being motherless, she also has to find the courage to fight the fierce Voldemort.
- *Now and Then*. Comedy/drama movie, 1994. 100 minutes. Roberta lost her mother at a young age and grows up with her father and a house full of boys.
- *Save the Last Dance*. Drama/music/romance movie, 2001. 112 minutes. Seventeen-year-old Sara has dreams to become a ballerina. Her mother is killed in a car accident, and Sara puts her dreams on hold. Having to relocate to live with her father in a busy city, she turns to the clubs to express herself through dancing. Through dancing in a new and unique way, Sara begins to find her rhythm in life again.
- *Simply Irresistible*. Comedy/drama/fantasy movie, 1999. 96 minutes. Amanda lost her mother at a young age and has tried to keep her mother's

restaurant running, but she does not have the same culinary skills that her mother had. That is, until something magical happens to her.

- *Smallville*. Adventure/drama/romance TV series, 2001–2011. 60-minute episodes. Lana Lang and even Lucy and Lois Lane all lost their mother at young ages. It is neat to watch their stories unfold and to see the strong women they become despite losing their mothers.
- *27 Dresses*. Comedy/romance movie, 2008. 111 minutes. The story focuses on Jane, a motherless daughter who took over her mother's caretaker role of her father and younger sister after her mother died.
- *The Wedding Planner*. Comedy/romance movie, 2001. 103 minutes. Mary lost her mother at a young age and grows up living with her father.
- *You've Got Mail*. Comedy/drama/romance movie, 1998. 119 minutes. Kathleen lost her mother at a young age and has tried to keep her mother's bookstore alive. It works until the future love of her life moves into the neighborhood with a state-of-the-art bookstore and ruins her business.

Schoolwork and extracurricular activities can be challenging while you are still dealing with your loss. If you find you are having trouble coping, talk to a teacher, guidance counselor, or school official to get support. ©iStock / Antonio_Diaz

Books on Mother Loss

A note about fiction: Sometimes reading fictional stories that cover topics similar to what we are dealing with in our nonfiction lives can help us learn more about what we are going through. Reading about fictional characters can not only help us understand what we are thinking and feeling, but also show us how the characters handle their situation; then we can decide whether that is a good choice for us.

Here is a list of novels on mother loss you might find helpful:

- *Alone at Ninety Foot* by Katherine Holubitsky. Pamela's sister died and then her mother took her own life afterward. Pamela's father avoids talking about what happened and tries to just "move on" with life. On the other hand, Pamela finds herself constantly thinking about her mother's death while trying to deal with everyday life.
- *The Beginning of After* by Jennifer Castle. Laurel loses her whole family in a tragic accident. She is trying to make sense of everything and piece together her new life post-loss, and she finds herself now connected to the boy down the street, David, who lost his mother in the same accident.
- *How to Be Brave* by E. Katherine Kottaras. Georgia's life changes when her mother dies. She realizes that she has a choice, however—be strong through her pain or get lost in it. She decides to be strong and to live her life to the fullest. Georgia makes a list of all of the things she wants to be brave enough to try that she may have been too afraid to attempt before.
- *I Never Told Her I Loved Her* by Sandra Chick. This novel involves the journey of a girl who lost her mother and has guilty feelings about fighting with her before she died. The daughter wishes she could take back the things she said.
- *Someone Else's Life* by Katie Dale. Seventeen-year-old Rosie's mother dies from Huntington's disease. While grieving, Rosie's pain intensifies when she learns she has a 50 percent chance of inheriting the disease herself. After she tells her mother's friend she is going to be brave enough to get tested,

a midwife tells Rosie the hard truth—she was switched at birth, and who she thought was her mother, wasn't her mother at all.

- *The Survival Kit* by Donna Freitas. Rose's mother dies and leaves behind a brown paper bag filled with items to help Rose cope afterward. Rose frequents the items and wonders why her mother chose the items she did. While Rose is coping, someone seems to keep distracting her in the meantime.

- *We Are Okay* by Nina LaCour. Marin's mother, a surfer, drowned when Marin was young. She never knew her father. Her grandfather raised her and kept many secrets from Marin, who struggles emotionally with her grieving.

You might also want to read memoirs—true stories written by women who have lost their mothers. One example is *The Long Goodbye* by Meghan O'Rourke. The author lost her mother to cancer and recorded her inner mourning life. She also talks about how caring for her sick mother strengthened their bond in the end.

Fatherless Daughters: The Importance of Having a Father

Fathers are important to daughters, and losing a father at a young age can cause daughters to miss out on a lot. For example,

> a daughter needs a dad to teach her to believe that she deserves to be treated well, to teach her to accept the differences in others, and to teach her to weigh the consequences of her actions and make decisions accordingly. A daughter needs a dad to make the complex simple and the painful bearable, to tell her that all is not hopeless, even when she feels it is. She needs her dad to join her journey when she is too afraid to walk alone, as well as to teach her the meaning of integrity, and how to avoid the crooked path.[7]

Losing a father is a challenge to say the least. The journey ahead of you is going to come with a lot of obstacles and ups and downs. The best thing you can do is prepare yourself and push forward. After all, you know deep down inside, that is probably what your father would want you to do.

"When my dad died, I was actually there to witness it. He had gone running at about seven o'clock at night, and came home. As I remember it, I was in the kitchen, and then I heard this thunk of something heavy falling to the floor. I turned around, and my dad was lying on his face on the rug in the entry-room. I ran over and was shocked and very scared. My mom told me to run and get a pillow, and I did, because her voice had this note of fear and urgency in it that I had never heard before. I came back, and she had rolled my dad onto his back. I will never forget it. He looked almost asleep, with the white pillow under his head, but there was a cut, maybe an inch long just above his right eyebrow from where he hit his head on the tile floor, and it was slowly oozing this thick, bright, red blood. The rest of the memory blurs. I remember my mom on the phone talking with the 911 lady and practically shouting frantically. Sometime, the ambulance got there. My mom took me into my parents' bedroom. I was sitting on the bed and crying, because a loud buzzing noise was coming from downstairs, sounding almost like that of a car tire pump. Then, I somehow was at the hospital, sitting on a white bench, my mom beside me. Then a man came up, and at first, I did not recognize him as my pastor. He asked me if I wanted to see my dad. I said no. I spent the night at my best friend's house. It was the first and only time we ever had a sleepover."—Carissa™

There is no way you could ever prepare for your father's death. Your father may have had a sickness or a disease that could very well have somewhat prepared you for his death, while other times, a sudden tragic accident may have taken your father's life away unexpectedly.

When you lose your father, you can handle it in two different ways. On the one hand, you can develop healthy coping mechanisms and get involved in positive and constructive activities such as clubs, sports, or volunteering; journaling; and/or going through counseling. On the other hand, you can turn to drugs, alcohol, or other destructive activities that can harm you physically, mentally, and/or emotionally later on down the road. Which will you choose?

"I lost my father when I was seventeen years old in December 2014. I was attending boarding school while my two younger brothers attended school by our home. The night before my final exams, my adopted brother called to wish me good luck on my finals. He sounded emotional over the phone, but I didn't think very much of it. The next morning at school, I was called in to see the Dean. When I went into one of the Nun's quarters, I saw my mom, the head of the school, my two brothers, and the Dean. My mom was crying and suddenly said, 'Sweetheart, daddy had a heart attack last night—daddy died. I am so sorry.'

"The first thing I did was look over at my youngest brother, Tristan, who was extremely close with my dad, and offered my condolences to him. I knew how close they were, and he was my first thought when my mom told me what happened.

"The whole situation was so surreal to where I even thought it was a joke at first. I didn't even know how to comprehend what I just heard. At my school, we had 250 girls attending there at that time, and everyone saw how upset my family was. The other students started crying as well, and it hurt them to see my family in so much pain. After my family told me what happened, I went back to my dorm, packed, and drove home. I ended up missing my final exams.

"When I got home, my adopted brother told me he was at my dad's hospital bedside the previous night. He had his left hand on the phone calling me, with his right hand holding my dad. He wanted me to have that connection one last time with my father before he left. When we arrived home, there were also a ton of people waiting and making funeral arrangements already—it was very overwhelming. I even saw people who I hadn't seen in years in my living room."—Catherine"

"My dad's death was very sudden. He lost control of his truck on a gravel road late one night and hit a tree. We were told he died instantly. Around 4:30 a.m. a lady with a clipboard came to our house and told us he had been found dead. I don't remember much from that day, except that it felt like a dream. And when I think back to that day now, it still seems like a dream. I remember a few sensory details, the smell of coffee, the feel of my blankets in bed, my mom's skin, but no timeline of events."—Mahala°

While learning about yourself on your grief journey and what works and doesn't regarding coping mechanisms, you might become interested in conducting personal research on the matter. There are some helpful tools out there: websites, books, TV shows, and movies that can help you cope. These resources can provide support in various ways: novels might have fictional characters you can relate to, nonfiction books such as this one can provide practical tips and information, movies and TV shows can depict parentless situations or situations with a parent that you miss. These can all help you feel like you are not alone and give you comfort during your grieving process.

! Notable Fatherless Daughters

Did you know that celebrities, athletes, and other notable women have also lost their fathers at a young age? Some of them thought their life was over and were worried about their future without their dads. Yet, they somehow managed and pushed forward (something your father would want you to do). They have even grown into strong and successful women today. If they could do it, so can you.

Here are a few famous women who lost their fathers at a young age:

Kate Beckinsale (1973–)
- Actress
- Father died of a heart attack when Kate was five years old[p]

Queen Elizabeth I (1533–1603)
- The Queen of England
- Father, King Henry VIII, died when the future queen was a teenager[q]

Bindi Irwin (1998–)
- Television personality
- Father, the wildlife expert Steve Irwin died after he was stung by a stingray while filming Bindi's new television series; she was eight years old[r]

Gabrielle Reece (1970–)
- Model, athlete
- Father died in a plane crash when Gabrielle was five years old[s]

Julia Roberts (1967–)
- Actress
- Father died of throat cancer when Julia was ten years old[t]

Barbra Streisand (1942–)
- Actress, singer
- Father died from complications of an epileptic seizure when Barbra was fifteen months old[u]

Movies with Father Loss

Here are some movies about fatherless daughters that might help you cope when you're feeling down:

- *Fantastic Four*. Action/adventure/sci-fi movie, 2005. 106 minutes. Scientist Sue Storm lost her father at a young age and later becomes a superhero who helps not only her community but the world.
- *Freaky Friday*. Comedy/family/fantasy movie, 2003. 97 minutes. Anna loses her father, which has now led to a lot of mother-daughter rivalry. Anna's mother wants to remarry, and something happens where both mother and daughter experience what it is like to be in the other's shoes.
- *Lara Croft: Tomb Raider*. Action/adventure/fantasy movie, 2001. 100 minutes. Tomb raider Lara Croft was very close to her father, whom she lost at a young age. Despite how hard life is without him, she manages to fight through her pain by trying to protect the world from harm.
- *Pirates of the Caribbean: At World's End*. Action/adventure/fantasy movie, 2007. 169 minutes. Elizabeth loses her father at a young age, years after she already lost her mother. Now she has to navigate the next step in her life without him.
- *The Princess and the Frog*. Animation/family/fantasy movie, 2009. 97 minutes. Aspiring restaurateur Tiana loses her father and continues to pursue a dream she and her father had together when he was alive.
- *Saving Mr. Banks*. Biography/comedy/drama movie, 2013. 125 minutes. *Mary Poppins* author P. L. Travers lost her father at a young age. When Walt Disney turned her story into a movie, the truth about her father's life and death spilled out in the process.
- *Twister*. Action/adventure/drama movie, 1996. 113 minutes. Jo loses her father to a tornado when she is a little girl. She grows up to find ways to better track tornadoes to create warning systems so a twister doesn't take another father away from his daughter.

Books on Father Loss

Books can also help you cope with the loss of your father. Here are some nonfiction and fiction resources on fatherless daughters that might help in your journey.

Nonfiction

- *Daughters without Dads: Overcoming the Challenges of Growing Up without a Father* by Lois Mowday Rabey (1995)
- *Father Fiction: Chapters for a Fatherless Generation* by Donald Miller (2010)
- *Fatherless Daughters: Turning the Pain of Loss into the Power of Forgiveness* by Pamela Thomas (2009)
- *Fatherless Daughters Project* by Denna Babul and Karin Luise (2016)
- *Fatherless Women: How We Change after We Lose Our Dads* by Clea Simon (2001)
- *Longing for Dad: Father Loss and Its Impact* by Beth Erickson (1998)
- *Lost Fathers: How Women Can Heal from Adolescent Father Loss* by Laraine Herring (2005)
- *On Grieving the Death of a Father* by Harold Ivan Smith (1994)

If you like memoirs, you might try *H is for Hawk* by Helen McDonald. The author's father suddenly and unexpectedly died. She was an experienced falconer and never attempted to try and train a dangerous predator, a goshawk, until she felt the goshawk's fierceness mirrored her own grief.

Fiction

A note about fiction: Sometimes reading fictional stories that cover topics similar to what we are dealing with in our nonfiction lives can help us learn more about what we are going through. Reading about fictional characters can not only help us understand what we are thinking and feeling, but also show us how the characters handle their situation; then we can decide whether that is a good choice for us.

Here is a list of novels on fatherless daughters you might find helpful:

- *After* by Kristin Harmel. Lacey's father dies in a car accident that Lacey feels was her fault. She keeps rehashing that morning and how she took her time getting ready. If she hadn't done that, she feels her mother wouldn't be grieving anymore, one brother wouldn't drink anymore, and her little brother would still have two parents. She tries to push forward by helping others.

- *How to Save a Life* by Sara Zarr. Jill has been isolating herself from everyone around her ever since her father died. When her mom decides to adopt a baby, Jill can't help but feel like her mother is trying to replace one family member with a new one. This book is an intertwining tale of the two lives of girls who must learn how to push forward in life.

- *Kissing in America* by Margo Rabb. Sixteen-year-old Eva lost her father two years ago and found consolation by reading many, many romance novels. The romance novels served as a distraction for her, until a real-life romance sparked between her and a boy named Will. This boy could relate to Eva's grief, and Eva fell for him. Then suddenly he moved away, and Eva is not handling it well. She then goes on an adventure of a lifetime to learn some hard truths about life and love.

- *Tiger Eyes* by Judy Blume. Davey's father was shot and killed. Now her mother is moving them away. On her new adventure she meets a new friend who helps her try and work through her grief and move forward in life.

- *The Truth about Forever* by Sarah Dessen. Seventeen-year-old Macy witnessed her father's death and is now trying to learn how to grieve and move forward with her life, while being a teenager at the same time.

To all of the daughters out there who have lost one or both of your parents: Life is going to change for you now. It is not going to be easy to adjust, but with support, love, and patience, you can learn how to have happy days again. You might not be so happy now, but know that one day you will probably get to a point where you can live with your loss and continue on with your life—something your late parent would have wanted for you.

SONS

Losing one or both of your parents as a teen boy is tough. You probably expected your parents to be around well into your thirties, forties, and maybe even fifties, and now one of them is suddenly gone. "We spend a lifetime looking to our parents for answers," says psychotherapist Sherry E. Showalter, author of *Healing Heartaches: Stories of Loss and Life*. "They're the repositories of knowledge about our history, our upbringing, family traditions, the names of all those faces in old photos. With their passing so, too, goes the information and insight that hasn't already been transmitted or recorded."[1] To lose one or both parents is a life-changing event, one that will significantly impact the rest of your life.

As a result of your loss, you may have a lot of questions and feel really confused, like your whole world just turned upside down. Although you may not feel it, know that this is 100 percent normal. No one expects you to quickly pick up the pieces of what feels like a shattered world. Grief does not work that way. The one thing you can know for sure is that you do not have to deal with your grief alone, and that you are not the only teen guy who has lost a parent.

As you have probably figured out, life without your mother or father is a whole new ballgame and it's not going to be easy. Your parent will always be in your heart and memories, but sadly he or she is no longer down the hallway from your room, or in the backyard mowing the lawn when you need to ask him or her for advice. You are going to have days where you are coping well with it, and other days where you are really struggling and don't know how you are supposed to get through one day to the next. This is normal. Psychotherapist Shelley Gilbert summarizes her grief research: "Losing a parent young is a tragedy. You have to acknowledge how tragic it is."[2] If you accept early on that you are going to have good days and bad days, and if you welcome all challenges that arise, then you are on your way to getting on the right track to the journey that lies ahead of you.

Fatherless Sons: The Importance of Having a Father

A father-son relationship is one of the strongest bonds you will ever experience during your lifetime. So, the pain you felt when you heard the news and the pain

"My father and I were very close. He used to play catch with my brother and I almost every evening after he got home from work. He coached my baseball teams, came to all my school events, and was very involved in my early childhood. I remember feeling very close to him as a child.

"The day my dad died changed my life forever. I was with him when he passed away. He and I were driving home from a baseball game on a weekday night when we decided to stop at a Burger King and get something to eat. He asked me to wait in line while he went to use the restroom. He had a very severe history of asthma and allergic reactions, and when he returned from the bathroom he was very disheveled and could barely speak. At eight years old, I was uncertain as to what was going on, but now looking back, it's clear that he was having a severe asthma attack that was causing him great distress. I remember him telling me to get into the car and that we were going to drive to the hospital. So, as afraid as I was, I got in the car like he told me to and we started driving erratically in the direction of the hospital. About two minutes into the drive, I remember him telling me to roll down the windows to get more air into the car. Those were the last words I ever heard my dad speak. Shortly after, he lost consciousness at the wheel and crashed the vehicle into the side of the road. I tried waking him with no success. At that point I got out of the car and flagged down others for help. I remember one kind lady stopped and stayed with me until my mom made it to the accident scene. Not very many people had cell phones in 1995, so it took some time for 911 to be contacted. After the emergency crews arrived, they tried performing CPR on him with no success. They transported him to the hospital and he was pronounced dead after continuous attempts to resuscitate him. I remember being in a state of shock when we were told that he was gone. As a child, you just assume that when people are sick they are going to get better and everything will go back to normal. It took some time for it to sink in that he was really gone and that I would never see his car pull back into the driveway after school, or play catch with him again in the front yard.

"His death has impacted my life in more ways than I can explain. Growing up as a young man without a dad is very difficult. In many ways, I felt like I was on my own. My mom was tremendous, but she couldn't relate to me as a young boy like my dad could. His death ended my 'magical' childhood and began my 'responsible' childhood. What I mean by that is before he died, I didn't think about things like death, sadness, or grief on a regular basis. As far as I knew, my parents were going to live forever and be there to help me throughout my whole life. Before, I was concerned with things like baseball, Pogs, and the Teenage Mutant Ninja Turtles. After, I was concerned with things like grief counseling and expressing my feelings. Looking back, I remember feeling different than other kids because I was never completely in a carefree state after my dad died. I was always the responsible kid that just couldn't fully let loose."—Thomas[a]

you still feel now—you have every right to feel the way you are feeling. Your time with your father was cut short, when you still depended on him. And now you are probably trying to understand why, how it happened, and what you are supposed to do next. A father is supposed to be there to guide you; not just show you how to fish or throw a spiral football, but how to grow up to become a good man and take care of a family of your own someday—just like his father before him showed him. According to author Gregory E. Lang, "A son needs a dad to prepare him for being responsible for his own family. . . . A son needs a dad who will show him that love is unselfish, and who is willing to make sacrifices for his family."[3] Now it is up to you to pick up the pieces where your father left off teaching you. The importance of having a father may haunt you for your lifetime, but you can be thankful for the amount of time you did have with him.

"My father's death was completely unexpected. He went for a hike in South Mountain park early Sunday morning and had a heart attack while out on the trail. That afternoon, my mom went to go pick him up at the trailhead, learned what had happened, and had to tell us when she got home."—Eric[b]

Not having a father around can make your life journey tough. ©iStock / eelnosiva

Helpful Ways to Cope with the Loss of Your Father

Knowing how to deal with the loss of your father is like knowing how to throw a spiral football as soon as you're born; it's not natural. It takes time, a lot of mistake making, a lot of trial and error to see which ways work best for you and to learn how to deal with your emotions. You're probably not going to get the process right on your first try. As you move forward with your life without your father, you will identify triggers that are going to upset you. You have to be patient with yourself.

It is important to find healthy, positive ways to express yourself. If you need a distraction because the pain hurts too much, especially at first, find constructive ways to take out your emotions. Play sports, pick up a hobby like camping or fishing, join clubs at school, volunteer at your church—stay busy, but in a healthy way. Drinking, experimenting with drugs, or partaking in any other risky behavior is not going to do you any good. These behaviors will lead you down a path that could in fact alter your life forever in a negative way if you end up doing any permanent damage. Your dad would not want you to do anything destructive, so stay on the positive path.

Counseling or peer support groups are another way to cope in a constructive way. These will give you a chance to see that there are other sons out there who are going through similar grief roller coaster rides. Clinical thanatologist Dr. Alan D.

Famous Fatherless Sons

Far too often the public thinks that celebrities or other people in the spotlight have perfect lives. All we see in the tabloids and on the news is how lavish their lifestyles are, what nice expensive cars they have, and how they don't have to worry about what "ordinary" people have to worry about. However, this is simply not the case. In fact, there are many celebrities, athletes, and even past presidents who lost their fathers at a young age and who have grown to be successful despite this setback. Some on this list might even surprise you.

Julius Caesar (100–44 BCE)
- Roman general and statesman
- Father died when Caesar was sixteen years old[c]

Confucius (551–479 BCE)
- Chinese philosopher, teacher, political figure
- Father died when Confucius was three years old[d]

Bill de Blasio (1961–)
- Mayor of New York City
- Father committed suicide when Bill was eighteen years old[e]

Travis Hamonic (1990–)
- Professional hockey player
- Father died from a heart attack when Travis was ten years old[f]
- Received 2017 NHL Foundation Player Award for his D-Partner Program for kids who lost a parent

Thomas Jefferson (1743–1826)
- Third president of the United States
- Father died when Thomas was fourteen years old[g]

Nelson Mandela (1918–2013)
- First black president of South Africa, Nobel Peace Prize laureate
- Father died from lung disease when Nelson was nine years old[h]

Jason Schwartzman (1980–)

- Actor
- Father died of pancreatic cancer when Jason was fourteen years old[i]

J. R. R. Tolkien (1892–1973)

- Author of the Lord of the Rings series
- Father died when J. R. R. was four years old; mother died when he was twelve[j]

George Washington (1732–1799)

- First president of the United States
- Father died when George was ten years old[k]

Wolfelt advises, "Peer support groups are one of the best ways to help bereaved teens heal. They are allowed and encouraged to tell their stories as much, and as often, as they like. In this setting, most will be willing to acknowledge that death has resulted in their life being forever changed."[4] (A thanatologist studies death.) Ask your school guidance counselor for a peer support group you can join, or look for a counselor outside of school. Paul Young, author of the bestselling book, *The Shack*, shares, "Let people in. We are not designed to try and make our way alone through loss. Healing comes through community and relationship."[5]

Sometimes we turn to books or movies to help us cope with life circumstances. Whether it's a book about father loss, a novel that has a character who reminds you of your dad, or a movie that shows a father spending quality time with his

"One movie that I connected with as a child was *Patch Adams* starring Robin Williams. I always felt a connection with Robin Williams because not only did he look like my dad, but I remember my dad having a similar gentle demeanor with children. I always seemed to like whatever movie he was in because it gave me a brief feeling of being around my dad again. The day that Robin Williams died was somewhat personal to me because it felt like I was losing a bit of my dad also."—Thomas[l]

An Interview with Author Violetta Armour

Violetta Armour, author of the fatherless son novel *I'll Always Be with You*, answers questions behind her idea for the book.

Michelle Shreeve (MS): Is this your first book? If so, what gave you the specific idea to write this particular book? A personal loss?

Violetta Armour (VA): This is my first book and my original idea was to write a young adult novel where a teen undergoes a huge change in his/her life and learns how to make that a positive experience. I thought the loss of a parent would be a huge change and also if that teen felt they were responsible for that loss, it would be even more challenging.

MS: Describe the characters in your book.

VA: There are three main characters in the book. Teddy, age sixteen, is getting a driving lesson from his dad when a drunk driver hits them broadside and the father dies. Although he was not responsible for the accident, Teddy experiences terrible survival guilt as well as grief. The other two main characters are Teddy's mother, Mary, and Rosetta, the late father's high school girlfriend. The story is told in their three voices with alternating chapters and they are all experiencing grief in their own way. Teddy's grandmother also plays a significant role in helping Teddy heal.

MS: How can teens relate to your book?

VA: Teens can especially relate to this book, because Teddy has many challenges. In addition to grief, his family has moved across the country to get away from the intersection where the accident occurred. So, he has to start all over with new friends, new basketball tryouts. This book would be an inspiration to teens who have not only lost a family member, but perhaps are grieving for the loss of friends when they have to move. Teddy finds many ways to come through this difficult period, which other teens might want to emulate.

One teacher in Florida said she will keep the book on her shelf to give to any teen in her class who has suffered a loss, because she feels the way Teddy comes through his grief in a positive manner will be an inspiration to others.

If you are interested in learning more about the book, would like to purchase the book, or would like to contact the author, check out her website at violetta-armour.com. The website will give you a link to her blog (serendipity-reflections.blogspot.com/), which has many other book reviews. The book is available in all formats (e-book, paper, hardcover) at Amazon.com and as an audio book at Audible.com. You can also check your local library.[m]

Give yourself time to grieve and time to heal. ©iStock / lolostock

Movies with Father Loss

Here are some helpful movies that either talk about a father loss situation or just have a good old-fashioned feel-good father-son story.

- *Fantastic Four*. Action/adventure/family movie, 2005. 106 minutes. Johnny Storm lost his father at a young age and tends to deal with his emotions in a comical way so that everyone around him thinks he is irresponsible. An accident in space allows him to show the world the responsible hero he truly can be.
- *Harry Potter and the Sorcerer's Stone*. Adventure/family/fantasy movie, 2001. 152 minutes. Harry Potter's father was killed by a dark wizard and Harry is now forced to navigate through life without him. Along the way he learns he is chosen to not only defeat the dark wizard who took his father's life, but also try and save the wizarding world.
- *Iron Man*. Action/adventure/sci-fi movie, 2008. 126 minutes. Tony Stark lost his father at a young age and later inherited his father's business. Tony must figure out a way to find his own path, despite the path his father was leading his business on.
- *Star Trek*. Action/adventure/sci-fi movie, 2009. 127 minutes. Captain Kirk lost his father right after he was born; dad was trying to save his crew. Now Kirk has to try and navigate his way through life and find his place in the world on his own. He struggles with trying to make his father proud of him and trying to fill his father's shoes at the same time.

son, reading and movie watching can help you cope with the loss you are experiencing in real life. You might also find comfort in watching a movie you used to watch with your dad.

Another helpful way to cope is to enjoy a relatable movie or book with a friend or even a bunch of your family members. Remember, you don't have to go through this alone, and you shouldn't if you have the chance to surround yourself with people who care about you.

Books on Father Loss

Here are some nonfiction books that might answer some questions, provide comfort, or just give you some things to think about in your father loss situation.

- *Father Fiction: Chapters for a Fatherless Generation* by Donald Miller (2010)
- *Fatherless Sons: Healing the Legacy of Loss* by Jonathan Diamond (2006)
- *Fatherloss: How Sons of All Ages Come to Terms with the Death of Their Dads* by Neil Chethik (2001)
- *On Grieving the Death of a Father* by Harold Ivan Smith (1994)
- *When Your Father Dies: How a Man Deals with the Loss of His Father* by Dave Veerman and Bruce B. Barton (2003)

If you want to read an inspiring true story about someone else's father loss, you might like *Son of Elwood: On Becoming Fatherless* by Tom Bickimer. The author describes what grief feels like for a sixteen-year-old boy experiencing father loss. He also shows that he has learned to deal with it at times in a humorous and spiritual way.

Motherless Sons: The Importance of Having a Mother

A son and his mother represent one of the strongest bonds experienced during a lifetime. According to author Gregory E. Lang, "A son needs a mom to teach him that embarrassment is not a reason for quitting, to teach him to play fair, and to believe in himself even when it seems no one else does. . . . A son needs a mom to make sure that faith is the light that guides him, to tell him that anything is possible if done for the right reason, and to tell him that remaining faithful is his promise and obligation."[6]

Your time with your mother was cut short, as you weren't finished learning from her. And now you are trying to understand why, how it happened, and what you are supposed to do next. Grief educator Carol Staudacher, author of the book *Beyond Grief*, shares, "You are now forced to cope with the loss of parental love

"On December 3, 1993, I woke up and it was daylight. This was uncommon as my father used to get my sister and I up early. When I saw that it was daylight, I knew that something was wrong. I checked my sister's room, and my sister wasn't in there. I looked out her window and saw that my dad's car was still in the driveway. That's when I put two and two together. I then went out to the living room and I saw my sister and dad crying. At that point, I didn't need an explanation—I already knew what happened.

"For more than twenty years, I was angry because I felt like someone should have told me how she really died. Now, I am a parent myself, and I understand why they hid the truth.

"My last words to my mother still haunt me to this day. On the last night my mother was alive, I went down to the hospital cafeteria with a family member. When we came back up to my mother's room, everyone had left for the night. The last words I said to my mother were, 'I'll see you later, bye.' I never got to tell my mother that I loved her on her last night here on earth. Now, that is exactly why I cannot say 'bye' to anyone on the phone anymore. Sometimes it slips because it is such a natural thing to say, but for the most part, I try to avoid it. It's easy to end a phone call if you ever get mad or frustrated, but now how I see it is, you don't know if that person is ever going to be there ever again. If I catch myself saying 'bye' to someone, I actually get pretty mad at myself afterwards."—Mike[n]

and attention that was given uniquely to you, and that you depended on, possibly even took for granted."[7] A mother is there to guide you—not just to show you how to treat a woman or have manners but also how to grow up to become a good man and take care of a family of your own someday. The importance of having a mother may haunt you for your lifetime, but you can be thankful for the amount of time you did have with her.

Helpful Ways to Cope with the Loss of Your Mother

Knowing how to deal with the loss of your mother is not a cut-and-dried process. It takes time, a lot of mistake making, a lot of trial and error to see which ways work best for you and to learn how to deal with your emotions. You're probably

"My mother and father both, for the first part of my life, worked at relatively moderate paying jobs, my father assisted in ads at the city newspaper, and my mom was a manager at a Dollar General store. My mom, one night, was told to assist in unloading a truck filled with heavy items. (I don't recall) and had ruptured one of her spinal disks. She was placed on unemployment, and went through a myriad of surgeries, none successful. Due to the side-effects of the surgeries, she was required to take prescription drugs, but due to their side-effects, she needed to take even more to counter the insomnia, lack of energy, and other sicknesses. Due to the large amount of prescription drugs she required (I remember her saying it was around 100 different portions of pills a day), one of the chambers of her heart was no longer functioning. After getting it checked out, and the doctor telling her she did not need to go to hospital care, and that it was nothing to worry about, she died two days later of congestive heart failure.

"I was the last one to speak to my mother before she passed away, and I distinctly remember making fun of her for always falling asleep. Her large amount of prescriptions made her almost narcoleptic and she muttered something and fell asleep. Part of me wishes that I was able to say goodbye, but knowing the nature of the relationship between my mother and I, I think she would've preferred the last thing I said to her to be a joke, rather than something overly emotional."—Aedan°

not going to get the process right on your first try. As you move forward with your life without your mother, you will identify triggers that are going to upset you. You have to be patient with yourself. It is important to find healthy, positive ways to express yourself.

If you need a distraction because the pain hurts too much, especially at first, find constructive ways to take out your emotions. Play sports, pick up a hobby like camping or fishing, join clubs at school, volunteer at your church—stay busy, but in a healthy way.

You know, deep down inside, that your mom would not want you to do anything destructive. Stay on a positive path. Take your tragedy and turn it into something positive that can help others. Start a club at school, volunteer at church to help other parentless kids, or start a nonprofit organization. Channel your

Famous Motherless Sons

Although you may feel like you are the only son out there who has lost his mother, you are not alone. Even some famous sons lost their mothers at a young age.

Many celebrities, athletes, and scholars do not usually like to talk about their loss as it is a very sensitive subject.

The following famous sons lost their mothers young and were still able to grow up and be successful. You can too.

Oscar De La Hoya (1973–)
- Boxer
- Mother died from breast cancer when Oscar was seventeen years old[p]

James Ellroy (1948–)
- Author
- Mother was murdered when James was ten years old[q]

Larry Fitzgerald (1983–)
- Professional football player
- Mother died from breast cancer when Larry was twenty years old[r]

Prince Harry (1984–)
- Prince of Wales, pilot
- Mother, Princess Diana, died in a car accident when Harry was thirteen years old[s]

John Lennon (1940–1980)
- Singer, songwriter
- Mother was hit and killed by a car when John was seventeen years old[t]

Bernie Mac (1957–2008)
- Actor, comedian
- Mother died of cancer when Bernie was sixteen years old[u]

Paul McCartney (1942–)

- Songwriter, singer, animal rights activist
- Mother died from an embolism when Paul was fourteen years old[v]

Dylan McDermott (1961–)

- Actor
- Mother was murdered when Dylan was six years old[w]

Prince William (1982–)

- Duke of Cambridge
- Mother, Princess Diana, died in a car accident when William was fifteen years old[x]

experience and your pain into something positive for the greater good. Sometimes by helping others, we can also help ourselves.

At some points during your grieving journey, you might not have anyone available to help you through it. In these cases, books (nonfiction and fiction), movies, and TV shows can be sources of information and comfort.

The Ways Prince William and Prince Harry Try to Make Their Late Mother Proud

Losing a parent can often create a void, and instead of going down a wrong path to fill that void, many are doing wonderful things for others. For example, Prince William and Prince Harry lost their mother, Princess Diana, when they were teenagers. Throughout the years, both young men have been involved in countless organizations, charitable causes, and more, trying to do good in the world. In an interview with *People* magazine, Prince Harry shared that he feels his late mother inspires his work: "Whether I know it or not, there's all sorts of things I end up doing and places I find myself where I do think, 'Wow, this is bizarre that I've ended up on this path, this route.' There's other times when I think, 'All I want to do is make my mother incredibly proud.' That's all I have ever wanted to do. What would she think nowadays? Would she be content, proud, happy with the way I'm carrying out my life?"[y]

In 2014, Prince Harry's advisers created the Invictus Games, an international Paralympic multisport event in which wounded, injured, or sick armed forces personnel and associated veterans can participate.[z] Prince Harry himself served in Afghanistan, so this charity is dear to his heart to be a part of. During his interview with *People* magazine, Harry shared, "When she [Princess Diana] died, there was a gaping hole, not just for us but also for a huge amount of people across the world. If I can try to fill a very small part of that, then job done. I will have to, in a good way, spend the rest of my life trying to fill that void as much as possible. And so will William."[aa]

Prince Harry also started another charity, Sentebale, to help children who were orphaned by HIV/AIDS in Africa. He is also involved in about twenty other charities, including the Foundation of Prince William and Prince Harry, which he cofounded with his brother, where they offer guidance and support to disadvantaged young people. William is involved in around twenty charities as well, including one he started with his wife called the Royal Wedding Charity Fund, which helps other charities close to both of their hearts.

Both Harry and William are doing what they can to try and make a difference in the world, while also trying to make their late mother proud of them at the same time. They are great role models to all parentless sons who struggle with figuring out what to do with all of the anger, grief, and frustration caused by the loss of their parent. If William and Harry can turn their tragedy of parent loss into a positive cause, know that so can you.

Movies with Mother Loss

Here are some movies about motherless sons you might find helpful:

- *The Amazing Spiderman.* Action/adventure movie, 2012. 136 minutes. Peter Parker lost his mother at a young age and now has to navigate life without her. While growing up, he tries to learn more about her, as she was taken away from him at such a young age.

- *Batman vs. Superman: Dawn of Justice.* Action/adventure/sci-fi movie, 2016. 151 minutes. Both Batman and Superman think they are enemies because of their past history together. However, they discover that their mothers both share the same name. Although Batman already tragically lost his mother, he steps up to help Superman save his still living mother.

- *Finding Nemo.* Animation/adventure/comedy movie, 2003. 100 minutes. Nemo and his father lose Nemo's mother in a tragedy when Nemo is young. Now it is just Nemo and his dad. Nemo is trying to learn how to live life without his mother. His dad struggles with how to move forward as well.

- *Guardians of the Galaxy.* Action/adventure/sci-fi movie, 2014. 121 minutes. Peter Quill watched his mother die from cancer right before his eyes. Right after her death, Peter gets taken from his home and every single person he ever knew. Now all he has are the memories of his mother to hang onto.

- *Harry Potter and the Goblet of Fire.* Adventure/family/fantasy movie, 2005. 157 minutes. Neville Longbottom lost his mother to a dark wizard. Another dark wizard affiliated with his mother's murderer comes back to bring up painful memories for Neville. A strong person, Neville stays true to himself and continues to try and just honor his mother.

- *Ratatouille.* Animation/comedy/family movie, 2007. 111 minutes. Linguini loses his mother, and a letter she wrote to a head chef opens the door for Linguini to get a job and support himself. While learning more about his past, his late mother, and who his father really is, Linguini also meets a new friend named Remy to start a new adventure.

- *Tarzan*. Animation/adventure/family movie, 1999. 88 minutes. A tragedy takes Tarzan's mother away, and now Tarzan must grow into a man without her. Gratefully, he was taken in by a group of gorillas, which has made him more part of the jungle than a traditional human.
- *Thor: The Dark World*. Action/adventure/fantasy movie, 2013. 112 minutes. Thor has to deal with the pain of dealing with one of his enemies who killed his mother just seconds after Thor arrived at the scene. His mother was protecting the woman that he loved, but now his mother is gone. Thor, his father, and their kingdom say farewell to the Queen and try to learn how to move forward with their grief while saving their world at the same time.
- *Tron: Legacy*. Action/adventure/sci-fi movie, 2010. 125 minutes. Sam Flynn loses his mother at a young age and tries to move forward in life with just his father. When his father goes missing, Sam's world is rocked to the core. He learns a lot about himself and that he would go to the end of the world to bring his father back, knowing that the loss of his mother has already left him with a void.

Books with Mother Loss

A note about fiction: Sometimes reading fictional stories that cover topics similar to what we are dealing with in our nonfiction lives can help us learn more about what we are going through. Reading about fictional characters can not only help us understand what we are thinking and feeling, but also show us how the characters handle their situation; then we can decide whether that is a good choice for us.

Here is a list of novels on mother loss you might find helpful:

- *The Boy in the Black Suit* by Jason Reynolds. After a seventeen-year-old suffers a parental loss tragedy, he stumbles across someone who has had it way worse than him while working at a funeral home. The girl who has dealt with more than he has can help bridge the gap upon learning what he needs to move forward with his life.

- *The Lost Boy's Appreciation Society* by Alan Gibbons. After losing his mother, and dealing with his own grief, John is also struggling with his father and brother, and how they are all coping with their mother's death and life afterward.

- *Wipe Out* by Mimi Thebo. Billy's mother just died and he is trying to cope with his grief. His father is not coping too well with his wife's death, so Billy moves in with his Aunt Mary in the meantime. His late mother was a surfer, and Billy embarks on a journey of trying to learn more about her, cope with his grief, and move forward with his life.

THE NEW FAMILY DYNAMIC

Change in Roles

When a parent dies, the household will never be the same, no matter how hard you and your surviving family members try to make it the way it was before. You and your surviving family members are now entering a state of change. Dr. David Schonfeld, director of the National Center for School Crisis and Bereavement, suggests that coping with these changes involves balancing the past and present: "The goal is to balance continuing bonds with the deceased parent (preserving positive elements that can be preserved). An example being adopting a goal held by the deceased parent as the child's own, transitional objects and sharing memories and stories. Balancing doing this while also creating new relationships with living family members and supports."[1] It might be hard to adjust at first, but as time goes on, hopefully you will feel you are getting better at adapting. Remember, if you find yourself still struggling, don't be afraid to tell an adult you trust. It will be hard for anyone to help you if you don't let them know you are having a hard time.

Changes will come in many forms. You might get new responsibilities. Maybe before your parent died, you were able to be a kid; now, you might need to look after your younger brother or sister. You may never have had chores when your parent was still alive. Now, you might have to take out the trash, wash dishes, vacuum, or do weekly tasks to help out around the house. You may not like your new responsibilities, but this is part of your new reality. Try not to fight it or resist it; just accept it. Consider it as training for when you will become an adult one day and live on your own. You might as well get an early start.

If both parents were working before, your family will most likely experience a drop in income now that only one parent is working, and this can impact you and your siblings. Maybe when your parent was alive you could always get the new-

"The loss of both my parents carried significant life changes. With my mom, we lived in a rental home and I had to immediately vacate the home. My mom had previously wanted me to go with my older brother (nineteen years older) if anything were to happen to her, so my dad was not prepared for me to beg him to let me live with him instead. He never could tell me no, so he quickly made arrangements with my uncle who was renting out a house, and I went from living with my mom for fifteen years to living in a new house with my dad, who I had only spent hours at a time with on the weekends. To say the least, it was a learning experience for both of us. I think the experience of starting over, moving into a new house, and building a different type of relationship with my dad distracted me from the loss of my mom. With my dad, we also were living in a rental home, and although the landlord agreed to let us stay, the trauma of finding my dad's body in the home was enough to make me never want to go back to that house. I also did not want to take my son back there and watch him go to that room and ask for my dad. My ex-boyfriend's family took us in until I could find us a new place to live and my son thought it was all just a long fun sleepover. They understood how important it was to me to keep him happy and we all did everything we could to keep ourselves together and make it a positive environment. It was not easy finding us a place to live because it was my first time on my own, so I had no rental history and not very much income either, but I finally found us a house and we moved immediately. My family helped pack up the old house and I explained to my son that he and I were moving into a new house of our own. Again, I think the process of moving into a new house and adjusting to the new household dynamic helped to distract me from the feeling of loss. This time around, seeing my son happy was a big factor in helping me through as well. I think those changes of home and routine lasted through the first week, month, and year of losing each of them. As far as how my life has changed since then, I would say it made me more independent and confident in myself because I had to be.

"I would say the biggest impact the losses had on my life came after my dad's passing, when I realized that I was now without both of my parents. I was not close with most of the rest of my family, and my son's father was not in the picture, so there was a feeling of being completely on my own. Even if you don't see eye to eye with your parents, you never realize how much influence they have on your decision making. In people's lives, it is usually their parents or their spouse that they turn to when having to make any big decisions. They count on those people to step in and tell them if they are making a horrible mistake or overlooking important details. There is a sense of comfort that is taken for granted when you are able to just run ideas past someone who you know has your best interest in mind. Suddenly, I found myself single and orphaned with the sole weight of decision making on my shoulders. Is this a good rate for car insurance? Should I set up pest control services? What does this rash mean? Am I being a good mom? Without anyone there to guide me or reassure me, I began overanalyzing and second-guessing every decision in my life. It was exhausting. I had to learn how to trust myself and how to be confident in my own decisions."—Kaylene[a]

est video games or the most popular clothes. Now that your mom or dad is gone, your surviving parent might have to make cuts to the extra stuff you used to get.

Your surviving parent might not be around as much as they used to be, especially if he or she has to work more. Or your surviving parent might be home more and want to spend a lot more time with you. Perhaps you are finding that you are attached to your surviving parent more now that your late parent is gone and possibly he or she seems more attached to you. Expect change. If you welcome change instead of trying to resist it, you will be able to adjust more smoothly than if you do the latter.

Grief-Stricken Surviving Parent

In some cases, you might be doing OK dealing with your grief, but that doesn't mean your surviving parent is. Your surviving parent could really be struggling with his or her loss, the new responsibilities, and managing the new dynamic of the household. "When family members are also struggling, this can create challenges for children. The death of a family member can result in depression in a parent, increases in fighting or domestic violence, financial stresses, and other problems."[2] If your surviving parent is having a hard time, you might have to step in and be more responsible than you used to be, especially if you are the oldest of your siblings. Whether it's getting your younger siblings ready for

Abandonment

Abandonment is the condition of feeling or being left, completely and finally; it is the sense of being utterly forsaken or deserted. Chances are that when your parent died—and perhaps to this present day—you may have felt a deep sense of abandonment. You probably were questioning why your parent was taken away from you, why he or she left you, why it happened to you, and many other questions. Feeling abandoned by one parent may make you extremely terrified that your surviving parent or primary caregiver is going to leave you too. If you find that you are constantly worried that your surviving loved ones are going to leave you after your parent died, especially to the point where it is debilitating you daily, please tell a trusted adult immediately so you can get the support you need.

You might not like all the changes in your household, especially if your responsibilities increase and your free time decreases. Remember that you're not the only one in your family having a hard time, and fighting such changes can make things more complicated for everyone. ©iStock / shironosov

Attachment

Attachment is the condition of being emotionally connected to something or someone. Because of your strong attachment to your late parent, you most likely felt a significant amount of pain—and probably still feel it to this day—when he or she died. Your parent was a part of you, still is, just like you are a part of him or her. According to an article in *Psychology Today*, "Our responses to loss depend in large measure on the type and the intensity of our attachments to the person or thing that is lost. Attachment makes life worth living, and attachment makes sure we are in pain when we face loss. Attachment is simply an affectional tie between one's self and another person or thing. We have all sorts of attachments to people, and objects (e.g., souvenirs) and ideas (such as expectations and hopes). And, the more we feel attached, the more it affects us when we lose that person or thing."[b]

Attachment doesn't just have to do with your late parent, however. Now that your mom or dad is gone, you might feel strongly attached to your surviving parent or caregiver, mostly in fear that you will lose him or her too. In return, your surviving parent might be more strongly attached to you as well.

school in the morning, making everyone breakfast, or playing with your siblings to give your surviving parent a minute to grieve, be ready to help your surviving parent if need be.

It will probably be hard to watch your surviving parent grieve. He or she might not process the situation in the same way you do, so try to remember that everyone grieves differently. Helen Fitzgerald of the American Hospice Foundation shares, "It may help you to remember that every person experiences grief differently, and that losing a spouse isn't the same thing as losing a parent. You shouldn't assume that you know exactly how your father [or mother] feels. Try to be understanding and patient."[3] You can help your parent by taking care of things around the house without being asked. This will give your surviving parent more time to grieve, which might help your whole family develop a new system more quickly.

Movies That Show Families Coping with Loss

- *We Bought a Zoo.* Comedy/drama/family, 2011. 124 minutes. Based on a true story, widowed father Benjamin decides to try and re-open a zoo with his children to get a fresh start after the passing of his wife. As there were many obstacles involved with reopening a long-closed zoo, dealing with their grief and learning to try and move forward helped give them the strength to pull off re-opening the zoo after all. The positive distraction brings them all closer together as a family, a family that is trying to grieve its past but look forward to its future.

- *The Boys Are Back.* Drama, 2009. 104 minutes. A sportswriter loses his wife, and is now trying to raise his children as a single father.

- *Louder Than Bombs.* Drama, 2015. 109 minutes. Famed photographer Isabelle Reed dies and leaves her family behind. Two years later, her family is still struggling to cope with life without her.

Youngest Child

If you are the youngest sibling, your role may not change much at all, or it could change significantly. If you were already making your bed every day and cleaning your room, then you will probably keep these same responsibilities. But if your late parent helped you take out the trash or made your lunch for school, you might have to do your chores by yourself and make your own lunch.

Another change might be that you now have to go to someone else for advice and guidance—your surviving parent or an older sibling. You may have gone to your late parent in the past; now you have to adjust to the way someone else handles conversations like these. Keep in mind, however, that your surviving parent and older sibling are also adjusting to changes—such as having you come to them for guidance—and they are also grieving in their own unique ways; just like they are being patient with you, try to be patient with them. This is a period of change and adjustment for everyone in many different ways: "Over the course of mourning, the surviving parent has to adjust to single parenting, the child has to adjust to all the changes in daily life because of the loss of the parent, and the family has to find a way to talk or not to talk about the parent who died."[4]

Family Timeout and Grief Temperature Check

According to the Moyer Foundation, "We all grieve differently and experience different emotions during our grief journey, even if we are grieving the same death of someone."[c] To help people explore how grief is a different experience for each individual, the Moyer Foundation created an activity called the grief puzzle. Here's how it works:

What You'll Need

- Construction paper or butcher paper
- Scissors
- Colored pencils, markers, or crayons

Steps

1. Cut a large piece of paper into puzzle pieces (make sure that everyone has at least one puzzle piece).
2. Each person chooses a prompt (from the list in the next section) to represent on his or her puzzle piece.
3. Using pictures, drawings, designs, or words, everyone colors their own puzzle piece to represent their answer to the prompt.
4. When everyone has completed their puzzle piece, assemble the puzzle as a group.
5. Take turns sharing about your different puzzle pieces.

Puzzle Piece Prompts

- If grief was a color . . .
- If grief was a song . . .
- If grief was an animal . . .
- If grief was a flavor . . .
- If grief was a building . . .
- If grief was a sound . . .

Interview with Dave, the Author's Surviving Parent

Meet my dad, Dave. When my mother passed away in 1993, my dad suddenly became a single father of two children while dealing with his own personal grief at the same time. Let's see what one surviving parent's perspective is like to give you a better idea of what your surviving parent might be going through. Remember, everyone's experience is different.

Michelle Shreeve (MS): Can you describe what it was like when your wife, the mother of your children, was sick? What was going through your mind leading up to the very end?

Dave (D): When she got out of the hospital in 1993, I had felt that she wasn't going to make it to Christmas. I think she felt that too, but we never talked about "the end." On Wednesday morning of her last week, I went to her room (we moved her to the kid's playroom, because she didn't want to keep waking me up in the middle of the night), and we talked for two hours. She thanked me for everything. I think at that moment she knew where she was. At the end of our talk, she told me she wanted to leave the house and go back to the hospital. I think she did that because she didn't want to die in our home where we would still all live in afterwards. I didn't want her to go back to the hospital, but reluctantly, I took her per her wishes.

I visited her during the day when the kids were at school, would pick up the kids from school, and take them back with me to the hospital. She wasn't in the ICU but had flu-like symptoms. She was dealing with pneumonia now at this point. She hadn't been sleeping and was finally able to get some sleep the morning she died. Around 3:00 a.m., I woke up and called the nurses station to see how she was doing. I told them to have her call me. I fell back asleep and at 5:15 a.m., her father called and asked if I had talked to the hospital yet. I said "No." He said, "Don't bother, she passed."

I went next door and explained the situation to the neighbor, and asked if they could come over to watch my kids so I could go to the hospital to sign papers and identify her. I wanted to come home and be there for my kids before they woke up, as that was really important to me.

Michelle came into the living room first and sensed that something was wrong. Mike, my son, came into the living room about thirty minutes later, saw us crying—basically he knew automatically already what happened.

If I would have known that was going to be my wife's last night, I never would have left the hospital the night before.

MS: Can you describe the day you found out the news of your wife's death? The first week, funeral planning, breaking the news to your kids? How did you feel? How did you cope and grieve?

D: After I told my kids what happened and after they picked up my wife and took her to the funeral home, I never wanted to leave my kids alone. I involved my kids with picking out the casket, the pillow inside the casket, the material in the pillow—everything; my kids were a part of the entire process. We looked at the funeral home together and realized it could only hold about 250 people. At that point I realized it wasn't going to be big enough. So, we decided to move it to the very church that we got married in.

Every aspect of the funeral was set to my wife's specs—she was a classy lady who deserved nothing but the best. I went to my friend who was a hairdresser and asked if he could fix her hair and make her look beautiful like he always did for her. He and I were both crying while he fixed her hair.

Neighbors and people from the school made us dinners those first few weeks to help out. For me, I had to think about my kids. It was hard.

MS: Can you describe what it was like to suddenly be a single dad with two kids after you just lost your wife? Was it overwhelming? How did you deal with your emotions? Did you have help?

D: She passed on December 3rd, so holiday plans were already set. We were already scheduled to go to L.A. to be with her family at her brother's house. Everyone was calling us and ringing our phone off the hook—come here for the holidays, come here.

Many times, I just wanted to check out of my life for good: it was anger, hurt, I was upset—all sorts of emotions. Anytime that I started thinking about checking out, I would look down the hall and see my two kids and be reminded why that wasn't an option.

I worked sixteen hours a day when my wife was alive, and she still took care of our kids and worked from home while she was dying. Back then, I looked at life like it was a race. I felt that when my wife died, she handed me the baton and said, "I did the first twelve years with our son and nine years with our daughter, and now it's your turn." Each time I would think about checking out, I reminded myself about the baton she left with me.

Especially in the beginning, I thought I wanted to get away from everyone and have it just be me and my kids. So, I thought about taking us on a cruise—it wasn't at any means a vacation. I also needed to be alone. So, my kids would hang out at one end of the ship while having free range wherever they wanted to go on the ship, and I would be in the back of the ship. They would do their kid stuff while I did my adult stuff, and they always knew where to find me. I would always be in the back of the ship in the morning, because I would reflect on where we have been in life, and I would end up in the front of the ship by the afternoon, to see where we were going in life. Then we would meet up together to have breakfast, lunch, and dinner.

I would think a lot while we were on the cruise ship when I was alone—everything that happened, what direction we were heading in now, how I'm supposed to do this being a single parent. I had a lot of selfish anger. I didn't suffer one bit compared to how my wife, Kathy, did. I tried to separate my thoughts. Now I'm a single dad and this is what I was dealt with.

The one thing I told my kids, is I sat them both down, and told them I can never replace their mother, nor could I ever be their mom, but that I would try to be the best dad ever for the both of them.

MS: How hard was it to raise two kids when you missed your wife so much?

D: I made the commitment to not check out and to stay and raise them, and I held true to my commitment. I sold our family business when my wife was sick at the end. For the next sixteen months, I didn't work and went through five bank accounts. I never left my kids. I woke them up in the morning, made them lunches, took them to school, and then would come back to the house. At the house, I would do paperwork regarding the legalities when a spouse dies. I would cry all the time and would wait for her to come walking back through the front door. It was my daily routine, and then I would pick the kids up after school, go to all of their sporting events, PTA teacher conferences. I would even get calls from other fathers who would be mad at me. Their wives would comment to them, "Why can't you be more like Dave? He's always involved and is at all his kid's events." The other dads and I would just laugh.

I focused on my kids. At one point, my kids were trying to get me to go on blind dates and try to get me back in the world. They knew I was hurting. I wanted to make them a priority first and make sure they had everything they needed. I cried every day. I tried not to do it in front of my kids, but I'm sure they sensed it, and even at times, heard me cry.

MS: Want to share about your remarriage?

D: I was never in a mind-set where I was ever trying to replace my wife. I thought it was just going to be me and my kids for the rest of my life. I never thought I would meet someone else. I met Trish and we had some really fun times together.

One night, I sat my kids down and asked what they thought about her moving in. They knew I was seeing her. I asked what they thought about her, and to see if it was ok if she moved into our house. I emphasized that Trish was not going to replace their mom. One of my kids asked if we had to call her mom. I told them they didn't have to and that she didn't want to be their mom, and to just call her "Trish."

I never passed on my parenting duties to Trish. I still did the parenting—I never thought that Trish was here to fill the gap. I never passed the buck to her.

Trish did something very special for us. She made a picture collage of my late wife, Kathy, that included a poem on top, *Death Is Nothing at All*. That really comforted me, and each time I would walk by the poem I would read it. It served as a reminder for me as to why I can't check out.

MS: How did the household change after your wife's death? Chaotic at first? Did you guys eventually find a new rhythm?

D: The foundation was already set—discipline and chores, back when my wife was alive. We pretty much maintained the same format. We would rotate chores and had a chore list. We tried to maintain the household as close as possible to how my wife did everything.

I remember reiterating to my kids that I can't replace their mom, but I will try to be the best dad I could be. There was no, "Wait until your mom gets home" to ask about decisions that needed to be made. It was only me now. I was the judge, jury, and executioner. I told my kids I would try to be fair and that they just need to be patient with me, because normally my bark would come out first. I didn't want to let my kids out of my sight, so if they asked if they could spend the night somewhere, I would go through a checklist in the back of my mind before I would tell them the answer. Have they been good? Did they do their chores? I could never say, "Let me check with your mother" anymore. The format of our household changed, but the foundation was already there. We were just down one key person.

MS: Did you have help? Refer to any books? Counseling? Support groups for you or the kids?

D: We had a family therapist we continued to see. If my kids ever needed the therapist, I let them see her anytime. Our therapist already knew my wife for ten years by that point. My kids could talk to her anytime. The therapist recommended some books and we got some—I just never realized they weren't books for kids, but were mostly for me. I never went to any support groups. I had the therapist and she knew our family well and she understood us. I just tried to keep moving myself forward and keep seeing how my kids were doing and determine where they were at.

I realized during all of this, there's a lot more good people out in the world than there were bad. The teachers, neighbors, the school, other children's parents were always there for us; they cooked us dinners, helped give us all a break, and would let my kids stay at their house. It was surprising because you don't really know how many good people are really out there.

MS: What advice do you have for teens who just lost a parent and now only have their surviving parent, other guardian, or caregiver to rely on?

D: Never go to bed, leave the house, or hang up the phone upset no matter how upset you might be, no matter what happened, without saying "I love you." When my wife passed away, we told her we loved her the night before, and her eyes weren't open and so she didn't get a chance to acknowledge what we said.

Hug your surviving parent or guardian and understand that might be your last hug. Stay close to them. No one ever tells the surviving parent or guardian they're doing a good job more than what a hug from their kid does. If you need something or are hurting, make sure you tell your surviving parent or guardian. With two parents, two people can sense stuff going on with their children easier than just one parent can. Make sure you always communicate with them.

MS: Do you have any advice for surviving parents or guardians out there?

D: What worked for me that might work for them is the relay race baton: now it's your turn to carry your family through. Make sure you communicate, as you are all hurting in different ways, but are hurting about the same person. Make sure you have access to a family therapist or church or something that works for you. Remember there's more good people than bad—most people who are real friends are there to support you. You don't want to ask for help, but you need to vent every now and then. Don't be afraid to tell family and friends in your life how you're feeling; it helps you.

MS: Any advice for surviving parents who remarry? Incoming stepparents of grieving spouses and children?

D: I would not want to be a stepparent ever and I do not envy a stepparent. I don't think my kids ever treated her like a parent, just Trish. Don't get remarried to have a new parent help you out with parenting. You are the parent. Only get remarried because you want to be with that person. It also depends on the age of your children. Never lose sight of the fact that you, the surviving parent, are the real parent.

MS: Anything you would like to add?

D: We all make mistakes along the way. Things could have been done better. We can't fix yesterday, don't know if tomorrow will come, so enjoy life and live for today is my motto. Enjoy everything you have because you don't know what tomorrow will bring, if there even is one.

The pain never goes away and always stays in your mind. Twenty-four years have gone by and I can watch a movie, experience a grief trigger about my late wife, and just start crying all of a sudden still to this very day.[d]

It might take some time for everyone to adjust to their new roles and responsibilities, so make sure you have someone to talk to about your own personal grief, in case your older siblings or surviving parent are not available. If you are having trouble finding someone to talk to, try writing in a journal (I highly recommend the Deconstruction/Reconstruction journal from the Dougy Center that you can find on tdcbookstore.org). If you can't get your thoughts out to a person right away, at least you can get them out on paper in the meantime.

Also, be aware that as the youngest child, you might have a harder time coping than your older siblings. This is completely normal for several reasons. According to Dr. David Schonfeld, pediatrician and childhood bereavement expert,

The death of a parent during the first five years of life (when children are most dependent on their parents) as well as death during adolescence (when adolescents are seeking independence with ambivalence), are times when complicated grief [when feelings of the loss of your parent are debilitating and don't improve even after time passes] is most likely. Younger children need particular attention to re-establishing a sense of safety, consistency, and a nurturing relationship with surviving family members. They also need more explanation to understand what death means, since their limited understanding often contributes to feelings of guilt and shame and concerns about the death of others.[5]

"My siblings are all significantly older than me (all in their forties), but my relationship with all of them changed drastically after my parents passed away. My brother and I have the same mom, but different dads, and he is the only sibling that I somewhat grew up with. He was already out of the house when I was born, but I loved visiting him and looked up to him when I was young. He did not handle my mom's death well at all, and I gradually lost respect for him as he let his life spiral out of control and we drifted apart to the point where we barely speak to each other anymore. I think I resent him for not trying to take care of me as my big brother when I was going through losing each of my parents. In the case of my two sisters, we have the same dad, but different moms. I didn't know that my sisters even existed until I was about twelve. I still don't know all of the details, but my dad had lost contact with them when they were young. I could tell it was a sensitive subject, so I never asked my dad about them. It wasn't until he had passed away that they reached out to me via Facebook and one of them asked to come from California to the memorial service in Arizona. It was then that I met my oldest sister for the first time and she invited me to California to stay with her family and meet my other sister and their mom, my dad's ex-wife. It was a whirlwind of emotions going through meeting them, discussing the memories we had of our dad and getting to know this side of my family that I never knew anything about. Since his passing, I have made several trips to visit them in California and I am extremely grateful to be able to gain and hold onto this piece of my dad."—Kaylene[e]

Another reason younger children sometimes have a harder time after a parent's death is that they can't control their anxiety and comfort themselves as well as older children. "This does not imply that all children who lose parents are destined to develop lasting emotional problems, but younger children are more vulnerable if they do not receive optimal adult care."[6]

Older Sibling

If you are the oldest sibling, you have probably stepped up to help around the house and with your siblings. Your parent might need to pick up extra shifts at

> "When my dad died, my brother inherited a sense of increased responsibility, especially over me. He felt the need to be 'my dad' in many ways. He was twelve when my dad died, so it wasn't fair that he felt he had to be the 'man of the house.' He struggled with that responsibility the first few years, but as I mentioned earlier, he really did an amazing job of showing me respect and making me feel loved and cared for. I respect him more than just about anyone in the world."—Julie[f]

work now because he or she is the sole provider for your household, and you need to be there to pick up the slack. Whether or not your surviving parent or guardian asks for help, he or she is going to need it, so try to be as helpful as possible. Taking on more chores, helping younger siblings with homework, and so on may be tough; it will make you grow up faster—put you on the fast track to adulthood. Also, looking out for your younger siblings doesn't just mean making their school lunches or tucking them in at night. It also has to do with letting them come to you for advice, being open to talk about the death of your parent together, and paying attention to who they are hanging out with at school. Caring for siblings can also provide you with a positive distraction to take your mind off your late parent, especially during that first tough year.

Taking on the extra roles at home can add more to your plate; these new responsibilities combined with your academic or extra-curricular activities might be taking a toll on you. According to Dr. Schonfeld, "Parental death poses a unique challenge in regards to adolescents—impact on juniors and seniors, impact on academics, difficulty in considering leaving family/home for college or career—and it impacts those that are attending college [or planning to attend]."[7] If you are having trouble handling everything, don't be afraid to tell an adult. Then you will have someone to help you work out a game plan to try and make things more balanced.

> "When my mother died, I became a super protective brother of my younger sister. I noticed that I started being more aware of who she was hanging out with at school, who she was talking to, and I always kept a distant eye on her. I guess you could say I took a nurturing mother role on behalf of her to protect her after my mother died."—Mike[g]

Only Child

Maybe you are an only child. Now, it might just be you and your surviving parent, all alone in your home. Everything that you are used to is surely going to change, especially the way your household will be run. You may notice that your surviving parent is making some changes, not only in your household routine, but also with himself or herself. Just as you need positive distractions to help you cope, he or she might need that as well. Your surviving parent might decide to join a gym, start connecting with friends more, or need to cry more. Remember that your surviving parent is grieving just like you are, but he or she might need to do it in a different way.

In some cases, your surviving parent might be grieving steadily; he or she might even want to grieve alongside you. After a parental death, your surviving parent might start spending more time with you—even if you didn't spend a lot of time together before. It all depends on each individual situation and circumstances. "Single children won't have the potential support of siblings, but may have access to more of the time and energy of the surviving parent," says Dr. Schonfeld.[8] Be patient with your surviving parent, whether he or she is spending more or less time with you, and take this time to work on your own grieving. Through time, you and your surviving parent will get to a place where you both can feel like you are living again.

Do what you need to to grieve properly while letting your surviving parent do the same. Whether you work together to get over the loss or grieve separately, it will probably take an adjustment period to get used to the changes in your lives. ©iStock / KatarzynaBialasiewicz

When Your Surviving Parent Decides to Remarry

> "It's important that the stepparent should not be seen as a replacement for the deceased parent, and that children should be encouraged to share memories and stories of the deceased parent."—Dr. David Schonfeld[h]

There may come a day when your surviving parent wants to remarry. With remarriage, there is a chance that your family will grow, and you could inherit some new stepsiblings. Now your original family has become a new blended family. Acquiring new siblings can be fun and enjoyable, and at times hard and stressful. "As children move from a home with a single parent into one that now includes a stepparent and perhaps stepsiblings, they will probably have changes in the way their family functions. Routines will be changed and new chores may be in place."[9] Living with different personalities under one roof can take some time getting used to. It is important to communicate to your surviving parent how you are feeling.

If you are too afraid to talk to your surviving parent or stepparent about how you are feeling, you can always try to discuss the situation with a trusted adult at school, your congregation of choice, your coach, or a friend's parent. You can also try communicating in different ways. For example, you and your surviving parent and/or stepparent can do a family counseling session together. One thing that I did with my stepmother is that I would write her letters. I felt like I could get more of what I was feeling across in writing than in speaking to her face to face. She would also take me out to dinner frequently and let me vent or discuss whatever was bothering me, which really helped. Find what is comfortable for you and share it with your surviving parent and stepparent, so you all can communicate effectively.

> "The sibling dynamic most definitely changed, as I acquired three new siblings, all of whom were older than me. When I first met them, I was really excited to get three new siblings (like bouncing up and down excited), but they did not share my enthusiasm. As I said earlier, it was really rough adjusting to my new life. For kindness sake, let's just say that it has been basically the Cold War between the four of us ever since, until recently, and for the majority of the time, I might as well have been invisible."—Carissa[i]

When You Are Forced to Move in with Another Family Member

If one or both of your parents die, you might be in a situation where you must move in with extended family. Maybe your late mom or dad was a single parent, because your other biological parent was never in the picture. If you are still under age, you might be forced to move in with another family member. This means you not only have to deal with the death of your parent, but you must also deal with living in a new house, possibly going to a new school, and trying to make new friends. Each one of these life changes can be extremely stressful. Authors Schonfeld and Quackenbush call these changes "secondary losses"; that is, losses that result from the loss of the parent: "When children lose someone close to them, they experience the immediate and direct effects of that death. In most instances, especially if the deceased is a parent or primary caregiver, they also experience

"After she died, everything just sort of became a blur. I tried to stay as busy as I possibly could to distract myself from everything that happened. I filled my life with people and stuff and just tried not to think about my future or about what exactly did just happen in my life. I ended up moving in with a family friend that I at first called my aunt and later called mom. We instantly grew a bond with one another because she was like a second mother to me and since I was in need of a mother, it felt very comforting to have her in my life. At the same time, she had lost her daughter and was in need of that mother/daughter bond as well, and so I was like a second daughter to her. The timing was much needed as we both just lost a mother and a daughter pretty much at the same time.

"Although this is what we both needed, things changed a little bit as the months went on and a time of confusion started for me. There started to be custody and guardian issues and I felt like I was being bounced around with the people around me. Although the people around me were trying to show that they cared, I ultimately just felt like I was in a circle with five strings and I didn't know where to go or what to do. There was a lot of silent fighting that was going on and I felt like I didn't have a voice. After all, I was only thirteen, so how would I know what is best for me or how to express what I needed? I felt as though I was raising myself when all that I needed was a mother."—Joella[j]

Tips for Adjusting to a New Living Situation

It is always positive and healthy to have an emotional outlet, something you can do to relieve stress and give yourself a break.. This is especially true when you're dealing with a big loss like the death of a parent and other potential extenuating circumstances such as having to move away, attend a new school, adjust to a stepfamily, or move in with a family member. Since each individual is different, it is important to find the emotional outlet that works best for you.

Think about these questions:

Do you like to write poetry?

Do you like to record music?

Do you like to paint?

Do you like to volunteer?

Do you like to sing?

Do you like to sit quietly and read a book alone somewhere?

Do you like to cook?

Do you like to listen to music?

Do you like to tend to a garden?

What do you enjoy doing in your free time that gives you peace, relaxes you, makes you happy?

Has anyone ever told you how great you are at something? Drawing? Sculpting?

Take what you really enjoy doing and use that as a positive emotional outlet during your time of transition. This way, anytime you might be having a rough day, you have something to turn to, in case an adult you wish to talk to is unavailable. The more positive, healthy emotional outlets you have, the more options you give yourself in case you need them—if the adult you trust is unavailable, and you're out of watercolor paints, what next? It's good to have backups upon backups. Adjusting can be hard, but having emotional outlets can really help you get through this difficult time of transition during your life.

additional losses in their lives. Examples include changed relationships, moving, lifestyle, peer group status, shared memories, shared visions and plans for the future, and a sense of security and safety."[10]

If you find that you are struggling with all of these changes—moving to a new home, living with someone new, going to a new school, or other circumstances—don't be afraid to reach out to a trusted adult. Make sure you are trying to handle everything in a healthy and positive way to the best of your ability. If you feel like you are falling short with this and need some extra support, talk to your designated trusted adult for guidance, reach out to your teachers at school, counselor, or coach to get you the support you need.

No matter what your situation is, stay true to your emotions and your needs. If you are not getting what you need, then it is your responsibility to speak up and tell a trusted adult what's going on. People around you most likely want to help you, but they can't if you don't let them know what's going on. Staying true to your emotions and needs means you have to pay attention to how you are feeling, the thoughts you are thinking, the words you are saying. If you are sad, staying sad is not going to help you get happy. Engaging in a positive and healthy emotional outlet or letting a trusted adult know you are feeling sad—these are ways you can change your situation for the better. The same goes for if people around you are asking if you are OK. If you deny your feelings, and tell them everything is fine, then you are not staying true to your emotions, and thus, not getting what you need. Always remember, if you are having trouble handling all of the changes that are happening, don't be afraid to speak up and ask for support from either your surviving parent, your teacher, your guidance counselor, your coach, or any other adult with whom you can comfortably share your feelings.

SECOND PARENTS

No one can replace your parent: the way that your mother wore her hair or sprayed her perfume, the way that your father tied his ties or shaved his face. I won't lie, but those quirky things your parent used to do, the little things you didn't think twice about, are the things that you are probably going to miss the most about him or her.

There may be times when someone will remind you of your late parent, whether because she is wearing the same perfume your mother did or because he ties his shoes the same way your father did. These moments can be bittersweet. They may make you smile and feel good inside, but they also may make you realize how much you miss your parents. Let's talk a little bit about this.

When You Come across Someone Resembling Your Parent

Sometimes after losing a parent, you may have experiences of receiving a "gift" from him or her. It might happen at the moment when you least expect it, but when you need it the most. You might come across someone who closely resembles your late parent. Perhaps her voice is as beautiful as your mother's was, and as soon as you hear this person speak, your heart drops. Maybe it is someone who knew your parent when he or she was alive, or maybe it is someone who didn't know your mom or dad at all. You might find yourself wanting to spend more time with that person. Or perhaps you met a man who throws a baseball in the exact way that your father used to. This new man also happens to be your best friend's father, which explains why you find yourself hanging out at your friend's house a lot more than you used to.

There is no need to freak out if this ever happens to you. Instead, embrace it, because the person might be the closest you come to being with someone who resembles your late parent. If you have regular contact with this person, you might start thinking of him or her as your second parent.

It Happened to Me: A Note from the Author

I have had many second parents over the years; some knew my mother, and some did not. I remember a few years ago, I actually searched in my mother's yearbook to see if I could find someone to talk to who knew her when she was young. After all, my mom didn't get very many chances to tell me stories about her childhood, so I thought it would be neat to meet someone who was a child with her, who grew up with her, and later went to high school with her. I actually found a few names and then started researching the names on Facebook. I ended up connecting with two people. The two women have been kind enough to share some memories they had of my mother when they were all young as well as some letters they exchanged with one another, and one of the women (thank you, Debbie) was kind enough to send me a little keepsake package of some mementoes from when my mother was alive. She sent me some photographs and some memorabilia from my mother and father's wedding, which she attended and was a part of. That meant so much to me.

I have a few other second parents that I am still in contact with to this day: my high school basketball coaches; many of my friend's parents, who have guided me along the way for the last two decades; and many "work moms" I have met and kept in touch with over the years. Many of my second parents have helped me get through some difficult times in my life. I am very grateful to have had so many help me along the way.

What Is a Second Parent?

A second parent, or an alloparent, is someone a who takes you under his or her wing, as if you were his or her own child. They might also possess certain qualities or characteristics that remind you of your late parent. Look at your life right this second; you might already have a second parent in your life. Maybe it is your soccer coach or the pastor at your church or your friend's mother. Perhaps the person in your life wears her hair in the same style as your mother did or throws a football in the same spiral fashion that your dad did. Or maybe it's your friend's mom, who always invites you over for dinner on Friday night, or your buddy's

"My grandmother (my mom's mom) is literally my second mother. She tells me that I am her second daughter even though I am her granddaughter. I tell her about everything that I would have told my mom, to her. I call her at least once to three or four times a week, and have some really great twenty-minute conversations. I tell her about school, boys, friends, and everything in between. She is my everything and I love her so much."—Adriana[a]

dad, who always invites you to watch baseball games at their house. You might not have someone like this in your life already, but that doesn't mean you will never get one—it just might take some time.

Having second parents in your life can help fill the void you might feel after losing a parent. When you initially lost your parent, you probably walked around each day feeling like you had a huge hole in your heart. It may have felt, and still feels, like something's missing. The feeling will probably never leave you completely, but a second parent can help fill the void. Dr. David Schonfeld, childhood bereavement expert and director of the National Center for School Crisis and Bereavement shares, "A second parent is another caring and consistent adult in the child's life who can help provide important support to children; to the extent they [may have been] close to the deceased parent, they can assist with the preservation of continuing bonds (telling stories, listening to stories), anticipate and minimize grief triggers (e.g., be present on family holidays, attend events with children that were attended in the past by the deceased parent, etc.); minimize secondary losses (e.g., an aunt can help a daughter prepare for a first date and minimize the loss of advice that would have been provided by the mother)."[1]

Is a Second Parent a Replacement Parent?

No one could ever replace your parent. You can, however, have people who resemble your late parent and who can comfort you by displaying traits that remind you what you miss the most about your parent.

You might feel guilty if you become very close with your second parent, as if you are replacing your late parent. Don't feel guilty. If anything, see it as an opportunity to share things about your late parent with your second parent. By sharing what your late parent was like and what you used to do together, your second parent might be able to fill the void by participating with you in some of these activities.

"Throughout the whole process and my life today, there have been many women who stepped up to the plate as a mother figure in my life. My grandma, my dad's mom, moved in with us right after the accident to take on the motherly duties of the house. Throughout the years my grandma has always been a mother to my sister and I, being there for us whenever we needed her and walking us through the fun teenage stuff like periods, shaving, and boys. Our aunt, my mom's sister, has always been a mother figure to us as well, loving us, teaching us, and treating us like her own kids. My mom also had a best friend whose daughter was my best friend, so any time we spent with them she always made sure we were taken care of, and still does."—McKenna[b]

Second parents are like mentors to us. If only heaven had a phone and we could just pick it up and call our late parent and ask him or her for advice. That would be nice, but that is not reality. Since your parent can't be here, think of a second parent as a surrogate, someone to whom you can turn for advice.

Second Parents Come in Many Forms

Second parents can be anyone in your life. They can be your coach, teacher, pastor, friend's parent; your aunt or uncle; your employer; or even your neighbor. They are people you can talk to, ask for advice, turn to on your hard days, or someone who is your friend and will listen to you vent or share stories about your late parent. Child and adolescent psychiatrist Dora Black shares, "For optimal emotional and social development to occur, children need a warm, secure, affectionate, individualized, and continuous experience of care from a few caretakers who interact with them in a sensitive way and who can live in harmony with each other."[2] The caretakers you

"There were several men from our school (coaches and teachers) and church who also stepped up at various times to help my family and whom I looked up to as second fathers. I really was blessed to be surrounded by so many people who cared for me and my family. They truly fulfilled the Biblical mandate to protect and provide for the widow and her children."—Julie[c]

"My boyfriend and I are two of the few teenagers I know who have lost a parent. It is nice to have my boyfriend to talk to, as he can also relate to the topic of parent loss. I find it easier talking to people my age who went through a loss like I did, as opposed to adults or counselors or looking for a second parent, because they understand me better."—Ella[d]

have in your life right now might be acting as your second parents. Consider them angels from the sky, as if your parent sent them down to you.

You may gain more than one second parent as the years go on. Honestly, the more second parents you can accumulate, the better; if one is busy on a day you need to talk, you're likely to find someone else to talk with when you are having a hard day. Second parents are another part of your support system, and it's best to get more support than you think you need. There will be days where you think you are doing just fine, and then bam—a grief trigger happens, and you break down emotionally out of the blue. Having many positive people around you who love and care for you will really help you get the support you need as you are growing up.

Changes with Your Second Parents

Nothing stays the same forever. Sometimes you may have everything going the same for you for a few years, and then suddenly life changes in some way. Maybe your friend moved away for college and his mom, your second parent, decides to move away to be closer to her child. Now, you feel like you just lost your second parent. Or maybe you are the one leaving for college, which means you have to move away from your second parent. No matter the case, know that things with your second parents may change over the years. Some may stay in your life forever, while others may leave after a short while. Be thankful you have them for the time that you do and don't take their presence for granted. You never know when your time may be up with them.

"My social studies teacher had an uncle who died of suicide as well, so we have that in common, in terms of if I had to choose someone on the outside who was like a second father to me."—Chase[e]

It Happened to Me: A Note from the Author

Half of my growing up years were spent in California, and the other half in Arizona. When my mother died, we were in California, and everyone I went to school with knew my mother. So, when she passed away, a lot of people stepped up and tried to be a second parent to my brother and me. Teachers, coaches, our friend's parents, our family members, family friends, neighbors—there were so many. This was great at first. Having so many second mothers helped distract me in a positive way. They all tried to make my life feel normal, despite the turmoil I was frequently feeling.

The hard part is that I grew attached to a lot of these women, and then things would change: some of my second mothers moved away or they started to get too busy to spend time with me, and it would often sting when that happened. It was especially agonizing when I moved to Arizona in 1997 and had to say good-bye to all my second mothers. It was like feeling the loss of my mother all over again. We all did our best to stay in touch, but they had their own families and lives to attend to, so I could only talk to them or correspond with them so much.

When we moved to Arizona, we only knew two people at first, but they knew my mother, as we all lived in California together at one point. So, I instantly bonded with the two of them as if they were second parents to me. As I started going to school and meeting new people and starting friendships, I noticed I was doing it all over again: I was growing attached to those I felt were second mothers to me. That was fine at first, because I knew we weren't moving out of state again anytime soon. But then I made the transition from middle school to high school, and I lost some of my second mothers through the transition. The transition to college was even worse, and again when I moved into adulthood.

I was a tomboy growing up and played sports all of the time. Throughout my middle school, high school, and college years, and even to this day still, I always preferred hanging out with guys; there have only been a few select girls whom I considered friends. During middle school and high school, I stopped looking for a second mother.

During and after college, I even got to a point where I started pulling away from all women in my life, not trusting them and guarding myself against them. Why would I want to get close to women, when they kept leaving me or hurting me over and over?

Looking back, I can see that having second mothers benefited me a great deal. They helped me during my difficult transitional phases; they did girly things with me like shopping and putting on makeup, and they gave me life advice in general. Bless all of their hearts, they would always reassure me that my mother would be so proud of me, which I really needed to hear and really appreciated them telling me that.

A Warning about Second Parents

It is normal to develop a very strong bond and emotional attachment with second parents. Along with the new bond comes a warning I must convey to you. There may come a day when something terrible happens to your second parent, something that may devastate you and rock your world, such as your second parent moving away or even dying. You need to be prepared for that before you let in a second parent wholeheartedly.

Think about it. You are going through your own parent loss situation, trying to navigate how to move forward in your life without him or her. In walks a second parent, whom you grow to love and care for in similar ways. With caring and love come emotional attachments and bonds. If one day that bond gets dam-

"My Grandpa Bill was my 'second father.' He was always at all of my sports games and would spend Saturdays with me and my siblings regularly. He would talk to me about making good choices, and working hard in school. I remember him taking me fishing often and him telling me he loved me, and that fishing with his grandson was his favorite thing to do in the world. He was a great man and a wonderful role model to me. He had colon cancer and battled for five years until he finally passed away in 2000. I was fourteen years old when he passed away and I went through a very similar grieving process as when my dad passed away."—Thomas[f]

Having an attachment to a second parent can be valuable but potentially fraught with emotions. It's important to maintain a healthy, positive relationship between the two of you. ©iStock / Highwaystarz-Photography

aged through something tragic such as death, those feelings of abandonment or loneliness or a deep longing for that parental connection can spring back up to the surface all over again, causing more emotional turmoil.

Here is the kicker part, the one that you really need to prepare yourself for: If you suffer the loss of your second parent, it will bring back memories and emotions of losing your actual parent. The pain may be worse or just the same as before. That's why you need to be aware that when you do finally come across and grow close to a second parent, there is the potential that you could lose him or her, too, someday. This is true of everyone in your life; every single person in your life right now can go at any minute, with or without warning. We have no control over whose time is up or who will still be here for us tomorrow. All we can do is make the most out of each day, spend as much time with our loved ones as we can, and never forget to say, "I love you," to one another.

This warning is not designed to convince you to avoid having a second parent. You can't be afraid to get close to someone in life just because you don't want to have the pain of losing him or her. By doing that, you simply would not be living a full life—something your late parent would want you to do. This is just a friendly reminder to prepare yourself and accept up front that the person you are getting close to could one day disappear. Make the most of your time with your second parent. I hope that you do not have to suffer a double loss, but it's safer to prepare than to be completely blindsided.

Being Territorial with Your Second Parent

Your second parent can bring back happiness you thought you would never feel again, ever since your parent passed away. You love spending time with your second parent, and you have developed a strong bond in which you feel like you want him or her all to yourself. But that might not be possible. If you have siblings, you had to share your late parent with them. Likewise, you might have to share your second parent with his or her biological children as well. This is another aspect of the second parent scenario that you need to watch for. Your second parent may be a mother or father to other children. Just like your late parent, who made you a priority, a second parent needs to make his or her children a priority. Being a mother or father to other children must come first.

If you want to play catch with your friend's father, who also happens to be your second father, ask if you can join them to all play catch together. You can't demand that he only plays with you, and not his son. You are most likely going to have to share your second parent with others. As long as you are willing to share your second parent with others in his or her life who also need attention, you will have a healthier relationship with your second parent.

Getting Your Chosen Second Parent Involved in Your Life

Let's say you feel like you are getting close to an adult you feel comfortable with, someone you consider to be your second parent. You want to spend more time with him or her, but you don't know how to ask. Try to get him or her involved in your life, rather than trying to get involved in his or hers. Since your second parent is an adult, his or her life is established, while yours is still changing and evolving. It is easier and better for an adult to adapt to your life and choose what he or she can be involved in—you can make the invitation to events and let him or her work it in.

Maybe you play soccer on the school team or perform in school plays. Maybe you play an instrument in the choir at your church, or you are on a city league skateboarding team. Invite your second parent to attend. Don't stop there, as you can invite him or her to your birthday party or even family barbecues for that matter. If you do have a bond forming with your second parent, he or she will probably be more than happy to participate in your interests and activities to

Watching movies or reading books can help you cope with the loss of a parent. Sometimes, a certain character can remind you of your late parent, which might bring you comfort. ©iStock / diego_cervo

Movies and TV Shows to Help You Navigate Your Second Parent Situation

As brought up in previous chapters, sometimes fictional situations can help teach us how to navigate our real-life situations. This can come in the form of books, TV shows, or movies. Fiction can give us insight into real-life situations; however, in the end, you are the one who is responsible for the decisions you make, which may differ from those made by characters in novels or movies.

With that being said, here are some movies and TV shows that deal with second parent situations:

- *Big Hero 6*. Animation/action/adventure movie, 2014. 102 minutes. Hiro and Tadashi live with their aunt in San Francisco. Tadashi is the big brother always looking out for his younger brother, Hiro. When tragedy strikes, Hiro has to dig deep inside of himself to discover his true potential.
- *The Blind Side*. Biography/drama/sport movie, 2009. 129 minutes. This movie tells the true story of NFL player Michael Oher, who upon being homeless and traumatized by his difficult upbringing, was taken in by a family on the other side of his world. He ended up being a first round NFL draft pick and credits most of his success to the family that took him in as one of their own.
- *Creed*. Drama/sport movie, 2015. 133 minutes. Adonis Johnson, son of the late Apollo Creed, is trying to find his place in the world. This is something he struggles with. Rocky Balboa, the former world heavyweight champion, friend, and former rival of Apollo Creed, decides he wants to step in and help Adonis find his way.
- *Full House*. Comedy/drama/family TV series, 1987–1995. 22-minute episodes. When sisters Michelle, Stephanie, and D. J. lose their mother, their father, Danny, is forced to try and raise the girls on his own. Danny's brothers want to help, and so the two brothers move into Danny's house and serve as additional surrogate parents for the girls.

- *Harry Potter and the Prisoner of Azkaban.* Adventure/family/fantasy movie, 2004. 142 minutes. Harry loses his parents young and meets a plethora of second parents throughout his growing up stages. Many are those who knew his parents well; some are at the school he attends. Others are his friend's parents. He even gets reunited with his godfather, who he becomes quickly attached to.

- *Lilo and Stitch.* Animation/adventure/comedy movie, 2002. 85 minutes. Lilo lives with her big sister, Nani, who takes care of Lilo as if she were her own daughter. The two struggle because they wish they could just be sisters instead of acting like mother and daughter. Stitch, a new friend Lilo makes, is able to offer a new perspective for both Lilo and Nani, which helps the two sisters, in unique ways, move forward in life.

- *The Lion King.* Action/adventure/drama movie, 1994. 88 minutes. When tragedy strikes Pride Rock and their leader is killed, young Simba blames himself for his father's death and runs away. He stumbles upon a warthog and a meerkat, who take Simba in as if he were their own child. They later become good friends as Simba grows up and discovers who he truly is.

- *No Reservations.* Comedy/drama/romance movie, 2007. 104 minutes. Zoe loses her mother to a car accident. With her father out of the picture, there is nobody left to take care of Zoe, except her Aunt Kate. Kate is childless and used to living alone. Both her and Zoe's worlds change to try and create a new one together.

- *Pete's Dragon.* Animation/adventure/comedy movie, 1977. 128 minutes. An orphaned boy, Pete, meets a magical dragon who instantly becomes his closest friend. Pete gets caught up with his not so nice adoptive parents and struggles with what to do next. Luckily, two other adults serve as surrogate parents to Pete.

- *Prince of Persia: The Sands of Time.* Action/adventure/fantasy movie, 2010. 116 minutes. Dastan is wandering around the streets of the kingdom when he does something noble that catches the king's eye. It catches the king's eye so much that he decides to take Dastan into his kingdom as if he were his own child. The king acts as second/surrogate father to Dastan for the rest of his childhood.

- *The Princess Diaries*. Comedy/family/romance movie, 2001. 111 minutes. Mia lives with her mother and suddenly finds out she is entitled to the royal throne. Her grandmother, the queen, takes Mia under her wing and shows her how to be royal material. Joe, the queen's right-hand man, also takes Mia under his wing as if Mia were his own child.

- *Raising Helen*. Comedy/drama/romance movie, 2004. 119 minutes. Bachelorette Helen loses her sister and brother-in-law to a car accident. Suddenly, Helen is now the guardian of their three children. Amongst her grief and the difficulties of letting go of her single lifestyle, Helen starts a journey to change her world and the world of three children, to create a new one for all of them to live in together.

- *Rookie of the Year*. Comedy/family/fantasy movie, 1993. 103 minutes. Henry lives with his mother, as his father passed away when he was young. His mother does a good job trying to be both mother and father at the same time. After a freak accident, Henry's world changes to where he eventually meets his ultimate second parent as a result.

- *Secondhand Lions*. Comedy/family/drama movie, 2003. 109 minutes. Walter lives with his irresponsible mother and when she decides to run off with the new boyfriend of the month, she drops Walter off at his rich uncles' house. Her plan was to try and get Walter to find out where the uncles' money stash was. All it did was make Walter realize he would rather be raised by his two uncles than his irresponsible mother.

- *Star Trek*. Action/adventure/sci-fi movie, 2009. 127 minutes. Kirk lost his father when he was born and has struggled to find his way ever since. A commanding officer of the Star Fleet sees something in Kirk and tries to show him the way.

- *Tron: Legacy*. Action/adventure/sci-fi movie, 2010. 125 minutes. Sam loses his mother young, and a little while after, Sam's father disappears mysteriously. Feeling completely abandoned by both of his parents, Sam struggles to move forward with his life. Sam's father's old colleague has always kept a close eye on Sam, to try and help him through his growing-up years. In fact, he even gets Sam and his father reconnected eventually.

support you. You can also talk to your living parent and tell him or her that you would like to invite your second parent over more. Your living parent can probably think of more ways to involve the second parent in your life.

In any relationship, "there is a potential for conflict . . . actually a certainty. Open communication (modeled by the adults and encouraged of the child) can be very helpful," says Dr. Schonfeld.[3] The best thing to do is communicate with your living parent regarding this.

STEPPARENTS

After the death of his or her spouse, your surviving parent may start to feel lonely. Feeling lonely may lead to the need and desire to have a partner again, and as a result, your surviving mother or father may decide to remarry. He or she may do this to fill the void of the special person that was lost. If your surviving parent goes through with it, suddenly you will have a new person living in your home, sitting, eating, and sleeping where your late mother or father used to be. This will most likely be a tough adjustment, on top of your new routine, new responsibilities, and new life without your mom or dad.

Your new stepparent could never replace your late mother or father, and the new person should never make you feel that he or she could. According to bereavement expert Dr. David Schonfeld, "No one can replace another person, but someone can help fill a role—you can't replace a parent, but a stepparent can help fill much of the role no longer filled by the absent parent. This needs to be done in a way that is respectful of the continuing bonds to the deceased parent, and the reality that each person is different and is likely to fill the role in a different manner. Try to embrace the unique strengths and contributions of the stepparent without trying to minimize the losses associated with the deceased parent."[1] Also, you should not be required to call this person mom or dad. If this is something your stepparent is trying to force you to do, perhaps you should talk to your surviving parent and explain how uncomfortable that makes you feel.

! What Is a Stepfamily?

A stepfamily is a blended family in which children come from one or both spouses' previous relationships. If your surviving parent remarries and your new stepparent has children, these will be your stepbrothers and stepsisters.

What Is Life Going to Be Like with a New Stepparent?

If getting a new stepparent fills you with lots of questions, there are many places to go for help and guidance. For starters, perhaps one of your friends has been living in a stepparent situation for a few years now. He or she can tell you about his or her experience of what having a stepparent is like. Remember, however, that your friend's situation may be different from yours in terms of which parent died, personality of the new stepparent and your own, the amount of time between your parent's death and the remarriage, and so on, but discussing your friend's experience might help you understand how to proceed with yours. Sometimes, gaining insight into other people's lives can serve as a potential guide on how we do or don't want to live our own lives.

If you don't have a friend in a stepparent situation or if you learn better by visually seeing things for yourself, there are some TV shows and movies to watch and some books you can read to learn more; some examples are provided at the end of the chapter. You can also search online, talk to your teacher or school guidance counselor, or talk to your surviving parent regarding any stepparent or stepfamily questions or concerns you might have.

When you get a new stepparent, it is probably going to take time for you to get used to each other. He or she might be just as nervous about being your stepparent as you are to have him or her as your stepparent. Your stepparent may be in uncharted waters, especially if he or she does not have children. You and your siblings might be the first children your stepparent has cared for. Try to be patient and give him or her time to get used to being a parent for the first time.

Even if your stepparent has his or her own children, it will probably take time for him or her to get accustomed to you and your needs, just like it will take time for you to get used to how your stepparent does things. Dr. Schonfeld suggests,

> Parents of teenagers have many years to grow to understand each other and to develop approaches of interacting well with each other—stepparents of teenagers whose parent has died have much less time and are trying to establish the relationship at a time of considerable stress for the adolescent. I would encourage open communication—not only about what doesn't work, but what has worked well. Verbalize what is important to each person, what the individual feels is important to them, what is likely to be seen as effective and supportive, and be flexible and patient. Grieving children are going to be upset about the death of their parent—no matter what the stepparent does. Don't misinterpret grief and associated feelings (e.g., anger) as always a sign of failing on the parent or stepparent.[2]

"I thought my stepmother did an exceptional job as a stepparent. Stepparenting is way undervalued and is really hard—especially for my stepmom, who walked into our family after a tragedy happened. Our situation was an extremely difficult one, and I really do think she did an exceptionally good job. I think her job was hard, because it is really hard to be an authoritative parent while walking the line of knowing you are not the real mother. My father was happy to marry her, I was happy for him.

"I wasn't mad at my dad for getting remarried. I think he timed it just fine after my mother passed away. Some parents don't have good timing after the death of another parent, to bring a stepparent into the mix. I think my dad timed it well considering everything that happened."—Mike[a]

If you have any concerns or if something isn't working well for you, talk to your stepparent as well as your surviving parent. This way, you all can work together to get on the same page to try and come up with a game plan to see what can work better for everyone.

Am I Replacing My Late Parent?

As time goes on and you start getting used to your new stepparent, you may feel guilty about getting along with him or her, because you think that means you are replacing your parent's memory with the relationship with your new stepparent. This is simply not the case. Your surviving parent chose to remarry, in most cases

"My father got remarried in 2009 about three years after my mother's death. In the beginning, I refused to call her 'mom,' and I was not the nicest person to her because I didn't want her to replace my mom, even though my dad said she would never replace my mother. After a while, I started to sweeten up to her and started to call her mom, even though it felt really weird to. Fast forward to 2017, and she is now like my best friend. We have some really great conversations, we go shopping together, and it feels good to have someone to do that girly stuff with that I would have done with my mother."—Adrianna[b]

because he or she was lonely or wanted to have another parent step in to help raise your family or simply fell in love again. No person, whether your stepparent or not, could ever take the place of your late parent. According to parenting expert Derek Randel, "Your new stepparent needs to respect the love that you still have for your late parent."[3]

You can think of your stepparent as a friend your late parent sent to you, to try and help you get to adulthood, since your parent cannot be there to do so. By getting along with your stepparent, you are not forgetting about your late parent, nor are you trying to replace him or her. You are simply doing what is natural to do. You are learning how to cope with your late parent's death, while trying to move forward toward your future. You can't stand still in life.

In some cases, your new stepparent could be someone your family has known for years. Perhaps he or she was friends with your late parent, a coach or teacher from your school, or your friend's single parent. Knowing the person before he or she becomes part of the family can result in stronger bonds between you and your stepparent.

> "My dad did remarry after my mother passed away, a few years after. Comparing our situation to others probably isn't very fair. My stepmom and my mom were friends. After my mother passed away, we lost touch with her for years. Until one day my brother ran into her, found out she had gotten divorced and we told our dad to take her out. Little did we know, they would not only end up dating, but would also eventually get married, making our family of three a family of six! Her and I had a roller coaster of a relationship for a long time. I was the typical mouthy teen who didn't want to be told what to do, especially by my stepmother who, "Was not my Mom!" (I said it to her all the time). But, she was never trying to replace my mom. In fact, she tried very hard to keep my mother's spirit alive. She always talked about her leaving the door open for me to talk to her about my mom if I wanted to. I will never forget one Christmas, I want to say it was our first Christmas together under one roof, she had an ornament engraved with my mom's name on it. And she put it at the top of the tree, right in front for everyone to see. She puts it on the tree every year. That was one of the days I will never forget and realized she wasn't trying to replace my mom or be my mom, she was just trying to be a mother and help raise me to be the woman my mother would have wanted."—Lindsay[c]

A Sister and Brother Perspective

Ella and Chase lost their father to suicide at the end of 2016. Their mother was already remarried at the time that it happened. Once their father died, Ella and Chase moved in with their mother and stepdad right away. Here are their feelings about their stepfather:

> **Ella:** I love my stepdad as he's awesome. I remember him telling us, "I'm not trying to take the place of your dad, but I am here for you." He is a great stepdad, and told me exactly what I needed to hear—that he wasn't trying to replace my dad. I already had a dad. My stepdad loves my brother and I like we're his own kids.

> **Chase:** I have a stepdad and he is really nice to my sister and me. He moved in with us about two or three years ago, and my mom married him last year. We can talk to him about anything.[d]

Is It Bad to Like My Stepparent?

Not at all! Don't feel guilty if you do, thinking you are not being loyal to your late parent. Your late parent would want you and your stepparent to get along because he or she would want you to have the extra support from your stepparent that your late parent can't give you. Keep in mind, that if you started out not really getting along with your stepparent, things can change as you get older. Also, just because you might not get along with your stepparent now doesn't mean you won't later.

As already stated, everyone's stepparent experience is going to be different, and that's OK.

How Age and Gender Play a Role

Many factors can influence your adjustment to a new stepparent situation: how close you were to your late parent, the time in between your late parent dying and your surviving parent remarrying, your personality and the personality of your new stepparent, and many more. Gender and age can also determine how smooth or difficult the transition is, and these factors might explain why you and your siblings are adjusting in different ways. For example, you might have an older brother who seems to be adjusting to your new stepparent just fine, but you are struggling; there is a reason behind this. Or you might have a younger sibling adjusting to the new stepparent better than you are; this is actually quite normal. According to Lynn Norment, "Younger children accept stepparents more readily than older ones. Gender is equally important, as men adjust more easily to step family life than women do, and children seem to accept stepfathers quicker than stepmothers."[4] So, by applying this information to your stepparent situation, perhaps you can see why you might be struggling or why your sibling might be struggling a little more than you. You can look at this as a handicap or as a challenge that you or your siblings need to try to work through.

Timing Is Everything

What people say is true—timing really is everything. Hopefully your surviving parent is thinking of you and considering your feelings about bringing in a new adult to the family dynamic. According to Ron Deal, president of Smart Stepfamilies, "It is recommended that the surviving parent wait at least two to three years before remarrying."[5] Not only does your parent need at least that amount of time to heal from the death of his or her spouse, but you need time to get to know the potential parent before the relationship takes the next step. Plus, you're still coping with your loss. Two to three years is just a guideline; every situation is different. But most likely, the more time you have to spend with and get to know the incoming new parent before the remarriage, the better. If you feel like your surviving parent did not wait long enough, don't be afraid to speak up. Speaking up could lead to more time for you or your surviving parent to make this big transition.

> "My mom did remarry in December of 2000. It was five years after my dad passed away. It was a very tough transition to see my mom with someone else. By that time, I was already a teenager dealing with teenage issues and I wasn't the most accepting of a new stepdad. Looking back, I probably should have been nicer to him considering he was marrying into a family with four children, two being teenagers."—Thomas[e]

Not Being on the Same Page as Your Stepparent

It is understandable if you are not particularly fond of your stepparent at first. You may feel like he or she is trying to replace your late parent, even if your stepparent says otherwise.

It's also OK to be angry. Many teens feel that way when a stepparent joins the family shortly after a parent has died.

There are probably going to be times when you and your stepparent clash. After all, you both are new to the situation and you need a grace period to learn how to get along with one another. Your surviving parent might be in a situation where he or she has to work a lot, and now you spend more time with your stepparent than you would like. This is normal and happens a lot in new stepparent situation families. You are probably going to have days when the communication between you and your stepparent is less than positive. You may even get extremely upset with your stepparent and you wish your late parent was present in your life instead of your stepparent.

As you already know, your stepparent is not your biological parent. The two of them might not look the same, act the same, talk the same, or have the same interests, ideals, or values. They will probably run the household differently too. Change is always hard to accept, but try to make the best of the new living arrangement. Until you are eighteen years old, your surviving parent and now your legal stepparent are in charge of you, so you have to play by their rules. I know it might be hard to accept and that you wish your surviving parent was still around so everything could go back to being the same as it was before, but you know you can't undo what happened. I'm sorry that those were the cards you were dealt, but one day, you will probably realize you have grown stronger as a person for everything you have lived through and survived.

If you find yourself in constant conflict with your new stepparent, tell your surviving parent, even though this might be hard to do. That way you all can work together to come up with a game plan to make your new life situation work.

> "My dad married my stepmother a year after he and my mother got divorced. Six years later, my mother died. My stepmother would say bad things about my mother, which caused a lot of problems for us later. Much of the time I think that she was trying to be honest with us about mom, but it did more damage that good."—Rebecca[f]

Hearing negative things about your late or surviving parent, or even stepparent, can make life at home more stressful than it already is. Try to take in only the positive. ©iStock / maxkegfire

Some of you might just need a little time to start accepting your stepparent. Some of you might need a little extra help and guidance, such as from support groups, counseling, or even the school psychologist. Both situations are normal. Whatever the case, find a plan that works best for you and your whole family; everyone must agree to give the solution a try.

How Do I Try to Get Along with My New Stepparent?

The best way to start a healthy relationship with your stepparent is to find common interests. Do you both like sports? To read? To cook? Finding similar interests can create a healthy foundation for you and your stepparent to build a relationship. If you are finding that you do not share common interests, perhaps take an interest in something the parent enjoys that you may not know anything about.

Obviously, you both have one thing in common already—your surviving parent. After all, your surviving parent is the reason why you and your stepparent have been brought together under one roof. Perhaps that is the starting point for you and your stepparent to build a relationship. You never know where it might lead.

Another reason to make an effort with your stepparent is that it's an opportunity to keep your late parent's memory alive. For example, if you and your

"My mother got remarried, about four or four-and-a-half years after my father died. My stepdad loves me very much. He even let me take my two cats to my new home (because earlier it had been discussed that we would give them away because all four of my new family members are allergic to animals). I distinctly remember that day. I was crying because I loved my cats, and he said I could take them with. Sadly, one ran away on the drive there, but a few years later, we got a new one by coincidence. It was pretty rough the first few years with my new siblings (as I was used to being the oldest and only child), but it has gotten better."—Carissa[g]

mother liked to go shopping together and do a girl's night every Friday night, why not give your new stepmom a chance and include her in the same ritual? This way you are getting to know your stepmom, while still honoring your mother. If you and your dad used to fish every fourth Sunday of the month, why not invite your stepdad along to continue the tradition?

At first, you might be feeling as if you are betraying your late parent by including your stepparent in the festivities you used to do together, but that's not the case; you are actually keeping your parent's memory alive. By doing these activities with your stepparent, you are not replacing the person you used to spend time with; you are making it easier to live with the new stepparent in your life. You have a stepparent whether you want one or not, so you might as well make the most of the situation. Fighting it won't change anything, as your surviving parent already decided to remarry and bring this new person into your life. Give your new stepparent a chance to get to know who your late parent was. Perhaps by learning more about your late parent, your stepparent can get to know you better, too. This will help him or her become a better parent to you.

It Is Important to Communicate

According to psychologist Dr. Jann Blackstone, "It's well known that all children need a 'safe place' to express their feelings—even the negative ones. If not, they tend to bury them and then act them out in destructive ways."[6] As mentioned, anger is one feeling you might have when a parent remarries—anger at the situation, at the stepparent, maybe even at your surviving parent. This is especially common when the surviving parent remarries right away after his or her spouse passes away. Although you weren't ready for a stepparent to enter your life, your surviving parent may be ready to move life forward. If you find yourself angry

It Happened to Me: A Note from the Author

My mother died in 1993, and a few years afterward, my father started dating. As an adult, I understand why he started dating again, but I was only nine years old when my mother passed away. Although my father was ready to move on and remarry, I was not. I wasn't done dealing with my devastating loss. Suddenly my father narrowed his dating down to one woman—a woman named Trish, who was about to become my stepmom.

I remember it being very awkward at first. My dad introduced Trish to us as his friend, so that is all that my brother and I thought she was. I wasn't ready yet to realize my father wanted to marry anyone again after my mother passed away. Their dating led to engagement, and in 1996, Trish officially and legally became my stepmom.

Things at home changed and I had a hard time adjusting. Now instead of carpooling with my friends to school, my stepmom changed our routine and started driving us. I was so used to my mother's cooking, and now my stepmom cooked a different way. She also had an accent, and my mother did not. I was used to smelling my mother's Lancôme perfume, and my stepmother wore something different; my mother dressed a certain way, and my stepmom dressed a different way; my stepmom even listened to a different type of music. There were just so many little changes that added up to a big overall change for me.

A year after they married, my father and stepmother decided to move our family to another state. This devastated my brother and me even more because we were forced to move away from everything we knew—friends, family members, home, places that reminded us of our mother—and go to a new state where we didn't know a single person.

Although that was a difficult time for me when I was growing up, now as an adult, I am close to my stepmother. I have come to understand how hard her job truly was back then, and I am grateful that she was a part of our family and still is to this day.

and rejecting the idea of having a stepparent enter your new family dynamic, let your surviving parent know as soon as possible. Your family can coordinate a plan of action to try to work through the frustration and hostility of the situation before it gets worse.

Even when you move past your initial anger, you still need to communicate. As you transition to accepting your stepparent, you will probably experience other feelings. There might be times when you still have trouble accepting your stepparent or the way he or she does things. This is OK. Just be open and honest about your feelings. If you are not comfortable using "mom" or "dad," speak up. If you are not comfortable showing affection, tell your stepparent. The more open and honest you are with your feelings, the better chance you have at making your relationship work in a positive way.

According to author Colleen Oakley, "Everyone should get a chance to share how they feel, what they like and don't like, and to share both positive and negative opinions. It is also good to make suggestions about how to make things better."[7] By doing so, you will stay true to yourself and your feelings. You might not have the power to change your existing parent's mind as to the final decision of bringing a stepparent into your house, but you will gain more support from your parent and even your new stepparent by being open and honest during this transition period.

Movie and Television Stepfamilies

Sometimes when we are experiencing something difficult in our life, we seek out examples from other people's lives to help us figure out how to handle it. Other times, we might turn to fictional characters to learn how to solve our problems, whether through movies or TV series. Here are some resources that can help you gain additional insight into your stepparent situation:

- *The Brady Bunch.* Comedy/family TV series, 1969–1974. 30-minute episodes. Two widowers fall in love and marry, while also merging their children to live together under one roof.
- *Cinderella.* Animation/family/fantasy movie, 1950. 74 minutes. Cinderella's mother died when she was young, and her father decided to remarry. Her new stepmother is mean, and so are her two stepsisters, whom Cinderella is now forced to live with.

- *Enchanted.* Animation/comedy/family movie, 2007. 107 minutes. A princess lost her mother, and her father remarried an evil woman. The queen is jealous of the princess and plots to get rid of her.

- *Snow White and the Seven Dwarfs.* Animation/family/fantasy movie, 1937. 83 minutes. Snow White has an evil stepmother, the queen, who his jealous of her. Out of jealousy, the queen plots to get rid of Snow White.

- *The Sound of Music.* Biography/drama/family movie, 1965. 174 minutes. A woman falls in love with a widowed father and his children. They all must learn how to adjust during harsh times in the world around them.

- *Step by Step.* Comedy/family/romance TV series, 1991–1998. 30-minute episodes. Two people fall in love and have to merge a total of six children between them under one roof.

- *Stepmom.* Comedy/drama movie, 1998. 124 minutes. A mother and father divorced, and as the mother is dealing with a terminal disease, the mother, father, and stepmother start preparing the children for life without their mother.

- *Yours, Mine and Ours.* Comedy/family/fantasy movie, 2005. 88 minutes. A widowed man and woman fall in love and go on the journey to merge a total of eighteen children between them under one new roof.

Ways to Adjust and Get Support

If you are having trouble communicating with your surviving parent or stepparents, you can always talk to your school guidance counselor, a coach, your pastor, a teacher, or even your friend's parents. There are also counseling services you and your family can seek out, as well as support groups and online websites where you can research information together as a family; check out the National Stepfamily Resource Center (www.stepfamilies.info/), and the American Psychological Association (www.apa.org/helpcenter/stepfamily.aspx) to get you and your family started. Your family might have counseling coverage depending on what type of insurance you have, so that is another helpful route to take. Don't think that you have to face your situation alone, because you don't. There is always support out there, as long as you are brave enough to ask for and seek out help.

Don't be afraid to ask for support. Your surviving parent, your stepparent, and other family members should be your allies. ©*iStock / lolostock*

A great way to help yourself cope with accepting your new stepparent is keeping a journal. Write down your feelings nightly before you go to bed, as that will give you a chance to recognize how you are truly feeling about your late parent's death and the change of having a stepparent in your family. Keeping a journal will also help you see how far you have come from when your stepparent first joined your family, to six months later, to a year later. The journal entries will tell your future self if things seem to be getting better with your stepparent, or if they are staying the same, or getting worse.

Some schools have a club that has to do with stepfamilies. Being in a club like this can really help because you can share what you are going through with peers who can relate. If your school does not have such a group, why not start one? You don't know how much it will help you to start a group that can help others. It will be therapeutic for both you and your peers, as it will help you all realize that you don't have to face the challenge of having a stepparent alone.

An Interview with Trish, the Author's Stepmother

Sometimes we have to step into another person's shoes to better understand how that person might be feeling about a particular situation. You may know what it feels like to be a stepchild to your new stepparent, or by reading this chapter you are getting the idea, but do you know what it feels like to be a stepparent? Here's one stepparent's perspective on what it is like to become a stepparent to a newly motherless teen. Perhaps this can shed some light on your situation.

Meet my stepmother, Trish. I asked her the following questions, and she responded with the following answers regarding her stepparent journey.

Michelle Shreeve (MS): What was it like to become a stepparent to two children who just lost their mother?

Trish (T): It was obvious that this entire family was grieving; however, I admired how well they were managing their grief and continuing to grow and live. My stepdaughter was only eleven and my stepson was fourteen. They'd lost their mother only a few years before I entered their lives.

My parents divorced when I was in my teens and my dad remarried, so at least I had gained experience from having a stepmom myself. I tried to draw upon my own experiences growing up, but that didn't really apply. My world was so completely different than their world, and it was a big adjustment for me to realize that I had so little experience in this new role.

There were times of confusion on all our parts and I think we worked our way through them without too much drama. I feel fortunate for that. I have heard some horror stories of kids acting out and doing terrible things. That never happened in our family, and I am so grateful for how they behaved so well.

MS: What was it like to be a stepparent in general? Was it hard? Was it easy?

T: For the most part, it was completely easy. One hard part was going to the grocery store. That was a complete shock to my system. We'd fill up two grocery carts, and I'd never experienced that kind of shopping before, even coming from a family of six. I have no idea how my mom did it come to think of it. Funny.

I enjoyed the chaos and becoming the taxi driver, darting all over San Francisco for sporting events and other interests. I enjoyed having someone around all the time, the noise and even the dog Andy. It was a very busy time of my life and I have no regrets.

MS: What advice would you offer a new stepparent who just got on board with raising two children who just lost their parent like you did? Anything that you recommend he or she do or not do?

T: I participated in visiting the grave site during birthdays and special occasions. I purchased my own flowers to show my respect. I enjoyed listening to the stories about their mom, and felt like I knew her. The walls were covered with photos of her, and I felt that was necessary for them to feel her presence still. I welcomed her into my life and our home and felt she was doing the same to me. That may sound strange, but it was how I felt. I think that is the best advice I can give. Be open and welcoming to the memories your family will share with you about their lost parent. Even if that means setting a place for her at the table sometimes.

MS: What advice would you give a teen who just got a new stepparent?

T: Any teen is going through the biggest changes of their lives, physically and emotionally. It is hard enough for a teen to deal with that issue alone, and all adults know this. They've survived it somehow themselves. The only advice I would give a teen is focus on school and what you are good at. You are not going to be a teen forever and as a matter of fact, it goes by pretty fast when you look back. Try to show a little patience with your new stepparent and don't overreact if they aren't fitting into the perfect image you had of your late parent. They never will. You'll have to accept your stepparent the way they are and do your best to be happy.

MS: Any advice you would offer the surviving parent of the children, who just married and gave their children a stepparent? How should they support the stepparent?

T: I was very fortunate that I had the support of my husband and he was always recognizing little things and encouraging me in a positive way. He was very good at telling his kids that I was not there to take their mom's place and to not be intimidated by me. I believe that is a key to a successfully blended family.

MS: Did you have lots of enjoyable moments being a stepmother?

T: Oh yes. I have many great memories. The first time I went to Disneyland with Michelle's dad and Michelle was magical. Then traveling on to visit my dad and stepmom in Yuma, with a little side trip down to Algodones, Mexico. Michelle negotiated her first purchase there and we were applauding how well she did buying this wooden toy if I remember correctly. Later we played golf and Michelle drove the cart for my dad. I remember her really enjoying that and especially taking my dad through a puddle to splash him. They were both laughing a lot and it was a great time. Unfortunately, she left her great purchase in the golf cart and was disappointed when she realized it after we had left Yuma.

I had another wonderful trip to Vancouver with Michelle visiting my family. We went up Grouse Mountain and had a snowball fight. She was experiencing some back pain along the way and we stopped to visit a very handsome chiropractor. We had a few laughs about that too.

I enjoyed receiving my stepdaughter's notes. She was so sweet about reaching out to me and I felt a good connection between us. I know I haven't mentioned much about my stepson, but I believe because he was older, we didn't really connect quite as much. I still enjoyed going to his basketball games and watching him play. We rarely missed a game if any and it was always a nice family outing.

This is just a small glimpse of the many good memories I have.

MS: What advice would you give for a stepchild and stepparent who are having trouble getting along?

T: I would suggest to the stepparent to step back and learn how the stepchild likes to communicate. That is the first step toward a nice connection between the two. With me, it became apparent that Michelle preferred to write, so we often wrote notes to each other. That helped us understand each other so much better.

MS: Did you research, buy any books, go to helpful seminars, and so on, to learn how to become a stepparent?

T: I have always read self-help books and feel that I am a work-in-progress, striving to be the best I can be. I don't recall reading anything specific about parenting, but I was reading and attending conferences such as Tony Robbins, Richard Carlson, and Eckhart Tolle.

MS: Anything you would like to add regarding stepparenting?

T: It's not for everyone, and you had better be sure it is something you are prepared to take on. One minute all you had to do is take care of yourself, and the next you're juggling four different schedules and yours is taking the backseat for a while. But to me, it was worth it and in retrospect, it was some of the best times of my life.[h]

Your household is never going to be the same. However, with the help of your stepparent and surviving parent, you can work together to come up with a new household that provides what each of you needs. ©*iStock / DGLimages*

Adjusting to a new stepparent will take some time. However, through communication and a lot of patience, you could grow to become best friends with your stepparent someday. All you can do is your best and hope that your stepparent will reciprocate his or her best back to you. You never know; maybe your late parent had a hand in who was sent to you to be your stepparent. The least you can do is to give the new person a chance.

TRANSITIONING THROUGH HIGH SCHOOL

Some of you might be making the transition from middle school to high school. Maybe you had a fairly smooth journey during middle school because you had supportive friends and family helping you get through those years without your parent. Or maybe middle school was very challenging for you because you didn't have your parent there to support you, and now you are stressing out about starting high school. You know high school will be challenging enough, not counting the obstacles related to your parent's passing. Whether you have support or not, know that this book can help guide you through your parent loss journey. You do not have to face this challenge alone.

You Are Not the First Parentless Teen to Attend High School

High school is a time of transition and transformation, as some of you already know. You will be busy getting involved in clubs and activities, sports, and academic groups. Your school and homework load will get heavier, you will meet new friends, and you will lose some of your old ones. You will be battling self-acceptance, self-confidence, and other obstacles along the way. Not having your parent to guide you may be challenging, but you can get through high school despite the loss. Many parentless teens have made it through high school without one or both of their parents, and they went on to college and to lead successful lives. If they did it, so can you.

Emotional Management 101

You need a strategy before going to high school, a strategy to manage your emotions as well as your work schedule. As some of you already know, high school is more demanding than middle school. You have six or seven classes and homework just like middle school, but the workload is harder. You also have a lot more options for extracurricular and social activities, which means your schedule could get really busy.

Just like you have to manage your time properly among all of your activities and classes, you must do the same thing for your emotions. Bonnie Rubenstein, professor of education at the Warner School of Education at the University of Rochester shares, "The fear of anonymity, unfamiliar surroundings and higher expectations all play a central role in the anxiety leading up to the start of one's high school career."[1] You will probably experience a whole bunch of different emotions throughout your high school journey, but you also have to deal with a parentless journey—something not a lot of your peers can relate to. It is your responsibility to come up with a strategy so you can properly handle your high school life.

Be aware that high school will probably be filled with grief triggers. The students in your classes might say things that remind you of the loss of your parent. Your teacher might require you to read a novel concerning the death of a parent. So many things will be said and done during high school that might serve as emotional triggers for you. If you don't figure out a way to handle them and manage them in a healthy and constructive way, you might experience negative consequences. You could fall behind on your studies and ruin your 4.0 GPA; you could get kicked off sports teams, lose friends—there could be a lot at stake. But, if you manage your emotions every single day, whether you think you need to or not, high school will be a lot easier for you to get through than if you choose to ignore your emotions.

How to Manage Your Emotions

One way to manage your emotions is to treat your parentless situation as a class. Just like you go home every day after school, take out your planner, and go over what projects you need to work on, what upcoming tests you need to study for, or how many pages of your class novel you need to read, you need to check in with your emotions and see if there's grief, anger, or anything else you need to deal with. Literally, act like your emotions are a class. If you have seven classes, you now have eight. Pick a time during the day that works the best for you, and try to consistently do something at this time that helps you manage your emotions and cope with the loss of your parent.

For example, you could give yourself fifteen minutes every night before bed to just cry if you need to. Maybe writing in your diary or journal before you leave for school will help keep your emotions at bay. Writing a letter to your late parent, especially at the end of your day, might really help you cope with his or her loss.

Dealing with your emotions requires time and effort, just like homework for a class. Make sure that you're taking the time you need to grieve, cope, or just vent. Seek out support just like you would ask your teacher for help with your homework. ©iStock / demaerre

In the letter, you can describe how your day went, how you felt, and if anything good or bad happened. Or, before you go to bed each night, you could flip through an old photo album of your parent. Watching a home video of your late parent before you go to sleep might help you sleep better, and it might help you feel as if he or she is still physically present in your life.

Whatever you choose, make sure you feel like you are dealing with your emotions in a healthy way. This is a good strategy that can really help you cope while you are attending high school.

The Absent Moments

As you have probably heard, high school is filled with moments that will last your lifetime. Some moments you might not be too proud of, but they are moments of your life, ones that will help shape you as a person. Some moments will make you laugh, cry, love high school, and, at times, hate high school. Some things that happen to you, good and bad, will help shape the path you take beyond your high school career. You will also have lots of different emotions flying around, so expect that to happen and don't be afraid when it does.

"It bothered me in high school, as I began dating, to not have my dad around for guys to ask permission to go out with me. I remember it was awkward knowing if they should ask my mom or my stepdad or my brother or no one. Definitely not having my dad around to give me away at my wedding was difficult. I am really blessed, however, in that my brother and my stepdad really stepped up to fill the role of a father figure for me. Because of them, I don't think I have as many of the emotional scars as I could have had."—Julie[a]

You are probably looking forward to the moments you have heard great things about—prom, homecoming, senior ditch day, graduation, and more. Perhaps you have seen the pictures of your parents' prom, your uncle's famous football catch that won the homecoming game, or your grandmother who was crowned homecoming queen. The pictures you see are happy moments, but remember, it's more about the moments we don't see, the ones that led to taking that picture, that really matter—those bumps in the road that got people to the point where they were able to take that happy picture.

You will have those happy moments, goofy moments, sad moments, and even angry or frustrated moments. They are all a big part of attending high school. However, you also carry the moment of your parent's death. As mentioned, this loss is like having an extra class—one in which you deal with the grief you feel from losing your parent at such a young age. This extra class is not something that every teen entering high school is automatically enrolled in. Some may join you in this particular class, while others may be attending classes of different struggles that you have never heard of or been through yourself. The extra class you need to concern yourself with is your own.

High school can be challenging enough, without adding dealing with your grief on top of everything. You are so busy studying, playing sports, playing an instrument, attending extra-curricular activities, meeting new friends, losing friends, dealing with bullying—you are about to carry a full load on your shoulders whether you realize it or not . . . and whether you are ready for it or not. High school is a moment in your life, a four-year one that you will either try really hard to remember, looking back decades from now, or you will try really hard to forget. Every person's experience of high school is different from others, and the one you need to concentrate on, with your given circumstance, is your own.

If you had not already thought about it, you probably have now: your parent will not be there for you during certain high school moments. He or she will not be there to help you get ready for the prom or learn how to drive a car. Your

Senior prom is a moment you will never forget, but it's also a moment in which you will probably miss your late parent. ©iStock / bwancho

parent won't be there to help you celebrate getting accepted at your college of choice or to hold you when your heart is broken for the first time. He or she won't be there to see you graduate and receive your diploma or watch you grow during this special time of your life. He or she will always be there in spirit, depending on your beliefs, but sadly, physically your parent will not be present for any of these moments.

Although it is hard to stomach that your late parent won't be able to witness all of these memorable moments, especially when your best friends have their parents celebrating with them, try to take this awful feeling and turn it into a positive one. Your parent may be absent for all future moments, but you can be thankful for the time you had with him or her. Your parent may not be here to meet your date for the prom, but maybe your parent was there to help you learn how to tie your shoes. Your parent might not be here to comfort you when you get bullied at school, but maybe he or she was there to catch you when you fell off your bike the first time. Some people never had a chance for those moments, because their parent died when they were an infant. Although you might feel it is unfair that you do not have your parent for your high school moments, remember there are probably teens out there saying the same thing about you, that it is not fair that you got to have your parent teach you how to ride a bike or tie a shoe, and they didn't. As hard as it is, be thankful for the amount of time you did have with your parent and know that although you feel like he or she is absent from your big life moments, he or she is still here with you, but in a different way.

> "Upon growing up and leading to my high school graduation, I felt as though I could have applied myself better to earn better grades. I felt as though I barely made it to graduation. The hardest part was watching my peers with their families, and the mothers fixing their daughter's cap and gowns, and the fathers standing around taking pictures. That was hard for me. Although I had support at my graduation, it wasn't the same without my late mother and father there. As a daughter, I know the intuition of my mother. I was searching for a mother figure and wondered why I could never fill that void or feel like a true part of someone else's family. Now that I think about it, graduation just felt like my body was there but my mind couldn't wrap my head around the fact that I was actually graduating and looking around knowing this is just one of the huge milestones in my life that my parents couldn't physically be a part of."—Joella[b]

The Jealousy Effect

You might think that you are not a jealous person, but when it comes to your magical moments and not being able to share them with your late parent, you will probably be introduced to jealousy. You don't mean to get jealous, but it is probably going to happen at some point. Maybe you are at the mall with your friends, and you see a mother and daughter shopping together. Although on the surface, you are happy that a mother and daughter are spending time together, you might start to feel jealous and that life is unfair because you can't spend time like that with your mother. Or maybe you go to a sporting goods store, and you see a father buying basketball equipment for his son, and you realize you will never have a moment like that with your dad ever again. Again, you might be happy for them, but then you also might start to feel jealous. At times, you might feel frustrated or angry because it is not fair that other sons and daughters still have their parent, but you don't have yours. It might be even harder to see your own friends hanging out with their parents, having a good ol' time. Ironically even if you see them fighting you may feel jealous, because you miss fighting with your parent. These feelings of jealousy and sadness are normal, according to childhood bereavement expert Dr. David Schonfeld, and he has this to say on the subject:

> The grieving child can discuss their needs and desires with friends and caring adults and identify solutions to meeting some of these needs (i.e., it would be better for grieving children to let their friends know that they would enjoy going shopping with their friend and their friend's mother, rather than experiencing jealousy and only communicating the emotion—friends will want to be able to help, without taking on too much responsibility/burden of support for the grieving child). But, even with these efforts, children are still likely to feel some sadness evoked by witnessing positive parent-child relationships of others that highlight their own loss of a parent. Open communication, journaling, expressive arts, engaging in creative activities or physical exercise, etc., are some means of addressing these feelings. When communicating these feelings to friends, it's helpful to also convey that the friend shouldn't feel guilty about making the grieving child sad—the sadness is from the loss of a loved parent, not the witnessing of a loving relationship that reminds the grieving child of that loss. These triggers ultimately remind children of treasured and important memories and feelings that help maintain the continuing bonds.[2]

No matter the case, be aware that these feelings might come up. If they do, remember this is normal. You are only human, and you are allowed to feel different

"One of the hardest things after experiencing something so tragic is that even though your world has stopped, the rest of the world doesn't. You still have to go to school, you still have to buy your friends birthday presents, and answer their phone calls when they want to complain about something. The rest of the world goes on like normal, but you feel like you're trapped in some dark, twisted alternate dimension. As time goes on, you adjust to your new life, but you will always carry around this little bit of darkness.

"Everything changes after you lose someone so central to you, especially at such a young age. When something so tragic happens in your own life you realize very quickly that you're not immune to death and tragedy. And the surviving people in your life that you once saw as your protectors and your support, are only human and are probably grieving themselves. No one was going to be able to take my pain away and certainly no one was going to be able to bring my dad back. You will have to do many things alone. There will be many nights that you will have to cry alone with no one to hold you. There will be many times that you will be berated for not finishing your homework or for skipping class with no one to stand up for you and everything you're going through. It is scary as a child to realize you can't always depend on adults to help you.

"I think one of the hardest things for me after my dad's accident, especially in my high school years, was learning to empathize with other kids my age.

"After you experience something so deeply traumatizing, it's hard to relate to your friends who come to you crying and devastated because their boyfriend of two weeks broke up with them. I think it's isolating realizing how different your life is now from everyone else's. I just remember feeling very cynical and starting to see myself as kind of a mean person for not caring about such seemingly stupid, normal things.

"It took me a long time to learn to respect other people's journeys. Eventually you learn that you can't tell someone they're not allowed to be sad about something just because someone else is sadder for the same reason you can't tell someone they're not allowed to be happy about something because someone else is happier. It's all relative, and your friend's emotions are genuine. Even if a two week break up isn't the most devastating thing you have ever experienced, it very well may be the most devastating thing they have ever experienced. You don't have to be able to relate to those feelings but you learn to respect them.

"Instead of starting to get jealous or angry, what if that was the moment you wrote in your diary? Or later when you go home, you pick up the basketball and shoot hoops, which is a pastime you and your father used to do when he was alive? Talking from experience, some parents and friends are really cool, to where they will let you in on the fun, and treat you like you are part of the family—like your friend's parent is like yours. This is very kind of them, but remember, at the end of the day, that is not your parent, so you can't get mad when they have to go back to their home with their family, and you have to go back to reality that you lost your parent. Second parents can be a positive outlet for you, just keep your jealousy in check at all times."—Mahala[c]

emotions from time to time. The important thing to learn is how to deal with them in a constructive, positive, and healthy way.

Bullying

In some very rare cases, losing your parent can open you up to mistreatment by your peers, otherwise known as bullying. The Centers for Disease Control and Prevention defines bullying as "unwanted, aggressive behavior among school-aged children that involves a real or perceived power imbalance. The behavior is repeated, or has the potential to be repeated, over time."[3] Teens tend to mistreat other teens who are different or have different circumstances than their own. People can be afraid of who and what is different from what they perceive is normal, and as a way to handle their emotions, they lash out in a negative way. Unfortunately, this means that since your parentless situation is not an average one, you might be subjected to bullying behavior.

What you are already going through is horrible all in its own, but if you are also getting bullied, this will definitely make your life more stressful than it already is. If you have been or are currently getting bullied, made fun of, or harassed because you lost one or both of your parents, please tell a school official or an adult immediately. Bullying is not right and needs to be addressed as soon as it occurs. Do not be afraid of what your peers will think of you if you tell an adult or school administrator. Being a victim of bullying while also dealing with your tragic loss is too much to juggle all at once. You need to tell someone immediately so the problem is stopped, and you can properly cope with dealing with the tragic loss of one or both of your parents.

Act as If Your Parent Is Still Here

Just because your parent is no longer physically around, doesn't mean you should just forget about him or her, stop talking about him or her, and try to move on. If this book has taught you anything so far, it is that you will never be able to forget or just simply move on. It doesn't work like that. You can learn how to move forward, but you will never get to a place where you can just get over your parent's death.

So, when you celebrate your seventeenth birthday, why not save a seat for your parent? Place your mother's favorite flower or your dad's favorite tie on the chair along with a picture, so everyone at your party knows that seat is reserved for your parent. At graduation, have your surviving parent bring a picture of your late parent, so when you guys all go to take pictures, a picture of your late parent represents his or her presence. Live as if your parent is still beside you. The trick is not to forget your late parent or to live life without him or her, but to move on with his or her presence still within your heart.

What's Going to Happen after High School?

At different points in high school, and especially as you near graduation, you will probably wonder, "What's next?" Maybe you have been overhearing some of the plans your peers want to pursue: one classmate is getting a scholarship to play soccer for an Ivy League university, while another classmate mentioned they plan on enlisting in the military right after they walk at graduation. Some of your other friends plan on attending the local community college or working at their family business. You realize there are so many different paths you can take and you start to wonder, "Which path do I want to go down?"

Thinking about your future can be both exciting and bittersweet at the same time. On one hand, you are excited for what your future may hold, and on the other hand, you realize you are growing up. Growing up means you are slowly moving away from your past and transitioning toward your future. When we start to think about what our future holds for us, it tends to make us reflect on what our life has been like up to this point. Just stop and think for a second about everything you have been through, how far you have come, and just be proud of yourself. Not only have you made it this far through high school, but you have

---

It Happened to Me: A Note from the Author

When I entered high school, lots of different feelings overwhelmed me, not just from dealing with high school, but also from missing my mother during my special life moments. It took me a little while to find a way to cope with her death while I was in high school. You want to know what worked for me? I wrote letters to my friends, and I played basketball. I played basketball literally from morning until sunset on the weekends and during summer breaks; during the week, I played right after school until the sun went down. I was always at the park playing basketball, riding my bike to the park to play, practicing at my house, or in the gym at school while at practice for the school team.

Writing letters was an outlet I accidentally stumbled upon. My friends would write letters to me asking for advice regarding their life situations. Some of my friends were having trouble at home either due to their parents' divorce, sibling rivalry, the loss of their parent, or boyfriend or girlfriend troubles at school. For whatever reason, they all confided in me and sought advice. I would leave school with a stack of twenty letters written to me, and by the time I returned to school the next morning, I had twenty letters that I wrote in response.

I still managed to maintain good grades on top of playing basketball and writing those letters. Writing all of those letters in high school actually led me to start an advice column in the local newspaper, which I continued for eight years. Looking back, that is what helped me cope with my mother's death in high school. I just needed to find a positive and healthy outlet that worked best for me.

---

done so while dealing with your grief at the same time. That is no easy task, as surely you have realized by now.

Whether it has been two months, two years, or ten years since your parent passed away, you really need to stop and reflect on how much you have been through and everything you have been juggling since your parent passed away. Being a teenager is hard just by itself—you have been getting out of bed, going to class, and starting to think about what your next life step is going to be. Your parent would most likely be so proud of you.

It Happened to Me: A Note from the Author

Before my mother passed away, my family owned a deli in California. I remember growing up in that deli and learning the ropes about owning a restaurant. It made me realize that I wanted to continue working in our family's restaurants when I got older.

Right before my mom died, my dad sold the deli. Running a business, raising a family, and caring for a sick wife was very challenging, so my father sold the deli so he could be home to take care of my mother.

After my mother died and we moved to Arizona, my father bought another restaurant. Again, I learned the ropes and worked in the family restaurant still thinking that is what I wanted to do when I got older. However, working in the family restaurant in Arizona was different than working in the family restaurant in California when my mother was alive. I started to realize that I didn't want to work in the family restaurant one day; instead, I really wanted to help people. That is when I started exploring helping professions, which later led to me studying psychology and striving to take steps toward being a psychologist. While on the path to becoming a psychologist, I realized I could reach more people and help them through writing, and that is when I finally decided that I wanted to be a writer, maybe even an author someday.

If my mother had not passed away, I could very well still be working in our family's restaurant. Only after she died did I develop the passion and desire to help others who have lost a parent at a young age like I did. It's hard to tell if I ever would have wanted to help parentless children and teens if I never became one myself.

No matter where life takes you after high school—whether it's to the workforce, backpacking in Europe, working on your family's farm, or off to college—remember to always tend to your grief. I really can't stress enough how important doing so is for your overall emotional, mental, and even physical health. Through high school it may help to look at your emotions as an extra class you have to prepare for. After you leave high school, it may help to have another analogy. One writer suggests looking at your loss situation as a *griefcase*, since "grief is the case that holds our emotions from the loss."[4] We carry our griefcase wherever we go

"My entire life is completely different, due to their deaths. I now live in Phoenix, Arizona, I have gone through a complete shift from a relatively introverted person, more interested in media than people, to a very outgoing social butterfly, as many of my friends have described me. Since elementary school, I have taken an interest in music, specifically percussion, and I was very good, but I had no drive, or motivation to practice or get better. After moving to Arizona, music sort of beckoned to me, and I have been aggressively pursuing it ever since. I plan to major in Music Performance in Percussion. I previously won 1st place in percussion for the Arizona Solo and Ensemble Competition in 2016, I conduct the marching band at my high school, I am an active member of the city Symphony, and have performed in numerous ensembles and concerts across the state. Without moving to Arizona, I don't think I ever would have been able to accomplish anything of that nature, and emerge as a leader in most things that I do.

"Overall, after the first two years, I no longer got worn down during anniversaries, or birthdays, but there were moments, and still are, that I'll remember a joke my dad made, or the smell of a candle that my mom had used, and it definitely shifts my mood from whatever it is at that moment, to sentimental—not so much sad, but sort of an in between bittersweet.

"As far as friendships, they are relatively normal. I do, however, experience large bouts of extreme loneliness, and lack a true sense of belonging. I feel like most of these feelings will subside as I progress into larger parts of my life, like college, and work.

"As far as relationships, I struggle with over-attachment. My parents, in an almost overprotective manner, were always there to overload me with positive reassurance, and as such, I was heavily attached to them. In the past, after progressing to a serious relationship, I find myself becoming attached rapidly, and becoming co-dependent on their acknowledgment and validation.

"The main issue to arise from their deaths is an adoption of their unhealthy ideology that 'everything is either this way, or that.' Or 'Black and White Thinking' as it's referred to. A lot of times, I feel like there are only two solutions to a problem, and they are drastically and diametrically opposite of one another. This leads to problems in finding a compromise, and being reasonable in situations that usually aren't life or death scenarios. Along with this, I have a tendency to overreact to stress and criticisms, but have found that as time goes on, they are less and less problematic to deal with."—Aedan[d]

in life, and as long as we remember to regularly tend to the contents of our grief-case—our sadness, anger, frustration, confusion, and other emotions that arise in coping with the loss of our parent—we will help ourselves stay on a happy and positive path. This doesn't mean that every day of your life is going to be super easy or smooth sailing, or that one day your grief will just suddenly disappear. Remember that there will always be grief triggers that can sneak up on us when we least expect them.

As you may have realized already, as each year goes by since the loss of your parent, it's not so much that the grief gets easier to deal with, but through your maturity, you get better at knowing yourself, identifying what your grief triggers are, and figuring out which coping mechanisms are good or bad, or which ones work or don't work for you. Just like we are all constantly learning more about ourselves and the world we live in each day, we will continue to grow and evolve within our own individual grief journeys. The journey never ends, but as you get older, you get wiser about carrying your griefcase around and dealing with what's inside.

Your Personal Goals Can Change

In considering your path after high school, it might be helpful to understand that your path in life can change after a parent dies. The goals or dreams you may have had while your parent was still alive might shift after he or she is gone. You may have started going down one path, but suddenly another path pulls you as a result of your parent's death. Oftentimes, it stems from the impact the death has on you or even what coping mechanism you tried to pursue. Either way, the death can change your entire life, and lead you on a path you never thought you would go down.

High school is definitely going to be a journey for you, and by adding the loss of your parent to your plate, you are going to have your hands full. Learn to tend to your needs and take care of yourself, and you will be better able to balance it all. If you ever feel like you are struggling to juggle everything, don't be afraid to reach out for some support.

FORGING AHEAD

As discussed in previous chapters, you will never fully get over your parent's death; you will most likely deal with grief in some form for the remainder of your life. According to childhood bereavement expert Dr. David Schonfeld, "The death of a parent is a life-changing experience and that is exactly what it does. Individuals never forget or 'get over' the loss of someone they care deeply about, nor should that ever be the goal. The work of grief starts out as a full-time job that may allow little to no time or energy for other pursuits. Over time, it becomes more of a part-time job that allows for increasing effort and attention to be placed on other life goals and relationships."[1]

As you have probably noticed, as the years move forward, you get better at managing your grief and knowing what triggers it, and you don't have such a hard time dealing with the loss every single moment of every single day as you did at first. You will always think about your parent, but life tends to keep pushing you forward, whether you want to move in that direction or not.

Remember the griefcase mentioned in the last chapter? That is something you need to take with you, no matter where life takes you after high school. Your new job or educational pursuit might make take you to other countries, or move you to another state, and keep you busy 24/7. You might meet someone special and decide to get married, and maybe even have a family someday. Wherever you go in life, remember to always carry your griefcase with you—and look inside regularly. You might think you won't need it, and you will probably stray from opening your griefcase for a few weeks, months, or even years. You will notice that when you do that, the loss of your parent and the emotions that come with it will creep back in your life, whether you want them to or not. "Grief denied is likely to surface unexpectedly and often at times when the individual is least prepared, most vulnerable, and most likely to become overwhelmed. It's better to approach grief directly and openly. The goal is not to deny strong feelings, but rather to learn coping skills to deal with such feelings that will make you more resilient to future adversity and resurfacing of difficult feelings."[2] Regularly tackling grief head-on is the healthiest route to take.

Not dealing with your grief will potentially bring your life to a standstill. You can't try and move forward until you place one foot in front of the other. Think of it like this: When you visit the beach, the warm sand feels good on your toes. When

Your life is what lies in front of you. You won't be able to fully experience and appreciate it until you learn to put one foot in front of the other. *©iStock / PeskyMonkey*

the waves come crashing in, the tide rushes past your feet. If you stand still, you start sinking slowly in the sand, simply because you are not moving anywhere. The only way to not sink, is to keep walking along the sand; in your case, that means dealing with your grief on a daily basis. Try to remember that going forward in your life.

How Dealing with Your Emotions Changes

You may have noticed that when you were younger, you felt like you needed to deal with your emotions a lot more often. As you got older, you learned more about yourself and became more familiar with how you deal with your emotions, the loss of your parent, and life in general. Some of you might think you are now an expert, like you have figured out your grief and solved it. Grief doesn't work that way. It is not a puzzle to be solved.

Remember that as you change and grow older, the way you deal with your grief will also change. When you were younger, writing in a diary or being involved on a sports team may have helped you cope. When you enter your early twenties, however, you may find you don't prefer a diary as your first coping method. Instead, you may want to meet a friend for coffee or go to the movies every anniversary of your parent's death. How you deal with your loss usually changes as you forge ahead in your life, and that's OK—as long as you still deal with it. Dealing with it regularly also helps you to never forget your parent.

Future Grief Triggers

As you move into adulthood, you will become more experienced in dealing with your grief; you will have probably learned what your triggers are and aren't. You may know that if you see a mother and a daughter at the mall together, laughing and having a great time, it will remind you of the moments you and your mother shared when she was alive, or the moments you missed out on because she passed away. Or you may know that if you see a father and son at the football game laughing and eating hot dogs together, it will upset you. It is good that you recognize those everyday triggers, but as you get older, you are probably going to discover new triggers you didn't even know were triggers, such as your wedding day, the birth of your children, getting a promotion at work, finishing a marathon, visiting Italy for the first time, or even when your friends and other family members start passing away (as you get older, this does happen). Just be prepared for new triggers as you enter adulthood.

When these new grief triggers happen, and they will, remember how you dealt with other grief triggers in the past when you were in school. You may not have handled them expertly at first, but you can probably admit that through time, you learned and got better at dealing with them. Hold on to how you handled your grief triggers in the past. You know what methods work and don't work for you. Deal with your new grief triggers the same way you dealt with your old ones.

Don't Be Afraid to Live Your Life to the Fullest

In some cases, you may feel what is called survivor's guilt. It will probably be the strongest around the time when you are the exact age your late parent was when he or she passed away. You might be scared and worried when the time comes because you wonder if you will have the same fate that your late parent did—like you will die at thirty-nine years old due to a sickness like your mother did or at twenty-seven in a car accident like your father did. And then when you make it past this age, you will probably be so happy and thankful—but then you might also feel bad. This is where the survivor's guilt comes into play, and this thought might cross your mind: why did I make it past thirty-nine, but my mother didn't?

You will most likely never know the real reason why your parent left this earth on the day that he or she did. Even if you find out he or she was sick or died from an accident, you will never know why it happened to him or her specifi-

An Important Warning

There will probably be a day, and you may have experienced this day already, when you lose your surviving parent. It may happen when you are twenty-three, thirty-eight, or forty-two, but it inevitably will happen someday. When this day happens, you will feel the grief from the loss of your first parent all over again, on top of feeling new grief from losing your surviving parent. Allow yourself to go through this grieving process. It will not be an easy time for you, but the healthiest way to make it through is to keep dealing with your emotions. You might need a few weeks of dealing with your emotions as when you were younger: reach out for support, write in your diary, pick up a basketball again, join the gym—whatever you have to do to stay on a positive and healthy path, do it. You might have been doing a great job dealing with the grief from losing your first parent over the past five, ten, or more years, and you can get through the second loss just like you got through the first one; this time it might be a better and smoother transition for you because you have learned about dealing with grief consistently and constructively.

cally, and not someone else. Do yourself a favor and don't spend time wondering about those questions. It is very painful to have questions like those that can't be answered. In fact, there's another way to look at it.

Live each day for yourself and for your parent. Instead of wondering why he or she died when you arc still living, give your parent the greatest gift of all—do everything in your power to live the fullest life you possibly can. Be happy, stay healthy, do goofy things, meet new people, try new things, travel the world—just live your life to the fullest. From the day you were born, that is what your parent wanted for you: for you to live a long, happy, and fulfilling life. Don't be sad that he or she isn't here to watch you live your life. The best way you could ever honor your parents is to live *your* life.

Those before You

Millions of teens worldwide share something in common with you. They, too, have lost their parent, and they know what you are feeling and going through

It Happened to Me: A Note from the Author

My schooling years were a little rough; as I mentioned before, I did not deal with my emotions. I thought I was doing just fine without dealing with my grief, and then it all crept up on me one day and my world turned upside down. Once I turned my life around, got back into school, and didn't stop until I graduated, a lot changed for me for the better. I let go and let God take over, met new friends, experienced new things, and actually started living my life—something I didn't realize at first that I wasn't doing.

After high school graduation, I lost touch with a good friend, who didn't come back into my life again until I was twenty-four. Like true friends always do, we picked up where we left off six years before. We became stronger friends, best friends even, and then started to date. Dating later led to getting married. I married my best friend and I couldn't be happier.

Was it hard knowing my mother wouldn't be at my wedding? Or would never meet my husband? Of course! I had my marriage grief trigger I warned you about, but then, remembering my griefcase, I decided to deal with my feelings head on. Instead of being sad that my mother couldn't be at my wedding, I made sure she was present anyway. My husband and I left an empty chair by the altar with a rose and her picture on it, signifying that she was indeed there at our wedding.

I made sure she was there, something she cried about to me before she died. I think she knew she was going to die, and during the last few months of her life, she cried about the fact that she wouldn't be able to see me graduate or to walk down the aisle someday. I remember comforting her as a nine-year-old child and telling her that surely she would. Now I know that I kept my promise, and she did in fact see me walk down the aisle.

I make sure that I still show my husband, friends, and family members pictures of my mom often. On Facebook, I have a photo album dedicated to her life where all who knew her can comment on her old pictures. I found some of the friends she went to high school with and befriended them. They have been kind enough to share pictures and old notes they shared with her. My mother collected duck figures, and her collection is now sitting in my kitchen, under the dish hutch that was hers as well.

There are ways to keep my mother's memory alive. I am thirty-three years old now, and my mother died when I was nine years old. She has been gone for twenty-four years, but it doesn't feel that way. I feel like I just saw or talked to her yesterday because I regularly look at her pictures, talk to my husband about her, or like comments on Facebook from old high school friends of hers when they write every so often. Keeping her memory alive has helped me live my life to the fullest, as if she were still physically here with me every day.

right now, because they have had similar feelings. They may not have had a parental death right this second, but whether it was two months ago, four years ago, nineteen years ago, or even fifty years ago, they have learned a thing or two about coping with their parental death along the way.

Here's some advice and helpful coping suggestions from others who lost their parent at a young age:

The advice I have for other girls out there who just lost their mother is that her death is not your fault. You didn't do anything wrong. Try to remember good memories you had with your mom and turn around and share them with your family members. Try to be as positive as you possibly can despite the overall situation. Remember how your mom made you happy and try to make your family happy in the same way that your mom made you happy. Also, find yourself someone to talk to and share your feelings with, like a friend or a counselor.—Taylor, lost her mother[3]

For a teenage girl losing her parents, I would tell her to take time for herself. I think it is important to take time to yourself to process your emotions before making any big decisions or risking taking out emotions on someone else. However, this does not mean physically being alone, which I would advise against. I would also share with her how much it helped me to keep myself in the "To-Do List" mind-set during the initial shock of losing them. Focusing on what I needed to do or get done step-by-step really helped me keep myself busy and distracted from everything going on around me. This gave me time for the wound to not be as fresh and then I felt more ready to face those emotions with a clear head and be able to move forward. Lastly, I would emphasize the importance of choosing what thoughts and memories to focus on. It is more beneficial to you to choose to focus on the good memories than on any feelings of guilt or regret that you may have.

Like I said before, keeping myself busy helped me the most. With my mom, I focused on school as much as I could. With my dad, focusing my energy and emotion on my son and his well-being helped me be able to move forward. For me personally, talking about it a lot right after it happened and crying about it didn't help me. That is just part of who I am though. Whether it was a break-up, or PMS, my dad always told me that crying about things wasn't going to fix anything. I knew he and my mom would both want me to be strong, so doing so made me feel like I was honoring their absence and showing them that I could be the person they wanted me to be.—Kaylene, lost both parents young[4]

My advice for a girl who just lost her father would be, I would tell her it's okay to cry. And sometimes, you just want to be alone, and I think that's okay, too. But, just remember that your friends and family love you and want to help you, even if they might not know how. Don't do it alone. You may or may not believe in Jesus like me, but I know that He loves you and has a plan for you if you love Him. You may not know why this happened and you might be angry. Just let it out and be honest with yourself, but don't take it out on others. And yes, the pain is new and fresh, but in time it will get better, trust me. It may not seem like it now. It feels like the world has just ended. But, it will get better. You will always have that hurt, but you will learn to deal with it as time goes on. But, for now, it is okay to cry. You should cry. Cry until you can't cry anymore. Pour out your heart. And then take a deep breath and let it go. Cry again if you need to. Yes, it sounds strange, but after you have done that, it feels better. Find someone you trust and who will listen to you and tell them how you feel. It doesn't matter if it's complete nonsense. Just let it out. And pray, talk to God, pour out your heart to Him: your anger, pain, guilt, sadness, everything. You might be surprised.

I went to a grief-share camp, but I don't think that really worked. I was saved and became a Christian. That is what turned my life around. But, for those who don't share my beliefs, I also started helping a friend from church. She owns horses, and she let me come and help her muck out the stalls and feed and groom the horses, and in return, sometimes I would get to ride them. My mom says that that is when I started smiling again, because I had been in basically a depression and oppression (I had lost everything I knew and was in a completely foreign place [forest to desert—big transition], and I wasn't happy or welcome where I now called home). I think just being around animals is healing, and being able to help someone else makes you feel good, too. For those who don't like animals of any sort, that's really a shame, but if you don't (and that's okay, we're all different), find something you do like. Maybe it's drawing, writing, reading, doing a sport, volunteering, whatever. And find others who like it, too. Also, find people who can relate to your loss, and share your feelings with them. Kind of like this book.—Carissa, lost her father[5]

Don't feel guilty talking about other things while the death is still current. It's all right to talk about football, or movies, or recipes, even if you're at the funeral. One of the things that helped me the most was sitting in the foyer of the funeral home, during my mother's wake, and talking to my cousin about videogames for an hour. It made me realize that all of the things in the world that I enjoyed, whether it was with or without my parents, still exist, and for me, the fact that a lot of things were exactly the same helped me realize that their death wasn't the end, and there were still so many things that bring joy in this world.—Aedan, lost both parents[6]

If a young girl just lost her father like I did, I think, first of all, I would want her to know that she is not alone—not alone in her experience or in her grief. I would want her to know that everyone grieves differently and in stages. Moving from grief to denial to anger and eventually into acceptance. I would let her know that the oppressive nature of the early grief does lessen, and even though you will feel the loss throughout your life, you will move into a place of acceptance and peace where the memory is more joyful than painful to remember him. Give yourself permission to grieve. I would highly suggest going to a school or church counselor to talk about how you are feeling and to receive some specific coping mechanisms specific to your situation. Each person's grief is so different, I think that is one of the hardest things to generalize what will work for everyone.

I think the feelings of anger are the hardest to move past. It is important to be able to express them in an environment that is beneficial. I think many children are afraid to talk to their moms about how they are feeling because they don't want to make their remaining parent's burden or grief any stronger. However, I would suggest that it is very healthy to talk frequently about your dad. Ask your mom to share memories. Ask her what your dad would think about the decisions you are making. Share memories that you had as a family. Work through the grief with your mom and your siblings. Also, cling to your faith, to your family and loved ones. Recognize that life is precious and fleeting. It is important to live each day to the fullest.

When I worked with a counselor in the first year after my dad died, we made up a chart for self-care activities (because I was neglecting myself).

I also had to draw pictures about how I was feeling. When you are very young, it is hard to find the words to express what you are feeling. Each day, I would have to chart with a simple picture/color how I was feeling (i.e., sunshine if I was feeling happy, clouds if I was feeling sad, etc.). I also had to keep track of the activities I needed to do each day to make sure I was taking care of myself. I also had to write about whether I was having nightmares and draw a picture of them. I believe I also had a box to check to see if I had shared with my mom that day how I was feeling. This simple tool was a wonderful way for a young child to express and move past some of those early emotions. If it was a teenager, I would probably suggest a journal to help express their emotions.

Talking to my friends about my dad's death honestly didn't help me much. None of them had any understanding of what I was going through. Some of them tried to be empathetic, but usually it just left me feeling worse. However, I do think it is important to find someone that you trust to share with in your grief.—Julie, lost her dad[7]

In life, we take so many things for granted, and you never know when somebody important to you is not going to be there anymore.

I am now thirty-five years old and it has taken me this long to be able to process what is really important to me in life. The little things are what truly matter and are what make a big difference in the long run. No matter how frustrated you get in a situation, ask yourself, what do you want that person to remember tomorrow if you were suddenly gone? When someone you care about is gone, and your last interaction was negative, for me, more than twenty years later now, it still haunts me to this day.

Too many people out there act like they know everything, and think they have all of the answers and the greatest advice. You are the only person who knows what is the best way to cope for you—whether you are twelve, twenty-five, or forty-two. You need to find a way that works for you, and only you know what way that is.

I am still struggling with the death of my mother. Perhaps if more people looked me in the eye along the way and offered help if I wanted it, rather than by telling me or trying to force me to cope with her death a certain way, I might have worked through these feelings years ago. Now, I am realizing what works for me, and I am dealing with my bottled-up anger.

My mother died on December 3, 1993, and every year on her death anniversary, I take a minute to think about her. I also look at the same picture of her and I. In the picture, she was smiling at me and wearing a red jacket, and I was making a goofy face looking back at her. This picture gives me peace and comforts me whenever I look at it.—Mike, lost his mother[8]

My advice for a teen who just lost his father would be, I would tell him to focus on all the good memories you have of him, and that it's okay to be sad sometimes.

Going back to school and getting back into a routine within a couple weeks really helped me a lot. I went out with my friends, and it gave me something to focus on, and helped me get back to a normal life.— Eric, lost his father[9]

Don't keep your feelings in. Talk about your feelings, good and bad. Tell someone, anyone. Keeping it in and pretending they're not there will only make it worse.

It's okay to be sad, it's okay to be angry, and it's okay to cry, I promise it's not just for babies. But don't let the anger and sadness rule your life. Your mom would want you to be happy and to live out her memory in the best of ways. The idea that nothing will ever be the same is crushing, and you're right. Life won't be the same as it was when your mom was here, but it will go on. The days will turn into months and months will turn into years and eventually you will go from crying every day to just missing her, and you'll go from questioning "Why did this have to happen?" to realizing how much the experience has shaped your life. You are stronger than you think and you will get through this. Losing a parent makes every difficultly in life more bearable because you've already been through the worst.

Your mom may not physically be with you, but she will always be in your heart. My favorite thing to do is to talk to her as if I'm on the phone with her. I tell her all about what's going on and my struggles and joys of the week. Talk to your mom. It might feel weird at first and you might feel like a crazy person talking to yourself, and whether or not she can hear you depends on what you believe in, but you'll feel a sense of peace when you fill her in on what she has missed.

It's been almost twelve years and I still struggle with a sense of jealousy towards girls that have their mom. It's bound to happen and it's going to hurt and you'll want nothing more than to have her back. No one will ever be able to replace your mom, but find someone who is a mother figure to you, an aunt, grandma, a friend's mom, and take advantage of the love and support they have to give, even though it's not your mom.

Ask your family members their favorite memories about her. It will keep her memory alive and will always put a smile on your face knowing that the life she lived was not put to waste.—McKenna, lost her mother[10]

My advice for a newly parentless teen would be, to not blame yourself. Whether the cause of death was foreseen or unforeseen. Don't think of the what if's, or should have's. Everything happens for a reason. Don't believe people when they say the pain will go away. It doesn't. It just gets easier to deal with as time goes on. Time really does heal. Talk about her every chance you get! Look at pictures, watch old home movies to hear her voice. Do not try to forget her. Keep her alive by sharing memories of your mom. And most importantly . . . CRY! It's okay to cry!— Lindsay, lost her mother[11]

The advice I would give to a girl who lost her parent would be that she won't be the same again, but to not blame herself for it. To take some time for herself and be surrounded with people who love you, like your mom, friends, or any close relative that can provide you strength and support to deal with the grief. Be with somebody you can trust and feel comfortable with, so you can cry and let it all out. Don't bottle up your feelings because you don't want to drag them down the road later and carry anger or guilt towards life. And also, find an activity that helps you release your anxiety in a way that you can express it, like writing or drawing.

I tried counseling and even went down the dark path of drinking and nothing worked. Until I started writing and using it to write and create my own music. This was a very important part of my healing process because I was able to tell my story.—Tiffany, lost her father[12]

I find peace now knowing that she is in a better place, and I feel as if she is watching over my daughter and me. From time to time, I still cry when I think about her. Actually, by writing this, it's the first time I have ever confronted a lot of the emotions that stemmed from the situation. Now, I mainly try to stay busy and work hard, because I know that she would be proud of what I am doing. I still struggle with anxiety, but instead of using medications, I try to cope with my anxiety through practicing relaxation techniques, as well as I talk out my issues a lot more now.

My advice, don't hold onto past issues. I held onto all of the negativity that I had against my mom, and in the beginning after she died, I could not grieve. I did not begin to grieve my mom until her memorial service, when I was finally able to let go of everything. There will be tears, there will be hurt. Some days you will not know how to get through the day, but it does get better. You don't lose that parent forever, but you do learn to live without them, while also keeping their memories alive in your heart. It has been two years since my mother died, and I still hurt, but I let it out. I have slowly learned to live with my emotions.—Erin, lost her mother[13]

My advice for a teenage boy who just lost his father to suicide would be this: anything you are feeling is normal. You are always going to think about it.

What comforts me when I am having my hard days is to look at old photo albums of my dad. On Saturday nights, we used to go to Trader Joe's, grab a Redbox movie, and then come home and make dinner. I really miss our tradition of doing that with him.— Chase, lost his father[14]

I like to journal to help cope, but I get busy sometimes and don't always get a chance to do so. With writing in my own personal journal, I can be myself and no one will judge my thoughts or what I write down at all. I started journaling before he passed away, and it definitely helps out a lot. I also made a playlist of all of my dad's favorite songs that remind me of him. That playlist has helped me cope a lot. It reminds me of the happy times I spent with him.

My advice for teens who lost a father to suicide would be this: you are going to be sad for a while, and you are going to want to give up. The trick is to not give up. You are never alone, and each day gets a little better. You are going to be sad, and that's okay. It's okay to cry and to not let your feelings get bottled up, because in the long run, it will benefit you better by letting everything out. Giving up is never the way out. It is going to get better. Always ask for help and don't be afraid to ask for help.— Ella, lost her father[15]

I grieve a lot through my dreams. I get to see him again and talk to him. It started to get hard though because after the end of each dream I had, I knew it wasn't real. I woke up the last time I had a dream crying, and I prayed to God to not let me have those types of dreams anymore because they were too painful. I haven't had any since. Now, I miss them and wish I could still have those dreams. That is the one prayer I regret.

I'm aware of how precious time is, I watch my words more now, and try to always say "I love you," at every opportunity. If my mom and I accidentally hang up before we say it, I will call her back to make sure she knows. I do that with my friends in different ways too. It also makes me upset when I hear other kids complain about their parents. They take their time with their parents for granted. Kids don't realize how lucky they are to still have both of their parents.

You need to let the grief drown you a little bit, and you need to be able to pull yourself out of that. Set a timer for yourself—if you know you are about to have an emotional episode, set a timer for ten minutes, cry as much as you want, and then when your time is up, go back to your day.

Have someone come and get you even. But be strict with yourself. It's totally understandable when you see something random and it becomes triggering, like a curtain that triggers a childhood memory of some sort. It will happen, randomly, when you least expect moments like that to happen. But it's okay. Let yourself feel the emotions. Do not let them build up.

I am very in touch with my emotions, and I feel like I have used healthy coping mechanisms throughout all of this. My family and I did not go to therapy after my father died, nor did we join any support groups. Instead, we constantly talk about my father as if he was still here, and we talk about him to this day in present tense. I still consider him being here. I talk about my dad in the present tense, because he still is and always will be, my dad.—Catherine, lost her father[16]

Have that special friend that will be there to remind you that you will have good days again and that they are around the corner. Also, positive distractions will help you cope a lot. In a lot of situations, you are going to feel lost, but know that it is okay to feel lost. Somehow your mom from above and God will point you in the right direction. It's also important for other girls to know that it's ok to be lost and confused about situations we are given.—Joella, lost both parents[17]

My advice for a teen who just lost his father would be, I would tell him to stay close to his family. Find a male role model that can help fill the void of his father's loss and stay away from drugs/alcohol. I would tell him the pain will eventually ease over time and that he should use this experience as fuel to help others as opposed to using it as an excuse to ruin his own life.

I tried therapy to help cope with his loss, but I didn't like talking to strangers. I knew they were trying to use techniques to get me to talk about my feelings and I didn't like to revisit them at the time. I kept a lot of sadness inside for a long time until I figured out how to turn my own experience into a sense of empathy for others going through the same or even tougher experiences. I've always tried to remind myself that though this experience was very hard for me, there is always someone else out there who has it much worse that I can help if I just reach out and share my strength with them.—Thomas, lost his father[18]

I would not say that everything is going to be okay. Everything is going to be different. This is when you start your new life and you will always miss your old life.

Things are going to be very dark for a very long time, until one day you will be able to pack all that darkness into a little box and only let it out sometimes. But, you will have to carry that box around with you for the rest of your life.

You are going to try to distract yourself by running away and saving the world. But you don't have to take care of everyone else. It's okay if you only ever save one person in your whole life, and it's okay if that person is you.

It is okay to run away sometimes, though. Take trips, meet new people, read all the books you can. But don't burn the bridges to your home.—Mahala, lost her father[19]

My advice for a teen who just lost her father would be, I would tell her to talk to her family and friends, let them give her support, but understand that they might not know the right things to say. I would advise her to talk to a grief counselor, or even try to find a grief support group. And that she should be patient with herself, and it is very painful, but that she will be all right.

I coped by going to an individual hospice counselor, which was very helpful. I also went to a hospice grief support group which helped me, but might not help other young people since it is typically for much older people there. I found that they were very good listeners with good perspectives, though. I journaled a lot which I think helped, especially to try to make sure I wrote down memories that I was worried I would lose. I spoke about my dad and my loss a lot which felt comforting to me. I went to a youth grief support group which was beneficial in that I could go with my family, but I did not think that the discussions were typically deep enough to give me much emotional development. I also went with my family to my dad's grave sometimes. I think that was also very good to do.—Beth, lost her father[20]

Grief is weird. Everyone wants to feed you. It felt so strange that the world kept moving while mine fell apart. People who hadn't spoken to me or my dad in years magically appeared and wanted to say how sorry they were and offered to help. And it's okay if you hate them for it. It's okay to be angry. It's okay to feel numb. It's okay to want to escape. People will say things like, "God needed another angel." Or, "It was their time." None of these things feel right and you'll want to scream at the well-meaning person for saying that anything about this is okay or meant to be. I felt like I was drowning. I kept the mantra that everything people did or said came from a place of love. It is my opinion that people say or do crazy things during the three major life events: birth, marriage/divorce, and death. And it is also in those moments that friendships and relationships can be irreparably broken. Try to be forgiving. Not just to those around you, but to yourself. Forgive yourself for being weak. Forgive yourself for being angry. Forgive yourself for not being capable to do much more than breathe. Forgive yourself for crying or not crying enough.

I felt that I had to be strong for my brother and put off my own healing in the process. After about a year, I sank into a depression. I started having panic attacks and I couldn't sleep. I finally went to my doctor and broke down on that paper-covered table. She wrote me a prescription for an anti-anxiety medication and a referral for a therapist. Talking about my grief and having someone who understood and did not judge me for it, was what I needed to heal. Therapy and time. Soon I felt like I was more prepared for the tough moments. The birthdays and holidays and anniversaries were easier to endure and I could prepare myself for the emotional storm that I knew were coming. I had some of his ashes put into a necklace so he is always close to my heart. I still miss my dad every day, but thankfully it's the happy thoughts that mostly hit me. It's seeing my dad's blue eyes on my son. It's the realization that I inherited his penchant for making silly songs always out of tune. I've never been able to decide if I'm religious or not, but spiritually I believe that he is somewhere, and he can see me and my little family, and that thought sustains me.—Christina, lost her father[21]

My advice for teens all depends on their own unique situation. When it comes to a suicide situation, remember that it is not your fault that your parent committed suicide. You must make sure you need to go through a grieving process, or else it will control your whole life, no matter how long it takes. Once it is their choice, it is their choice. It is not your fault. If you still have a surviving parent left, enjoy your time with them. When a parent dies, you must grieve, or else it will take over your life and affect you everything else you do.

Counseling has helped me over the years to learn how to cope in healthy and constructive ways. I have also attended survivors of suicide support groups, which has also helped.

After my mother died, I learned to never take my family for granted ever again. My family tried to always remind me of the good times with my mother after she died. For me, my coping mechanism was to become emotionally strong so that I wouldn't be torn down like this again. I became a stronger person after her death. I feel like losing her made me stronger than I would have been if she was still alive, and so, if she was still alive, I might have developed her bad habits because I most likely would have been exposed to it more than before.—Rebecca, lost her mother[22]

My advice for a teen who just lost her mother would be, I would first extend my sympathy to her. I would definitely tell her about my experience with losing my mother and how it affected me. I would tell her, even if I barely knew her, that I will always be here for her, if she ever needs someone to talk to, or even relate to. I would tell her to definitely communicate with others about how you feel because I think that communication plays a huge part after the death of a loved one. If you don't communicate and keep every feeling inside of you, it won't do any good for you and it will make the death of a loved one even harder. I would tell her to do things to keep her mind off the death of her mother whether that be going for a run, or hanging out with friends—anything will help.

I went to a family counselor after my mom died and I didn't find that beneficial, maybe because I was so young, although I started going to a different family counselor three years ago, and I still find every session extremely beneficial. I also have always wanted to start journaling, because my mom did journal when she had cancer (I have hers), but I always hated the word "journal" and "diary." Three years ago, I created a document that I titled *Dear Mom*, and whenever I want to write and tell her something, I turn on my computer and open that document, write the date, and I journal what has happened that day. I write it as if I am writing a letter to my mother, so I am always telling her about what's going on in my life and how much I love and miss her. I also gained inspiration from Anne Frank's diary because in her diary she wrote *Dear Kitty*, and I loved that idea of not just writing *Dear Diary* or *Dear Journal*. It makes my writing a whole lot more natural because I am writing to my mom.—Adriana, lost her mother[23]

My advice to a newly parentless teen, is to cry it out. Look at photographs. Listen to music. Visit favorite spots. Re-create meals. Cry some more. Spend time alone. Spend time with friends. Spend time with other family members. Speak your mind, but be mindful of others. The dead do not care about the living, and what I mean by that is your mom and/or dad aren't here to make this any easier—it is YOU that has to keep going without them now, and you have to make them proud and represent the child that they created and raised and taught. If you need time to work things out, whether it be alone, with anyone, with specific people, with a doctor, whomever—if you need time, tell someone, and take that time. Find someone you can vent to who will listen, and if you want assistance, then ask for it. Most importantly, you have to keep moving on and living your life. It is not disrespectful to continue with your life commitments, whether it be school or work or whatever. You have to keep going in order to keep some sanity. A sense of normalcy will help you to cope. Life has drastically changed, and anything that continues as it was is a blessing and a comfort. Some days will be harder than others. And that doesn't just go away with time. Everyone handles death differently, and what is easy for some can be difficult for others. There is no time schedule for grief. You may have certain times when memories of your parents come back stronger than others, and it might happen in the first couple of years, or might happen for the next twenty. Any amount of time you need to grieve is okay. It is only when your grief takes over your ability to perform daily routine functions, or when your grieving behavior becomes destructive, that you seriously need to consider some outside source(s) for help.

I wanted to die to be with my mother again. However, I never got to where I would try, or even think of ways to do so. I was five months into quitting smoking at the time, and I started again. I saw the open pack at her bedside, picked it up and lit one, said, "This is for you, mom." Bad idea. I have attempted to quit two other times since. I am currently at about 53 weeks without smoking. The day of her death, I also had a few drinks, and while I do imbibe occasionally, it is never a good idea to drink because you're sad.—Stacy, lost both parents[24]

My advice for a teen who just lost their parent would be to find someone to talk to. It will also relieve how expensive a counseling bill can get. Find someone you can share everything with and choose your friends wisely. If you don't choose your friends wisely, that can have damaging effects on you more than the loss can. Ask yourself what nursery rhyme can you relate to in order to try and better understand what you are feeling. Do you believe in God? Angels? Having a connection with someone or your beliefs can help you cope and settle the stuff you have brewing inside of you. Everyone deals with loss differently. Start thinking about your future right away. Get close to your relatives, but remember it is also important to branch out on your own. You can even pick a family member to be your best friend. Write down your thoughts or your life history in a diary, so you can look back and see if you have a pattern of good or bad choices. Realize that cause and effect will always be there. Don't jeopardize your life by turning to drugs and alcohol to try and cope with what you are feeling. Instead, learn how to give back to others in your own way—join a church, youth groups. There are lots of books out there than can cultivate your spiritual journey—sports, healthy and positive distractions such as playing the piano and other related activities. Don't feel pressured in any way. Talk to your loved ones each night and it will all become clearer for you.— D. B., identical twin, lost her father[25]

My advice for a teen who just lost their parent, be patient with yourself and give yourself a lot of time to grieve. The memories you have bring pain right now, but that won't always be the case. The memories will bring happiness to you eventually. Take each moment as it comes and know you have support. Reach out when you need to, and work on breathing when you feel hopeless pain. The pain will pass.—Nicki, lost her father[26]

No matter who our parents are, we all have this journey to discover who we are. To have understanding supportive parents who can genuinely support who you are, is ideal. But, many of us do not get that. We may lose a parent or parents, or have bad parents or parents who cannot support us, or we have parents who actually give us away. There are many things that can happen to a child that makes it hard to know a parent's love. But, we can become even stronger and much more understanding and compassionate people because of it. Losing a parent can make you a better stronger person yourself. Life is rarely ideal for anyone. The main help in all of this is: Forgiveness. Forgiveness. Forgiveness. If we can always forgive, somehow God just blesses you more because of it. That is the main thing I have learned—from your heart, forgive everyone.

My advice would be to everyone, follow your own heart and don't let other people's opinions make you angry, or try to be someone you are not. Get to know yourself and stay calm before you make decisions. When you make mistakes, forgive yourself and try again. Forgive others, as well.—Katie, lost both parents to a murder-suicide[27]

My advice for a teen girl who just lost her father would be how I would tell her it was okay to do or not do what she felt would help her get through this one day. I would tell her that she needed to figure out who in her circle would be a person she could talk to who wouldn't stop her from talking as much or as little as she wanted. I would tell her to think about her dad and even write down all of his attributes, what mattered to him, and what he hoped for her. I would tell her that if she needed to cry, it was okay, but also okay if she didn't cry. I would suggest that she might think about keeping a journal or writing letters to her dad so she wouldn't feel her communication with him was over.—Barbara, lost her father[28]

My advice for teens is that you should know that everything will be okay. Things will get better. At a young age, you think the world is going to end, and you probably have a lot of fear you are feeling right now. Talk about how you are feeling, as there are those of us who will listen to you. Having a support system is crucial while you are going through this, even if you keep most of your feelings inside.—Larry, lost his mother[29]

My advice for a teen who just lost their parent, first and foremost would be to fight for their right to take part in the funerals and even the last week of their parents' lives. And I do mean fight. My children lost their father in 1987, my youngest was sixteen at the time, and I would not allow the hospital to do anything with him until the children arrived to see for themselves how he was.

Have faith in your God. Talk to Him about your problems. Think everything out for yourself, but also listen to advice—then, make up your own mind. God does not need a lot of fancy words. Remember, He is your friend and you can tell him anything. By just saying things out loud to God, helps you make decisions that you might not make for yourself. God is love, and may God be with you always.—Rachel, lost both parents[30]

The advice I would offer a teen girl who just lost her mother, would be although the grief is overwhelming and you feel detached from life, try to find comfort in close family and friends. Talk about what you are feeling; don't hold it in or detach from them as I often did. Don't dwell on what you might think was bad behavior during your mother's final days. As you live the turmoil of the teenage years, try to imagine your mother's support and advice.—Ellen, lost her mother[31]

I would tell her how sorry I am, and how I feel her pain—literally. I would convey to her that her feelings, no matter how intense or deep, are completely legitimate. I would tell her not to allow anyone to minimize her experience, as they cannot understand it fully if they haven't lived it. Then, I would tell her some of my experience, what I did with my feelings in the situation, and how I would have done things differently. Overall, I would try to convey to her that despite the apparent circumstances, there really is a God who sees her pain, feels her emotion, and has not abandoned her. In fact, He loves her far more than she can imagine. He is in control, and has great plans for her and her future, and desperately wants to carry her through the next days, weeks, months, and years. If she will allow it, He will do all this, and more.

After my experience of being completely out of control of my father's death, I immediately began to take control of what I could at eleven years of age. I was always a good student, and decided that was one area I could control, such as my perfect attendance in 5th grade, or getting the best grades I could throughout my elementary and high school years. I went off to college, and grew to be a pretty controlling young lady, because my experience taught me that no one was truly going to be there to take care of me. If no one could protect me from such excruciating pain as losing my dad, I would have to take charge of as much as I could in my life, and create the best life I could that would minimize future pain and loss. As an adult, I have been forced to deal with the fact that coping mechanisms that work as a child don't always work as effectively as an adult. Many years of personal and family counseling, along with many friends and counselors along the way, have helped me process my incredible loss little by little.— Maggie, lost her father[32]

Seek immediate help. Try and find groups with kids her age to talk to because no one understands most unless they have been through it themselves. It really is like a dead mother's club. A club you would never want to be in but need the support from people who have. I can't explain it. I would especially have them seek advice on relationships moving forward. For years, I suffered from post-traumatic stress not realizing it. I still do, but am aware of what I'm doing now and my reactions to certain things.

I stayed busy and was constantly with friends. I pushed everything down and never talked about it. That did not work.—Autum, lost her mother[33]

I think the best advice I would give to a teen is to get professional help if at all possible. The sooner the better. That would have helped me immensely—an independent person that could help to explore ways to deal with the emotions, pain, sense of loss, etc. It seems like there are more avenues or opportunities to work with skilled professionals that understand grief, especially that's experienced by a child or young teenager. This person needs to be able to provide you with the set of tools to deal with people and situations that you just wouldn't expect to deal with. That was not an option for me—my relatives meant well, but they did not know how to help me.

Accept the fact that this change in your life tends to make you hypersensitive. And as a result, your interactions with others who do not share this same life experience are, for the most part, immune to what you are feeling, and therefore, they can seem like insensitive jerks at times. It took me until well into my thirties to realize that most people do not intend to be insensitive to you—they simply have no idea how certain actions, conversations, etc. can be hurtful to you. I have learned to give people the benefit of the doubt—I assume they will become more sensitive as we learn more about each other. I learned to tell people how things make me feel, but it is not easy for sure. The important thing to realize is to not take things personally and let it ruin a potential relationship. I try to gently "educate" people I interact with—once they understand, the interactions go much better. Not perfect, but better. I don't think it will ever be perfect.

The goal is to find ways to convert the energy spent on feeling sorry for yourself to that spent on ways to move forward and survive. Realize that the loss is real, by finding ways to hold on to the goodness from that lost relationship (physical or emotional). Learn from failure—failing is inevitable, but what we learn from failure is oftentimes more worthy than what we learn from success. You survived—so make the most of it. Make your parents proud of your survival. Be responsible for your own happiness.— Isabella, lost both parents[34]

Upon hearing a teen lost her father like I lost mine, I will gather her in my arms and hold her tightly, and tell her it is okay to cry and let her sorrow and anger out. I will tell her that I will be strong for her and that I love her, as her father did. I will stay with her and watch over her, knowing that what I went through as a child is the same thing she is experiencing. I will be there . . . engaged . . . observing . . . supporting her! A constant force of love, concern, and unwavering support for as long as she needs me. Not just hours, not just days, but forever.

I want her to have all the love and compassion that I never had. I withdrew from everything. I became a shadow; the Shadow Child. Quiet, shy, secluded, and not part of the rest of the family. Rarely seen and not heard, I had no voice and no one listened to me. I retreated into my own little world of drawing and painting, reading, climbing apple trees on our property, exploring nature, and tending my garden that my dad had helped me make. My companion was my little kitty Skoshi.—Laura, lost her father[35]

My advice for a teen who just lost her father would be, I would want to put her head on my shoulder and put my arms around her and just let her cry, sigh, lament—rage? I would want to pray for her and communicate to her that God is a forever-Father who will always be with her, and who can comfort and guide her. She can even safely rage at Him. I would encourage her to seek good, wise friends, but caution her not to put all her hopes in friends or to place her longings in a boyfriend. As a teen, she will be old enough to have memories to comfort her, as well as memories where forgiveness will probably be needed (toward herself, toward her father, and possibly toward others). There will be spiritual needs, as well as practical needs in caring for spirit, soul, and body. A Grief Share program might be helpful. In recent years, my mother's only sister told me that counseling just wasn't thought of at the time of my father's death, and she thought that it could have been helpful for some of us.

I coped by, I became an active, believing Christian as an adult. As a child, I believed in God, and I often prayed, but I felt like God was far away. So, for coping, I spent a lot of time alone. I suppose that's always been my bent, for it's still my preferred method. I don't get on the phone. I start praying and walk around and get busy.—Sharon, lost her father[36]

My advice for a teen who just lost his father would be, turn to your heavenly Father—He will lead/guide and teach you about life more than your earthly father ever could. God has a plan and a purpose for your life that will fulfill you.

I coped with my father's death by finding identity in sports and followed my brothers. I sought fulfillment through girlfriends, and later, careers, hoping to find a sense of purpose.—Rick, lost his father[37]

My advice to a teen who just lost her mother would be, I would tell her to be as strong as possible; that it will get easier. To remember all the good things about her mother and to try to be the best person her mother would want her to be; become someone her mother would be proud of. Seek out comfort and guidance from friends and other loved ones. To have faith, knowing one day they will be together again. That it's not only okay to grieve, but that it's healthy to. To stay away from self-destructive behavior.—Nancy, lost her mother[38]

Though I lost my mother before I became a teen, I'd advise any young girl or young woman who has lost a mother to seek out and foster strong relationships with other women of all ages. They can teach you the things your mother is not there to teach you. They can comfort you when you need a mother's touch. There will always be sadness and hurt and loss and the wonder of what could have been, but the stabbing pain won't come as often as time goes on. Remember the things she taught you, and try to pass those things along. Let her live on through you, and always try to make her proud. Teach your children about her. Talk to other people about their memories of her and be a collector of stories. Allow the women you choose to become close with to contribute—even unknowingly—to your mothering, which is important, even as you become an adult. Recognize their strengths and take from that for yourself. Be selective about the women you spend time with, for they will have a greater impact on you.

You don't have to go through this alone. There are millions of people all around the world who have lost one or both of their parents at a young age, and there are many support groups out there. ©iStock / veerasakpiyawatanakul

> They will help mold you into the woman, sister, friend, and wife you will become.—Kristen, lost her mother[39]

As you can see, there have been many other parentless teens who have made it to adulthood before you. We are a huge community out there, and you never have to face what you are feeling or going through alone.

My Parting Advice for You

You have overcome so much already; you are a strong young individual. Whether you lost your mother, your father, or both, you are strong for the mere fact that you are still breathing despite having lost your parent; you are still sleeping, eating, getting dressed and out of bed each day, not to mention all of the other important tasks you take on each day. I don't think a lot of people realize how strong someone really is who lost a parent young. They say they understand, but they really don't. Unless they lost their parent young, they will never fully understand what you have been through and what you have overcome. There's no need to ever be mad at them—they just don't understand. Just make sure that you understand, though, and be proud of the person you are becoming and the good

Interview with Author's Husband

Meet Chris, my husband. Although we have been friends for years, we didn't start dating until we were in our midtwenties, which was about fifteen years after my mother passed away. Here's his perspective on being on the outside and marrying into a grieving family. This might give you an idea of how parent loss goes with you into adulthood.

Michelle Shreeve (MS): How has the loss of your wife's mother impacted your wife to this day?

Chris Shreeve (CS): She always worries about making her mother proud. Other kids get to see and talk to their parents and can usually know if their mother approves of the choices they make or the person that they are becoming. Michelle is always so careful to judge what she does before she does it. As if her mother is always watching her.

I see her struggle with things in her everyday life that others take for granted. I'm sure that when women grow up with a mother, their mothers pass on the things that they have learned throughout life to make things easier for their daughters. Things like doing their hair, putting on makeup, picking out clothes, proper etiquette for being a lady, etc. No one stops to think about what it would be like to never have been taught these things and how difficult life would be to live without this knowledge. I see my wife struggle with these simple things on a regular basis. It isn't that she is incapable or unwilling to do or learn these things. She just never had the decades of guidance from her mother that most women get.

Michelle has so much compassion and empathy for others. She has the biggest heart of anyone I have ever met. I think her empathy and compassion are amplified with having to experience such a devastation of a loss at a young age. She always wants to help those who are hurting. I think she wants to try to keep others from feeling the pain that she felt, so she does everything that she can to try to help the person alleviate it. Even if it's just a little and only for a moment.

MS: What helps your wife when she might be having a grief trigger about her late mother?

CS: I always come back to faith. I remind her that her mother is always watching over her and that she can talk to her at any time. If Michelle is anything like her mother, then I know how proud of her she is. We reminisce about fun and happy moments that she remembers about her mother. We talk about her smile, her beauty, and her favorite things that she loved. Michelle also turns to books and movies for comfort.

From my relationship with Michelle, I have come to understand that the pain of the loss of this magnitude will never fully go away. I've been fortunate enough that I have never had to experience this type of loss yet, but I am so thankful that I have someone who understands what I will need when the time comes.

MS: Marrying into the family, how have you noticed each member grieving? Are they all grieving differently? Are they all the same?

CS: I have noticed that grief strikes people on different levels and in different ways. This is the same with Michelle and her family. They all lost the same person, but had a different type of relationship to her. Even though she was the mother to Michelle and her brother Mike, mothers have different relationships with their daughters than they do with their sons. Dave lost his wife, which is completely different than losing a parent. For this reason, I have seen differences in the way that they deal with their loss.

One similarity that I have noticed is that their pain has toughened them. Not in a bad way, but I've noticed that they are capable of coping with difficult situations that many others would panic or crumble at. They unfortunately have the knowledge that things can be much worse than what they think. Michelle is one of the strongest people I know. She is able to take on some of the most grueling and arduous tasks that I could never do.

MS: What's your perspective on marrying into this family regarding the loss they've suffered?

CS: I knew going into my relationship with my wife that there would be things that I wouldn't fully understand. I still don't. I knew there would be times that I wouldn't know what to do or say because I've never experienced anything close to what she or her family have gone through. It was tough for me at times because I always wanted to be able to say or do the right thing to make everything better when she was missing her mother, but I always came up empty. Now I realize that there is no magic phrase or action that I can say or do to make everything better. I just try to be there for her as much as I can be and hold her when it hurts.[a]

things you are doing with your life. Your late and surviving parents are, and so are your family members and friends who have supported you along your parent loss journey—and so am I. I am extremely proud of you.

Live each day as if it were your last. Talk to your late parent every single day for the rest of your life, as some people believe he or she will appreciate a quick "hi" and will always be watching over you. Don't be afraid to ask for help from your surviving parent or other trusted adult or caregiver on your rough days. Seek positive outlets, try to find common ground with your stepparent, give more hugs to your surviving parent, and help out around the house more. If your world comes crashing down because you aren't regularly dealing with your griefcase, know that you can't get any lower, and use that as an opportunity to rebuild your life. But this time around, make sure you regularly deal with your emotions. Reach out to new parentless kids, teens, and adults, and help them along their journey. Helping others with their parentless journey also helps you with yours.

As a fellow parentless child, I understand what you are going through. We are all in this together. You are never alone. I wish you the best of luck on your life journey. You got this!

Glossary

abandonment: the state of being left completely and finally, of being utterly forsaken or deserted

AIDS (acquired immune deficiency syndrome): disease in which there is a severe loss of the body's cellular immunity, greatly lowering the resistance to infection and malignancy

alloparenting: parental care provided by a person other than the biological parent

anticipatory dread: a grief reaction that occurs before an impending loss

attachment: the condition of being attached to something or someone in particular

bereavement: to be deprived of a loved one through a profound absence, due to a loved one's death

bibliotherapy: using books as therapy when one is going through difficult psychological and emotional trials

blended family: family that consists of children from other relationships merged into one new family created by the couple; also called a stepfamily

bullying: when someone uses superior physical or emotional strength to influence or intimidate someone; forcing someone to do something against what he or she wants to do

casket: coffin in which a dead person's body is placed before it is buried

catharsis: the process of releasing and finding relief from strong or repressed emotions

celebration of life: gathering to celebrate the accomplishments, memory, and life of a deceased person

cinema/movie therapy: supplemental therapy that uses movies as a method of self-help

complicated grief: when feelings of loss are debilitating and don't improve even after time passes; reactions include being absent mentally or emotionally and having excessive, distorted, exaggerated, or unending feelings of grief

complicated mourning: when a person gets stuck at one particular difficult point of the mourning process

cope: to face or deal with an event in one's life that a teen could be struggling with

counseling: assistance and guidance in resolving personal, social, or psychological problems and difficulties, especially by a professional

counselor: person trained to give guidance on personal, social, or psychological problems

cremation: an alternative to burying a deceased person, where the body is turned into ash

dysphoria: a state of unease or generalized dissatisfaction with life

eulogy: a speech or writing in praise of a person who recently died; usually included as part of a funeral service

extreme avoidance: refers to choosing behavior based on trying to avoid or escape particular thoughts or feelings

funeral: ceremony honoring the deceased

grief: deep sorrow, especially caused by someone's death

grief trigger: sudden reminders of the person who died that can cause powerful emotional responses

gurney: wheeled stretcher used for transporting hospital patients

HIV (human immunodeficiency virus): the virus that causes AIDS

magical thinking: irrational belief that one can bring about a circumstance or event by thinking about it or wishing for it

memorial marker: a marker that usually commemorates a site where a person died suddenly and unexpectedly

memorial service: a service that can happen before or after the burial or cremation that celebrates the memory of the deceased

mourning: the expression of deep sorrow for someone who has died

neurophysiological functioning: a branch of physiology and neuroscience that is concerned with the study of the functioning of the nervous system

over-identification: a process by which one ascribes to oneself the qualities or characteristics of another person

parentless teen: teen who has lost one or both of his or her parents

physiological: relating to the branch of biology that deals with the normal functions of living organisms and their parts

psychosocial: of or relating to the interrelation of social factors and individual thought and behavior

PTSD (post-traumatic stress disorder): a debilitating anxiety disorder that occurs after experiencing or witnessing a traumatic event

ritual: a sequence of activities involving gestures, words, and objects, performed in a sequestered place, and performed according to set sequence

scaffolding: when a parent or trusted adult demonstrates the problem-solving process, then steps back and offers support as needed

second parent: parental figure who steps in to treat a young person as one's own child, after the young person has lost one or both of his or her biological parents; someone who reminds the child of his or her late parent

secondary loss: a loss caused by change in relationships after a death, a change caused by moving, lifestyle, peer groups, shared memories, security and safety, plans for the future

somatic: of or relating to the body, especially as distinct from the mind

stepparent: adult who marries the surviving parent, after the young person has lost his or her mother or father

surrogate parent: adult looking out for the interests of a child other than his or her own

surviving parent: parent who is left after the late parent dies

survivor's guilt: occurs when a person perceives themselves to have done wrong by surviving a traumatic event when others did not survive

thanatologist: person who studies death, including the needs of the terminally ill and their families

therapeutic: a form of healing

therapist: a person skilled in a particular kind of therapy

therapy: treatment intended to heal or relieve

transition: process of going from one mental state to another in terms of parent loss

trauma: a deeply distressing or disturbing experience

traumatic grief: a type of grief following the death of a loved one under traumatic circumstances

viewing: when loved ones can see the deceased person one last time in the casket after the funeral home prepares the body; can be a form of closure

writing therapy: writing as an expressive therapeutic coping mechanism to channel one's feelings and emotions after trauma or loss

Zen garden: a miniature garden filled with sand and rocks; the sand is raked to represent the natural movement of water, and the motion of raking the sand can be very relaxing and therapeutic

Notes

Chapter 1

1. "Loss of a Parent," All Psychology Careers, www.allpsychologycareers.com/topics/loss-of-a-parent.html, accessed March 14, 2017.
2. Phyllis Cohen, K. Mark Sossin, and Richard Ruth, *Healing after Parent Loss in Childhood and Adolescence: Therapeutic Interventions and Theoretical Considerations* (Lanham, MD: Rowman & Littlefield, 2014), 6.
3. David J. Schonfeld and Marcia Quackenbush, *The Grieving Student: A Teacher's Guide* (Baltimore, MD: Paul H. Brookes), 125.
4. Coalition to Support Grieving Students, "Advice on Funeral Attendance," GrievingStudents.org, grievingstudents.org/wp-content/uploads/2016/05/NYL-3A-Advice-Funerals.pdf, accessed October 2, 2017.
5. Schonfeld and Quackenbush, *The Grieving Student*, 125.
6. Coalition to Support Grieving Students, "Advice on Funeral Attendance."
7. Schonfeld and Quackenbush, *The Grieving Student*, 61.
8. Coalition to Support Grieving Students, "Grief Triggers," GrievingStudents.org, grievingstudents.org/wp-content/uploads/2016/05/NYL-4D-GriefTriggers.pdf, accessed October 2, 2017.
9. Coalition to Support Grieving Students, "Other Reactions," GrievingStudents.org, grievingstudents.org/wp-content/uploads/2016/05/NYL-4C-OtherReaction.pdf, accessed October 2, 2017.
10. Allison Gilbert, email interview with the author, January 19, 2017.
11. Coalition to Support Grieving Students, "Providing Support over Time," GrievingStudents.org, grievingstudents.org/wp-content/uploads/2016/05/NYL-1C-Providing-Support-Over-Time.pdf, accessed October 2, 2017.
12. Cohen, Sossin, and Ruth, *Healing after Parent Loss*, 8.
13. Schonfeld and Quackenbush, *The Grieving Student*, 83.
14. Schonfeld and Quackenbush, *The Grieving Student*, 52.
15. "When a Parent Dies, What Helps a Child Cope?" *U.S. News*, March 14, 2014, health.usnews.com/health-news/articles/2014/03/14/when-a-parent-dies-what-helps-a-child-cope, accessed June 1, 2017.
16. Cohen, Sossin, and Ruth, *Healing after Parent Loss*, 122.
17. Schonfeld and Quackenbush, *The Grieving Student*, 65–66.
18. Schonfeld and Quackenbush, *The Grieving Student*, 85.
19. Schonfeld and Quackenbush, *The Grieving Student*, 83–84.

a. Erin, email interview with the author, January 12, 2017.
b. Mike, phone interview with the author, January 13, 2017.

c. Julie, email interview with the author, February 18, 2017.

d. Catherine, phone interview with the author, September 17, 2016.

e. Thomas, email interview with the author, March 3, 2017.

f. Lindsay, email interview with the author, March 1, 2017.

g. Eric, email interview with the author, February 27, 2017.

h. Catherine, phone interview with the author, September 17, 2016.

i. Aedan, email interview with the author, February 7, 2017.

j. Julie, email interview.

k. Aedan, email interview.

l. Moyer Foundation Staff, "Art Therapy for Grief: The Why and How from Art with Heart," MoyerFoundation.org, moyerfoundation.org/resources/art-therapy-the-why-and-how-from-art-wtih-heart/, accessed September 9, 2017.

m. "Beautiful Pain: Found Poems and Creative Healing," What'sYourGrief.com, whatsyourgrief.com/journaling-exercise-found-poems/ (accessed September 9, 2017).

n. David J. Schonfeld and Marcia Quackenbush, *The Grieving Student: A Teacher's Guide* (Baltimore, MD: Paul H. Brookes), 86.

o. Taylor, phone interview with the author, March 7, 2017.

p. Julie, email interview.

q. "Children and Grief," American Academy of Child and Adolescent Psychiatry, July 2013, www.aacap.org/AACAP/Families_and_Youth/Facts_for_Families/Facts_for_Families_Pages/Children_And_Grief_08.aspx, accessed June 1, 2017.

r. McKenna, email interview with the author, March 9, 2017.

s. Taylor, phone interview.

t. Mike, phone interview.

u. Chase, phone interview with the author, January 26, 2017.

v. Schonfeld and Quackenbush, *The Grieving Student*, 31.

w. Schonfeld and Quackenbush, *The Grieving Student*, 60.

x. "Loss of a Parent," All Psychology Careers, www.allpsychologycareers.com/topics/loss-of-a-parent.html, accessed March 14, 2017.

y. Julie, email interview.

z. Chase, phone interview.

aa. Ella, phone interview with the author, January 26, 2017.

bb. Julie, email interview.

cc. Aedan, email interview.

dd. Phyllis Cohen, K. Mark Sossin, and Richard Ruth, *Healing after Parent Loss in Childhood and Adolescence: Therapeutic Interventions and Theoretical Considerations* (Lanham, MD: Rowman & Littlefield, 2014), 2.

ee. Marjorie Dyan Hirsch, "Helping a Child Cope with the Death of a Parent," mil.ccs.k12.nc.us/files/2012/06/Children-and-loss-of-parent.pdf, accessed September 19, 2017.

ff. Tiffany, email interview with the author, March 6, 2017.

Chapter 2

1. Phyllis Cohen, K. Mark Sossin, and Richard Ruth, *Healing after Parent Loss in Childhood and Adolescence: Therapeutic Interventions and Theoretical Considerations* (Lanham, MD: Rowman & Littlefield, 2014), 118.

2. Coalition to Support Grieving Students, "Guilt and Shame," GrievingStudents.org, grieving students.org/wp-content/uploads/2016/05/NYL-4B-GuiltShame.pdf, accessed October 2, 2017.
3. T. B. Grenklo, U. Kreicbergs, U. A. Valdimarsdottir, T. Nyberg, G. Steineck, and C. J. Furst, "Self-Injury in Youths Who Lost a Parent to Cancer: Nationwide Study of the Impact of Family-Related and Health-Care-Related Factors," *Psycho-Oncology* 23, no. 9 (2014): 989–97.
4. Cohen, Sossin, and Ruth, *Healing after Parent Loss*, 74.
5. Harold Cohen, "What Causes PTSD?" PsychCentral, psychcentral.com/lib/what-causes-ptsd/, accessed October 2, 2017.
6. Maja Lis-Turlejska, Anna Plitcha, Aleksandra Luszczynska, and Charles Benight, "Jewish and Non-Jewish World War II Child and Adolescent Survivors at 60 Years after War: Effects of Parental Loss and Age at Exposure on Well-Being," *American Journal of Orthopsychiatry* 78, no. 3 (July 2008): 370.
7. Cohen, Sossin, and Ruth, *Healing after Parent Loss*, 284.
8. The Moyer Foundation, "For Kids and Teens: Understanding Suicide," MoyerFoundation.org, moyerfoundation.org/resources/for-kids-and-teens-understanding-suicide/, accessed September 9, 2017.
9. "Loss of a Parent," AllPsychologyCareers, www.allpsychologycareers.com/topics/loss-of-a-parent.html, accessed October 2, 2017.
10. Cohen, Sossin, and Ruth, *Healing after Parent Loss*, 56.
11. David J. Schonfeld and Marcia Quackenbush, *The Grieving Student: A Teacher's Guide* (Baltimore, MD: Paul H. Brookes, 2010), 58.
12. Darcie D. Sims, "Understanding Anger and Grief in Children," MoyerFoundation.org, moyerfoundation.org/resources/understanding-anger-and-grief-in-children/ (accessed September 8, 2017).
13. Cohen, Sossin, and Ruth, *Healing after Parent Loss*, 11.
14. Robin F. Goodman and Elissa J. Brown, "Service and Science in Times of Crisis: Developing, Planning, and Implementing a Clinical Research Program for Children Traumatically Bereaved after 9/11," *Death Studies* 32, no. 2 (2008): 154–80.
15. Schonfeld and Quackenbush, *The Grieving Student*, 92.

a. Kaylene, email interview with the author, March 3, 2017.
b. Kaylene, email interview.
c. Lindsay, email interview with the author, March 1, 2017.
d. Stacy, email interview with the author, January 17, 2017.
e. Taylor, phone interview with the author, March 7, 2017.
f. Adriana, email interview with the author, February 19, 2017.
g. Christina, email interview with the author, February 27, 2017.
h. "Orphans and Vulnerable Children Affected by HIV and AIDS," USAid.gov, www.usaid.gov/what-we-do/global-health/hiv-and-aids/technical-areas/orphans-and-vulnerable-children-affected-hiv, accessed October 2, 2017.
i. Jordan Thaler, "Information Packet: Parents with HIV/AIDS and Their Children in the Child Welfare System," HunterCUNY.edu, March 2005, www.hunter.cuny.edu/socwork/nrcfcpp/downloads/information_packets/parents_with_HIV_AIDS.pdf, accessed March 14, 2017, and Baryl (name changed), in-person interview with the author, July 9, 2016.

j. Phyllis Cohen, K. Mark Sossin, and Richard Ruth, *Healing after Parent Loss in Childhood and Adolescence: Therapeutic Interventions and Theoretical Considerations* (Lanham, MD: Rowman & Littlefield, 2014), 245.

k. Julie, email interview with the author, February 18, 2017.

l. Beth, email interview with the author, February 27, 2017.

m. Lisa Capretto, "How Jane Fonda Uncovered the Truth about Her Mother's Death," *Huffington Post*, August 17, 2015, www.huffingtonpost.com/entry/jane-fonda-mothers-death_55cd098ae4b0bf5ab5bb56a6, accessed December 24, 2015.

n. Chase, phone interview with the author, January 26, 2017.

o. Ella, phone interview with the author, January 26, 2017.

p. Rebecca (name changed), in-person interview with the author, January 28, 2017.

q. Aedan, email interview with the author, February 7, 2017.

r. "Cleopatra VII," Biography.com, www.biography.com/people/cleopatra-vii-9250984#legacy, accessed October 20, 2015.

s. "Sylvia Plath," Biography.com, www.biography.com/people/sylvia-plath-9442550, accessed January 15, 2016.

t. "Jane Fonda," Biography.com, www.biography.com/people/jane-fonda-9298034, accessed January 15, 2016.

u. Yvonne Juris, "Mourners Remember Chester Bennington in 'Beautiful' Private Service for the Late Linkin Park Singer," *People*, July 20, 2017, people.com/music/chester-bennington-funeral-laid-to-rest/, accessed September 23, 2017.

v. McKenna, email interview with the author, March 9, 2017.

w. "Natasha Richardson," Biography.com, www.biography.com/people/natasha-richardson-425204, accessed September 23, 2017.

x. Katie, email interview with the author, February 16, 2017.

y. Elisabeth Kübler-Ross. *On Death and Dying: What the Dying Have to Teach Doctors, Nurses, Clergy, and Their Own Families.* New York: Scribner, 2014.

z. David J. Schonfeld and Marcia Quackenbush, *The Grieving Student: A Teacher's Guide* (Baltimore, MD: Paul H. Brookes, 2010), 36.

aa. Kaylene, email interview.

bb. Erin, email interview with the author, January 12, 2017.

cc. Joella, email interview with the author, January 13, 2015.

Chapter 3

1. Phyllis Cohen, K. Mark Sossin, and Richard Ruth, *Healing after Parent Loss in Childhood and Adolescence: Therapeutic Interventions and Theoretical Considerations* (Lanham, MD: Rowman & Littlefield, 2014), 180.

2. Maja Lis-Turlejska, Anna Plitcha, Aleksandra Luszczynska, and Charles Benight, "Jewish and Non-Jewish World War II Child and Adolescent Survivors at 60 Years after War: Effects of Parental Loss and Age at Exposure on Well-Being," *American Journal of Orthopsychiatry* 78, no. 3 (July 2008): 370.

3. "Loss of a Parent," All Psychology Careers, www.allpsychologycareers.com/topics/loss-of-a-parent.html, accessed March 14, 2017.

4. Gregory E. Lang, *Why a Daughter Needs a Mom: 100 Reasons* (Naperville, IL: Cumberland House, 2004), 3.

5. David J. Schonfeld and Marcia Quackenbush, *The Grieving Student: A Teacher's Guide* (Baltimore, MD: Paul H. Brookes, 2010), 93.

6. Michelle Hart, "Books That Helped Me Grieve for My Mother," BookRiot.com, bookriot .com/2017/07/13/books-that-helped-me-grieve-for-my-mother/, accessed August 31, 2017.

7. Gregory E. Lang, *Why a Daughter Needs a Dad: 100 Reasons* (Naperville, IL: Cumberland House, 2002), 20.

a. Phyllis Cohen, K. Mark Sossin, and Richard Ruth, *Healing after Parent Loss in Childhood and Adolescence: Therapeutic Interventions and Theoretical Considerations* (Lanham, MD: Rowman & Littlefield, 2014), 181.

b. "Coco Chanel," Biography.com, www.biography.com/people/coco-chanel-9244165, accessed June 15, 2015.

c. "Jacqueline Cochran," Biography.com, www.biography.com/people/jacqueline-cochran -9252061, accessed June 15, 2015.

d. "Marie Curie," Biography.com, www.biography.com/people/marie-curie-9263538, accessed June 15, 2015.

e. "Ella Fitzgerald," Biography.com, www.biography.com/people/ella-fitzgerald-9296210, accessed November 1, 2015.

f. "Ruth Bader Ginsburg," Biography.com, www.biography.com/people/ruth-bader-ginsburg -9312041, accessed June 15, 2015.

g. "Mary Todd Lincoln," Biography.com, www.biography.com/people/mary-todd-lincoln-248 868, accessed September 24, 2017.

h. "Eleanor Roosevelt," Biography.com, www.biography.com/people/eleanor-roosevelt-9463366, accessed June 15, 2015.

i. "Maya Rudolph," Biography.com, www.biography.com/people/maya-rudolph-21114517, accessed September 24, 2017.

j. "Harriet Beecher Stowe," Biography.com, www.biography.com/people/harriet-beecher -stowe-9496479, accessed June 15, 2015.

k. "Anne Sullivan," Biography.com, www.biography.com/people/anne-sullivan-9498826, accessed June 15, 2015.

l. Hope Edelman, phone interview with the author, April 26, 2016.

m. Carissa, email interview with the author, February 23, 2017.

n. Catherine, phone interview with the author, September 17, 2016.

o. Mahala, email interview with the author, February 16, 2017.

p. "Kate Beckinsale," Biography.com, www.biography.com/people/kate-beckinsale-20702025, accessed March 8, 2016.

q. "Queen Elizabeth I," Biography.com, www.biography.com/people/queen-elizabeth -i-9286133, accessed March 8, 2016, and "Henry VIII," Biography.com, www.biography .com/people/henry-viii-9335322, accessed March 8, 2016.

r. "Bindi Irwin," Biography.com, www.biography.com/people/bindi-irwin-241515, accessed March 8, 2016.

s. "Gabrielle Reece," Biography.com, www.biography.com/people/gabrielle-reece-21199595, accessed March 8, 2016.

t. DailyMail.com Reporter, "More Heartache for Julia Roberts as Her Mother 'Dies Aged 80 after Losing Battle to Lung Cancer' . . . One Year After Sister's Suicide," Dailymail.com, www.dailymail.co.uk/tvshowbiz/article-2960307/Julia-Roberts-mother-dies-aged-80-losing -battle-lung-cancer-one-year-sister-s-suicide.html, accessed March 8, 2016.

u. "Barbra Streisand," Biography.com, www.biography.com/people/barbra-streisand-9497402, accessed March 8, 2016.

Chapter 4

1. Paula Spencer Scott, "6 Reasons a Parent's Death Is a Special Kind of Loss," Caring.com, last updated August 14, 2017, www.caring.com/articles/death-of-a-parent, accessed March 14, 2017.
2. Susie Steiner, "Helping Children to Cope with the Pain of a Parent's Death," *Guardian*, May 4, 2013, www.theguardian.com/lifeandstyle/2013/may/04/helping-children-cope-death-of -parent, accessed March 14, 2017.
3. Gregory E. Lang, *Why a Son Needs a Dad: 100 Reasons* (Naperville, IL: Cumberland House, 2004), 9, 12.
4. Dr. Alan D. Wolfelt, "Helping Teenagers Cope with Grief," HospiceNet.org, www.hospice net.org/html/teenager.html, accessed March 14, 2017.
5. Quora, "Author of *The Shack* Shares Five Tips for Dealing with Grief," *Huffington Post*, February 14, 2017, www.huffingtonpost.com/quora/author-of-the-shack-share_b_14749380 .html?utm_hp_ref=grief, accessed March 14, 2017.
6. Gregory E. Lang, *Why a Son Needs a Mom: 100 Reasons* (Naperville, IL: Cumberland House, 2004), 6, 16.
7. "Loss of a Parent," All Psychology Careers, www.allpsychologycareers.com/topics/loss-of-a -parent.html, accessed March 14, 2017.

a. Thomas, email interview with the author, March 3, 2017.
b. Eric, email interview with the author, February 27, 2017.
c. Wilson Lee Flores, "Successful Men Who Grew Up Fatherless," Philstar.com, www.philstar .com/sunday-life/2012-06-17/817890/successful-men-who-grew-fatherless, accessed August 20, 2016.
d. Flores, "Successful Men."
e. Robert Krulwich, "Successful Children Who Lost a Parent—Why There Are So Many of Them," NPR.org, www.npr.org/sections/krulwich/2013/10/15/234737083/successful-chil dren-who-lost-a-parent-why-are-there-so-many-of-them, accessed August 20, 2016.
f. Barbara Barker, "Travis Hamonic Helps Youngsters Heal after Loss of a Parent," Newsday. com, December 13, 2014, www.newsday.com/sports/hockey/islanders/travis-hamonic-helps -youngsters-heal-after-loss-of-a-parent-1.9710330, accessed August 20, 2016.
g. Flores, "Successful Men."
h. "Nelson Mandela," Biography.com, www.biography.com/people/nelson-mandela-9397017, accessed August 20, 2016.
i. "Jack Swartzman," IMDb.com, www.imdb.com/name/nm0777512/bio?ref_=nm_ov_bio_ sm, accessed August 20, 2016.
j. "J. R. R Tolkien," Biography.com, www.biography.com/people/jrr-tolkien-9508428, ac cessed October 11, 2017.
k. Krulwich, "Successful Children."
l. Thomas, email interview.
m. Violetta Armour, email interview with the author, February 13, 2017.

n. Mike, phone interview with the author, January 13, 2017.

o. Aedan, email interview with the author, February 7, 2017.

p. "Oscar De La Hoya," Biography.com, www.biography.com/people/oscar-de-la-hoya-9542428, accessed March 25, 2017.

q. Andrew Anthony, "James Ellroy: Haunted by His Mother's Ghost," *Guardian*, August 21, 2010, www.theguardian.com/theobserver/2010/aug/22/observer-profile-james-ellroy, accessed March 25, 2017.

r. Elliott Wiley Jr., "Fitzgerald Overcomes Painful Offseason," ESPN.com, August 26, 2003, www.espn.com/college-football/news/story?id=1601791, accessed March 25, 2017.

s. "Prince Harry," Biography.com, www.biography.com/people/prince-harry-9542035, accessed March 25, 2017.

t. "John Lennon," Biography.com, www.biography.com/people/john-lennon-9379045, accessed March 25, 2017.

u. "Bernie Mac," Biography.com, www.biography.com/people/bernie-mac-9542611, accessed March 25, 2017.

v. "Paul McCartney," Biography.com, www.biography.com/people/paul-mccartney-9390850, accessed March 25, 2017.

w. "Dylan McDermott," Biography.com, www.biography.com/people/dylan-mcdermott -9542247, accessed March 25, 2017.

x. "Prince William," Biography.com, www.biography.com/people/prince-william-9542068, accessed March 25, 2017.

y. Simon Perry, "Prince Harry: Finding My Purpose," *People*, May 16, 2016, 54.

z. Invictus Games Foundation, invictusgamesfoundation.org/foundation/story/, accessed October 2, 2017.

aa. Perry, "Prince Harry," 54.

Chapter 5

1. Dr. David Schonfeld, email interview with the author, September 18, 2017.

2. David J. Schonfeld and Marcia Quackenbush, *The Grieving Student: A Teacher's Guide* (Baltimore, MD: Paul H. Brookes, 2010), 60.

3. Helen Fitzgerald, "Helping a Grieving Parent," American Hospice Foundation, 2000, americanhospice.org/working-through-grief/helping-a-grieving-parent/, accessed June 1, 2017.

4. Phyllis Cohen, K. Mark Sossin, and Richard Ruth, *Healing after Parent Loss in Childhood and Adolescence: Therapeutic Interventions and Theoretical Considerations* (Lanham, MD: Rowman & Littlefield, 2014), 121.

5. Dr. Schonfeld, email interview.

6. Cohen, Sossin, and Ruth, *Healing after Parent Loss*, 49.

7. Dr. Schonfeld, email interview.

8. Dr. Schonfeld, email interview.

9. "What Your Child Is Experiencing When You Remarry," HealthyChildren.org, February 6, 2017, www.healthychildren.org/English/family-life/family-dynamics/types-of-families/Pages/What-Your-Child-is-Experiencing-When-You-Remarry.aspx, accessed June 1, 2017.

10. Schonfeld and Quackenbush, *The Grieving Student*, 74–76.

a. Kaylene, email interview with the author, March 3, 2017.
b. Mitchell A. Levick, "Attachment, Grief, and Complicated Grief," *Psychology Today*, October 29, 2011, www.psychologytoday.com/blog/am-i-normal/201110/attachment-grief-and-complicated-grief, accessed October 10, 2017.
c. The Moyer Foundation, "Activity: Grief Puzzle," MoyerFoundation.org, moyerfoundation .org/resources/activity-grief-puzzle/, accessed September 9, 2017.
d. Dave, phone interview with the author, October 12, 2017.
e. Kaylene, email interview with the author, March 3, 2017.
f. Julie, email interview with the author, February 18, 2017.
g. Mike, phone interview with the author, January 13, 2017.
h. Dr. David Schonfeld, email interview with the author, September 18, 2017.
i. Carissa, email interview with the author, February 23, 2017.
j. Joella, email interview with the author, January 13, 2015.

Chapter 6

1. Dr. David Schonfeld, email interview with the author, September 18, 2017.
2. Dora Black, "Bereavement in Childhood," *BMJ* March 21, 1998, www.ncbi.nlm.nih.gov/ pmc/articles/PMC1112822/, accessed June 2, 2017.
3. Dr. Schonfeld, email interview.

a. Adriana, email interview with the author, February 19, 2017.
b. McKenna, email interview with the author, March 9, 2017.
c. Julie, email interview with the author, February 18, 2017.
d. Ella, phone interview with the author, January 26, 2017.
e. Chase, phone interview with the author, January 26, 2017.
f. Thomas, email interview with the author, March 3, 2017.

Chapter 7

1. Dr. David Schonfeld, email interview with the author, September 18, 2017.
2. Dr. Schonfeld, email interview.
3. Kate Bayless, "8 Boundaries Stepparents Shouldn't Cross," *Parents*, www.parents.com/par enting/dynamics/step-parent-boundaries/, accessed January 16, 2017.
4. Lynn Norment. "Stepchild/Stepparent: Must There Always Be Conflict?" *Ebony* 36, no. 3 (January 1981): 83. MasterFILE Premier, EBSCOhost, accessed January 16, 2017.
5. Ron L. Deal, "10 Things to Know before You Remarry," Smart Stepfamilies, www.smart stepfamilies.com/view/10-things, accessed January 16, 2017.
6. Jann Blackstone, "Remarriage after the Death of Their Parent," Bonus Families, bonusfami lies.com/helping-kids-deal-remarriage-death-parent/, accessed January 16, 2017.
7. Colleen Oakley, "9 Stepparenting Dos and Don'ts," WebMD, www.webmd.com/parenting/ features/tips-for-stepparents#1, accessed January 16, 2017.

a. Mike, phone interview with the author, January 13, 2017.

b. Adriana, email interview with the author, February 19, 2017.

c. Lindsay, email interview with the author, March 1, 2017.

d. Ella and Chase, phone interview with the author, January 26, 2017.

e. Thomas, email interview with the author, March 3, 2017.

f. Rebecca (name changed), in-person interview with the author, January 28, 2017.

g. Carissa, email interview with the author, February 23, 2017.

h. Trish, email interview with the author, March 6, 2017.

Chapter 8

1. Bonnie Rubenstein, "7 Tips to Help Teens Successfully Transition to High School," Fox News, July 29, 2012, www.foxnews.com/opinion/2012/07/29/7-tips-to-help-teens-successfully-transition-to-high-school.html, accessed June 2, 2017.

2. Dr. David Schonfeld, email interview with the author, September 18, 2017.

3. Centers for Disease Control and Prevention, "The Relationship between Bullying and Suicide: What We Know and What It Means for Schools," CDC.gov, April 2014, www.cdc.gov/violenceprevention/pdf/bullying-suicide-translation-final-a.pdf, accessed June 2, 2017.

4. Ron Kelly, "Organizing Your Griefcase," *Grief Digest* 13, no. 4 (2017), 4.

a. Julie, email interview with the author, February 18, 2017.

b. Joella, email interview with the author, January 13, 2015.

c. Mahala, email interview with the author, February 16, 2017.

d. Aedan, email interview with the author, February 7, 2017.

Chapter 9

1. Dr. David Schonfeld, email interview with the author, September 18, 2017.

2. Dr. Schonfeld, email interview.

3. Taylor, phone interview with the author, March 7, 2017.

4. Kaylene, email interview with the author, March 3, 2017.

5. Carissa, email interview with the author, February 23, 2017.

6. Aedan, email interview with the author, February 7, 2017.

7. Julie, email interview with the author, February 18, 2017.

8. Mike, phone interview with the author, January 13, 2017.

9. Eric, email interview with the author, February 27, 2017.

10. McKenna, email interview with the author, March 9, 2017.

11. Lindsay, email interview with the author, March 1, 2017.

12. Tiffany, email interview with the author, March 6, 2017.

13. Erin, email interview with the author, January 12, 2017.

14. Chase, phone interview with the author, January 26, 2017.

15. Ella, phone interview with the author, January 26, 2017.

16. Catherine, phone interview with the author, September 17, 2016.

17. Joella, email interview with the author, January 13, 2015.

18. Thomas, email interview with the author, March 3, 2017.

19. Mahala, email interview with the author, February 16, 2017.

20. Beth, email interview with the author, February 27, 2017.

21. Christina, email interview with the author, February 27, 2017.

22. Rebecca (name changed), in-person interview with the author, January 28, 2017.

23. Adriana, email interview with the author, February 19, 2017.

24. Stacy, email interview with the author, January 17, 2017.

25. D. B. (name changed), in-person interview with the author, March 7, 2017.

26. Nicki, email interview with the author, February 20, 2017.

27. Katie, email interview with the author, February 16, 2017.

28. Barbara, email interview with the author, February 14, 2017.

29. Larry, phone interview with the author, February 2, 2017.

30. Rachel (name changed) email interview with the author, February 18, 2017.

31. Ellen (name changed), email interview with the author, February 19, 2017.

32. Maggie, email interview with the author, March 10, 2017.

33. Autum, email interview with the author, March 12, 2017.

34. Isabella (name changed), email interview with the author, January 24, 2017.

35. Laura, email interview with the author, March 5, 2017.

36. Sharon, email interview with the author, February 16, 2017.

37. Rick, email interview with the author, February 27, 2017.

38. Nancy, email interview with the author, February 17, 2017.

39. Kristen, email interview with the author, March 6, 2017.

---

a. Chris Shreeve, in-person interview with the author, October 12, 2017.

Resources

Books

For Parents, Teachers, and Caregivers to Support Grieving Teens

Guiding Your Child through Grief by James P. Emswiler and Mary Ann Emswiler. This book helps adults know how to give children the support and help they need while grieving a loss.

The Grieving Student: A Teacher's Guide by David J. Schonfeld and Marcia Quackenbush. This is a very helpful guide for teachers and even parents trying to support a grieving child.

For Teens

Facing Change: Falling Apart and Coming Together Again in the Teen Years by Donna O' Toole. This book tries to help teens understand their loss, suggests healthy coping mechanisms, and recommends ways to work through their grief.

Grief Diaries: Surviving the Loss of a Parent by Lynda Cheldelin Fell and Heather Wallace-Rey. This book contains stories written by those who lost a parent and can serve as a resource for support—the stories can help you feel like you are not dealing with parent loss alone.

How It Feels When a Parent Dies by Jill Krementz. This book has real stories of young kids and teens who lost a parent: the feelings they have, the grief they experienced. It also has pictures of the teens with other family members.

I Will Remember You by Laura Dower. This is a guidebook through grief written for teens.

The Loss That Is Forever: The Lifelong Impact of the Early Death of a Mother or Father by Maxine Harris. This book offers stories from over sixty men and women who lost their parents at a young age and how they dealt with the trauma.

Never the Same: Coming to Terms with the Death of a Parent by Donna Schuurman. This book discusses how children and teens are never the same after their parents die, as well as how unresolved issues can negatively impact children and teens.

When Parent's Die: Learning to Live with the Loss of a Parent by Rebecca Abrahams. This book discusses the psychological and emotional toll losing a parent can have, and it explores more about the aftermath of losing a parent, how to cope, and more.

You Are Not Alone: Teens Talk about Life after the Loss of a Parent by Lynne Hughes. This book contains real talk from teens who have experienced parent loss.

Grief Camps

America's Camp: www.americascamp.org/. This camp is specifically for children who lost a parent or sibling in the attacks on 9/11 and for children or siblings of firefighters and policemen killed in the line of duty.

Camp Erin: moyerfoundation.org/camps-programs/camp-erin/

Comfort Zone Camp: www.comfortzonecamp.org/

C.O.P.S Kid's Camp: nationalcops.org/kidscamp.html. This camp is specifically for the children and surviving parents or guardians of law enforcement officers killed in the line of duty. Children must be accompanied by a parent or guardian at this camp.

Good Grief Camp: www.taps.org/national/2017/ggc. This camp is specifically for children of military moms and dads killed in the line of duty.

Magazines and Articles

"Going Back to School after a Death: 9 Tips." What'sYourGrief.com. whatsyourgrief.com/going-back-to-school-after-a-death/, accessed August 31, 2017.

Grief Digest Magazine: www.griefdigestmagazine.com. This is a helpful resource for finding grief books and literature to help you through your grieving process.

Hart, Michelle. "Books That Helped Me Grieve for My Mother." BookRiot.com, July 13, 2017. bookriot.com/2017/07/13/books-that-helped-me-grieve-for-my-mother/, accessed August 31, 2017.

Psychology Today—find a therapist page: therapists.psychologytoday.com/rms. If you are interested in speaking with a therapist, this is a good tool to locate one near your residence.

Stepparent Magazine: stepparentmagazine.com. This is great resource to get your stepfamily off to a good start.

Organizations

National Suicide Prevention Lifeline: suicidepreventionlifeline.org; 1-800-273-8255. The lifeline provides 24/7, free and confidential support for people in distress, prevention and crisis resources for you or your loved ones, and best practices for professionals.

Smoke Free Teens: teen.smokefree.gov/800quitNow.aspx; 1-800-QUIT-NOW. Whether you are having doubts, cravings, or just need help taking the big step, a friendly, supportive voice is just a free and confidential phone call away.

Substance Abuse and Mental Health Services Administration: www.samhsa.gov/find-help/national-helpline; 1-800-662-HELP (4357). This is a confidential, free, 24-hours-a-day, 365-days-a-year, information service, in English and Spanish, for individuals and family members facing mental and/or substance use disorders. This service provides referrals to local treatment facilities, support groups, and community-based organizations. Callers can also order free publications and other information.

Other Resources

Coalition to Support Grieving Students modules: grievingstudents.org/modules/. These modules provide information for adults wanting to know how to talk to a child regarding death- or crisis-related situations.

Teen Grief Handbook by Hospice of Santa Cruz: Hospice of Santa Cruz "has created a helpful 16 page booklet for grieving teens. The booklet starts by defining grief and explores many of the feelings that teens will experience. It explores some of the thoughts that they might be having and ends with constructive and creative ways to heal." You can download the handbook from the Moyer Foundation website at moyerfoundation.org/resources/teen-grief-handbook/.

Teen Grief Journal by the Dougy Center: "'Deconstruction/Reconstruction' is a teen grief journal put out by the Dougy Center, a children's grief center in Portland, Oregon. In a quick two-page intro, they cover all the bases that a teen should know about grief: it isn't linear, it doesn't have a clear beginning, middle, and end, coping is about figuring out what works for each individual, grief is about finding a new sense of self, remembering, memorializing, it looks different for everyone, not everyone was close to the person who died, other people say and do the wrong things. The journal has guided activities, allows teens to express themselves, but also offers prompts, flexibility, freedom, and guidance. It's a balance between writing, like a regular journal, but also venting and coping with grief, especially on the hard days. It's not just writing and expressing, but drawing, painting, collaging, and some pages where you get to choose what to do." The journal is available at tdcbookstore.org for $14.95. Read more about the journal at whatsyourgrief.com/teen-grief-journal/

Websites

Centering Corporation, centering.org/
Children's Grief Education Association, www.childgrief.org/schoolcounselors.htm
The Coalition to Support Grieving Students, grievingstudents.org/
C.O.P.S., nationalcops.org/
The Cove Center for Grieving Children, www.covect.org/
The Dougy Center, www.dougy.org/
Family Lives On Foundation, www.familyliveson.org/
Grief Digest Magazine, www.griefdigestmagazine.com/
Griefnet.org bookstore, griefnet.org/library/biblio/parentscaregivers.html
HelloGrief.org, www.hellogrief.org/
Hospice of the Valley, www.hov.org/our-care/grief-support/new-song-center-for-grieving-children/
The Moyer Foundation, moyerfoundation.org/
National Alliance for Grieving Children, childrengrieve.org/
National Center for School Crisis and Bereavement, www.schoolcrisiscenter.org/
New York Life Foundation, www1.newyorklife.com/nyl/v/index.jsp?vgnextoid=9b20f59594442310VgnVCM100000ac841cacRCRD
T.A.P.S., www.taps.org/
WhatsYourGrief.com, whatsyourgrief.com/

Who or Where to Turn to for Help

Bereavement support groups for families/children
Bookstores
Community-based mental health services
Health care provider
Hospice programs
Libraries
Pediatrician
Psychiatrists
Psychologists
School counseling services
Teachers
Therapists

Index

About the Author

When **Michelle Shreeve** was young and coping with her mother's death, a lot of her family members were coping with their own grief and understandably could not tend to her needs 100 percent of the time. As a child, Michelle had to find accessible coping methods. Michelle had access to the local Barnes and Noble to browse books to help her cope, as well as the school and public library. She also often rode her bike to the local video store to pick out movies that helped bring comfort when she missed her mother; she sought movies that featured fictional motherless daughters to help provide insight into her own loss. This is why Michelle included so many books and movies as suggestions to teens in this book.

Michelle later learned about bibliotherapy, writing therapy, and movie therapy, which can sometimes be used as supplemental tools for healing. Teens can get professional help, but many do not have access to money or the ability to drive a car to get counseling. Checking out books from their school library is often free, and teens nowadays have a lot more access to video games, movies, and TV shows that can help. The books and movies she suggests throughout this book are ones that helped her or her peers cope with parent loss while growing up. They are only a small sampling of the hundreds and thousands that are available.

This coping method helped Michelle so much when she was young that she even decided to write one of her thesis papers for her second master's degree on bibliotherapy and writing therapy and how these types of supplemental therapy can help teens and kids cope with parent loss. She is currently working on an academic study to gather more parent loss research to help the next generation of parentless children. She strongly feels that more research and resources need to be available for children, teens, and young adults who lost one or both of their parents young, and also so the world can better understand the aftereffects of traumatic parental loss.

Michelle holds two undergraduate degrees in psychology, as well as two masters' degrees: one in English and one in creative writing. She has written columns and journalism pieces, as well as movie and book reviews, for various newspapers, magazines, and online blog sites. Michelle has been a published freelance writer since 2008 and has been compiling lists on the side for years of notable people who lost one or both of their parents young and grew up to be successful or who gave something positive back to the world, as well as lists of nonfiction and fiction books and movies that can help the parentless grieve and cope.

In addition, Michelle has over ten years of experience in the education field; she has written for school newsletters, helped students enroll in college, tutored in English and writing, mentored children and teens, worked with special needs children, and worked at school libraries and a public library. She also has a marketing background, which she has used in working with publishers, authors, and various types of businesses.

Furthermore, Michelle has twenty-four years of personal parent loss experience, having lost her mother at nine years old. Over the years, she has tried to advocate on behalf of parentless children. She has mentored children and teens, reached out to newly parentless children and teens, shared her personal mother loss story on a local radio show, been featured in a global magazine regarding her parent loss experience, and had a parentless children national column for eight years. For nearly a decade, she also wrote a general advice column in the local newspaper, where she reached audiences throughout the United States, Canada, Mexico, India, and Sweden.

Originally from the Bay Area in California, Michelle now resides in Arizona with her husband, Chris; their dog; and their two cats. She is currently working on and wrapping up a few parentless teen fiction novels and parentless children's fiction picture books, as she hopes to write more regarding this subject to provide more resources for children, teens, and young adults in need of them. She can be reached at fortheparentless@gmail.com.